e-HR: using intranets to improve the effectiveness of your people

e-HR: using intranets to improve the effectiveness of your people

Bryan Hopkins
and
James Markham

GOWER

Published by
Gower Publishing Limited
Gower House
Croft Road
Aldershot
Hampshire GU11 3HR
England

Gower
Suite 420
101 Cherry Street
Burlington
Vermont 05401–44405
USA

British Library Cataloguing in Publication Data

Hopkins, Bryan
e-HR: Using Intranets to Improve the Effectiveness of Your People

    1. Personnel management – Computer networks.
    2. Personnel management – Computer network resources. 3. Intranets
    (Computer networks).
    I. Title. II. Markham, James.
    658.3'00285468

ISBN 0 566 08539 9

Library of Congress Cataloguing in Publication Data

Hopkins, Bryan, 1954–
e-HR: Using Intranets to Improve the Effectiveness of Your People

    Bryan Hopkins and James Markham.
    p. cm.
    Includes bibliographical references.
    1. Personnel Management – Computer network resources. 2. Intranets (Computer networks)
    I. Markham, James. II. Title.
    HF5549.A27H67 2003
    658.3'00285'768–dc21   2003048313

Typeset in Humanist521 on 10 point by Paul Newcombe and printed in Great Britain by MPG Books Ltd, Bodmin, Cornwall.

Contents

Chapter 1: Why put the 'e' in e-HR?

Chapter 2: How does intranet technology work?

Chapter 3: What kind of e-HR is right for your business?

Chapter 4: Delivering core HR services

Chapter 5: Managing people more effectively

Chapter 6: Improving collaboration and learning

Chapter 7: Enhancing employees' benefits

Chapter 8: Planning your e-HR implementation strategy

Chapter 9: Implementing IT systems

List of figures

List of tables

Acknowledgements

Many thanks are due to the following people who helped in the writing of this book by giving their time and sharing their knowledge with us.

- Sarah A Kent, Corporate HR Information Systems Project Officer, Sheffield City Council

- Richard Brady, HCM International

- Michael Harrison, Selima Software

- Derek Rowley, BT

- Alex Petrie, Inch-Perfect Ltd

Also, acknowledgements are due to the following organisations that have allowed screen prints from their products to be used:

- Selima Software, www.selima.co.uk

- Inch-Perfect Ltd, www.inch-perfect.com

- Centra, www.centra.com

- Journyx, www.journyx.com

A final thanks to Paul Newcombe for final desktop publishing and developing the graphics throughout.

Introduction

*Captain, we could route time and attendance through payroll and
realign the competency core with the Learning Management
System. That would give you all the HR information you need.*

Unnamed HR Manager, *USS Enterprise*

Writing a book about technology is difficult: books are expected to sit on shelves for
several years, but technology moves on and what is relevant and cutting edge at the time
of writing can be out of date by the time the book is available. Writing a book about a
subject like e-HR is even harder: organisations implementing it see it as giving them a
competitive advantage for a short time until others catch up and so are wary about
revealing too much about what they are doing, while businesses selling solutions are keen
to promote it as the best thing since sliced bread.

As writers we have therefore had to tread a path down the middle, as people who can see
real benefits of e-HR systems but who recognise that slowly, slowly really is the best way
to catch that monkey. There are a number of reasons for this.

Firstly, human resources is a human activity. Real people have to have a real involvement in
what organisations do to support what their employees do, and technology should never
be more than a tool to help this happen. Certainly as we were talking to people for our
research there was sometimes a degree of suspicion that we were part of a movement
that was seeking to computerise all human resources activity, and that our book would be
promoting a technical nirvana where such things as administration, training and appraisals
would be all done by sitting in front of a monitor. Well, we're not. What we do want to do
is to look at ways of how technology can make some processes easier, processes that are
often found to be time-consuming or uninspiring, such as transferring data from paper to
computer or travelling from one end of the country to another for a brief meeting. The
book also talks about how to make decisions about what e-HR functions will work for you,
a process that asks you to take into account a variety of factors. If, after, doing this you
decide that a particular e-HR solution will not be ethically appropriate, that is fine.

Secondly, it is difficult to predict what will turn out to be a technological blind alley. History
is full of stories about people and organisations that have blazed a trail doing something
that turned out to be the wrong something. That is not to say that we should never try
anything new: if we didn't, life would never have moved on and we would still be huddling
in caves hoping that someone else would come back with tonight's dinner. What we are
saying is that pioneering applications of technology should be treated with caution, by
sticking one toe in the water first and only going ahead with full-scale investment when the
technology has been proved to work.

That leads us on to another feature of this book, the distinction (or lack of distinction)
between what is available and what is still just an idea. New ways of using e-HR technology

are being introduced so quickly that it is impossible for a static medium like a book to capture the state of the art. So what you will find in this book is a mixture of descriptions about what current technology is and what the predictions and possibilities are. We have made no attempt to distinguish between them as we think that may limit our thinking about what e-HR can do.

e-HR actually reminds us of a set of children's building blocks. They may have been lying around in the nursery for years, being played with by different children, each one of them finding different ways to combine the same blocks. Then one day a new kid on the block thinks of doing something completely different with them that uses all the blocks to create a structure that has never been seen before. What we are seeing with e-HR is actually just a radically new way of using what has been around for some time. We have had HR information systems and other organisational databases around since the 1980s but until now it has proved difficult and expensive to link them together. Web technology provides us with the new kid on the block spark.

Biologists talk about 'emergent' properties of organisms, a term that describes how entities with their own individual qualities and abilities can become something completely different when they come together. Blood cells, liver cells and brain cells have their own unique properties as cells, but when they and thousands of other types of cell come together they form a living, breathing creature, one that is capable of doing things that none of the individual cells could do. E-HR systems are like this: by combining separate sources of information we can create a system that allows people to do things they have never been able to do before. And as emergent properties in nature may not be predictable by a simple linear addition of the properties of the individual organisms, so we cannot predict exactly just how e-HR systems may be used. All we can do is speculate and use our imaginations to think about what we could do. Therefore some of the ideas in this book are just that – what we might be able to do with the system. Of course, by the time you read this these ideas may be old hat and be standard features in off-the-shelf systems, but we hope that reading the book will stimulate your own ideas about what new ways of pulling together information would help you.

Who will find this book useful?

This book will be useful for anyone who is just starting to have some involvement with e-HR. You may have just implemented an e-HR system and be wondering how you can develop it, you may be looking to upgrade an existing client-server information system, or you may be planning to jump straight from a paper-based system into the brave new world of e-HR. Whatever sort of person you are, you should find this book of interest.

Do not feel you have to read the book from cover to cover. Each chapter covers a discrete aspect of e-HR, some of which will interest you more than others. However, you will find that there are significant linkages and overlaps between the content in Chapters 4 to 7. This is because, although the subject matter has been broken down into four separate areas for ease of presentation, in reality the integrating effect of e-HR means that all of them can be connected in some way.

What is in the book?

To help you find your way through the book, here is a summary of what each chapter covers.

Chapter 1 - Why put the 'e' in e-HR?

This chapter looks in general terms at what e-HR is and how it represents a quantum leap forward from existing uman Resources Information Systems (HRIS) technologies. It considers the general benefits that organisations can find from implementing e-HR systems but also looks at the challenges they present.

Chapter 2 - How does intranet technology work?

HR professionals diving into e-HR waters are going to find that they need to have a reasonable understanding of the basic underlying technology. The aim of this chapter therefore is to provide an explanation of intranet technology, so this will be useful for people with a limited understanding of the subject. It explains basic concepts such as TCP/IP and HTML, for example, then goes on to look at how intranet technology has evolved in recent years from sites offering fixed information to present-day portals that customise themselves to the user.

Chapter 3 - What kind of e-HR is right for your business?

This chapter will help you to start making some decisions about how e-HR may be able to help you. It takes you through a process that starts with the simple question 'Where are you now?' and then leads you on to think about where e-HR systems can add value to your business. It then explains what constraints you must take into consideration so that you can put together a blueprint outlining your e-HR plans and finishes off by looking at how you can prepare a business case that will justify the necessary investment.

Chapter 4 - Delivering core HR services

Many people's first exposure to e-HR systems is through what are described as self-service HR, where employees themselves are responsible for managing the information that is stored about them. The chapter looks at the benefits of such systems and also considers the challenges that they present. It describes the strategies you need to follow in order to make implementing self-service HR a success.

Chapter 5 - Managing people more effectively

In this chapter we look at how e-HR systems can support management processes. These include:

- e-recruitment, where on-line technologies are used to speed up and improve the efficiency of recruitment processes

- time and attendance systems, where on-line technologies can improve integration with other systems and make information available more quickly and easily

- reward management, where administrative tasks can be reduced considerably

- performance management, where the intranet can be used to manage a lot of the administrative effort required and make it much easier to access important information.

Chapter 6 - Improving collaboration and learning

There are a variety of ways in which on-line technologies can help both individuals and the organisation communicate with, and learn from, others. Not only can information be delivered to employees more easily and more effectively, it also becomes much easier to collect information from people. Document management systems make it possible for the content of all paper within an organisation to be widely available. The chapter also looks at on-line collaborative tools – applications that make it possible for people to work at their desktops with colleagues who may be many miles away using standard technology. One application of this is in e-learning, but the chapter also looks at other aspects of this subject including other ways in which learning can be delivered and managed.

Chapter 7 - Enhancing employees' benefits

Employees' portals can provide links to organisations providing useful services, such as financial services or on-line shopping. Such facilities can deliver benefits more effectively and be useful for improving employee motivation.

Chapter 8 - Planning your e-HR implementation strategy

After reading Chapters 3 to 7 you should have a good idea about how e-HR can help you. Once you have developed a business case to justify your decisions, you need to think about how you are physically going to implement the systems. This chapter looks at some of the different e-HR implementation strategies, such as upgrading existing systems, choosing suppliers, whether to rent or buy and how to ensure security.

Chapter 9 - Implementing IT systems

This chapter is somewhat different to the earlier chapters in the book as it looks at systems in general rather than specifically at e-HR. It considers the issues that you must take into consideration when implementing a new IT system.

chapter 1

Why put the 'e' in e-HR?

HR departments have been using computers for many years now. The ability to store, sort and retrieve large amounts of information has proved invaluable, and a large, specialised software industry has grown to meet these needs. But essentially all that has happened is that computers have replaced filing cabinets, the way in which HR works has not changed greatly. This book is not about computerised filing cabinets, but is about the brave new world of e-HR, a new approach to using technology for managing people, a technology that has its roots in the Internet revolution.

Hands up anyone who had heard of the Internet in 1990. Not many hands going up there, we would imagine. And even though you may have heard of it then, it is unlikely that you would have had a connection to it. But just a dozen years later the Internet and its kin, the intranet and extranet, seem to be occupying ever more areas of our personal and professional lives.

This technological revolution has brought a new prefix into the English language – 'e-'. We can hardly move without bumping into some manifestation of the e-revolution, whether it be e-mail waiting at our desks, e-zines to read or e-shops in which to spend our money.

The 'e-' stands, of course, for 'electronic', but we have had electronic devices with us for years, so why has the word suddenly taken on a new significance? It has happened because a number of technological innovations have been combined to offer a way of bringing together many hitherto separate aspects of the world around us. The written word, speech, music, television, video and even the humble refrigerator now have a common medium where they can be brought together and managed. The libraries of the world are available at our desktops and we can use our mobile phones to check the contents of our refrigerator at home (theoretically at least!).

Figure 1.1
Talking to our refrigerators

Just how much the e-revolution will change our lives will only become apparent as the years unfold, but we are already seeing huge changes in our working lives. This book aims to look at one aspect of this: how e-technologies are changing both

- the role of Human Resource (from now on referred to as HR) Departments and the people working in them, and

- how other people in the organisation will find alternative ways of working.

The technology bringing all these different possibilities together is, of course, the browser. Whether people are using Internet Explorer or Netscape and whether these are running on a PC, Apple Mac or UNIX system, what users can see and do is essentially the same. Standard office applications are increasingly being designed for use through a browser interface and so it makes a great deal of sense for HR applications to do the same. In this way, incompatibility between different systems becomes a thing of the past and people in different parts of an organisation – even if they are working in different parts of the world – can all easily access essential information using standard Internet technology.

 You can find more information about the technical aspects of intranets and web technology in Chapter 2.

This chapter looks at a number of different aspects of e-HR:

- What e-HR is

- What its benefits are

- What challenges it will present

- How to get the best out of e-HR

What is e-HR?

Let us set e-HR in context by looking at how HR systems have evolved over the years.

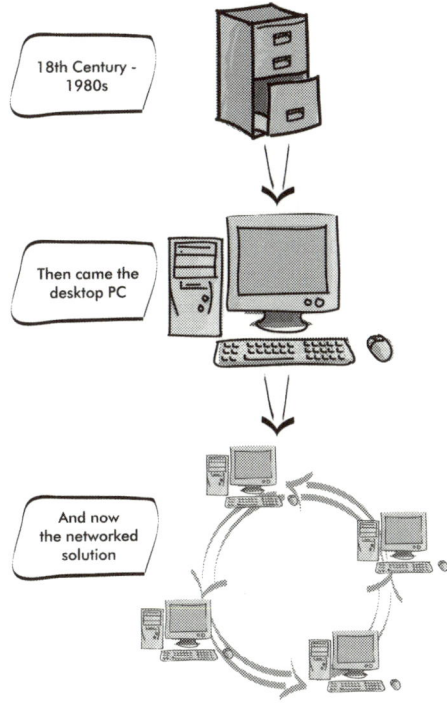

Figure 1.2
The development of HR information systems

In the beginning was the filing cabinet sitting in the corner of the Personnel Office. Drawers full of hanging files arranged in alphabetical order, the dust they collected only being disturbed by the Personnel Manager or an Administrative Assistant when an employee did something like change an address. Systems were very much about record-keeping, with such things as static information about employees, their addresses and other personal information. As organisations grew in complexity, other information about employees came to be recorded as well, such as training records and payroll information. However, these would usually have been kept by the appropriate functional department: the Training Manager would keep the training records and the Payroll Department the payroll information, and, as Rudyard Kipling might have observed, '... never the twain shall meet'.

Computer technology of the 1970s and 1980s moved things on, particularly the introduction of desktop PCs and networking in the 1980s. Databases specifically designed to meet the needs of Personnel came on to the market and many organisations started to transfer their paper records on to computer. Thus was born what are now known as Human Resource Information (or Management) Systems, HRISs (or HRMSs).

These systems were (and often still are) based on a technology known as **client-server**. This describes the relationship between the computer through which the data is accessed (the **client**) and the data on which the computer is stored (the **server**). Each different system had its own database structure and particular function which meant that the data could only be accessed by specially designed software which had to be installed on a client computer, as illustrated in Figure 1.3. Of course, each client installation required a licence, so to minimise costs organisations would only install the client software on the minimum number of machines necessary. Also, because each proprietary HRIS works in a different way, people using the system would have to receive special training. Both factors combined to restrict access to HR information. The client-server relationship meant that people might have several different clients installed on their computer, each talking to a particular database and each one completely unaware of the other databases.

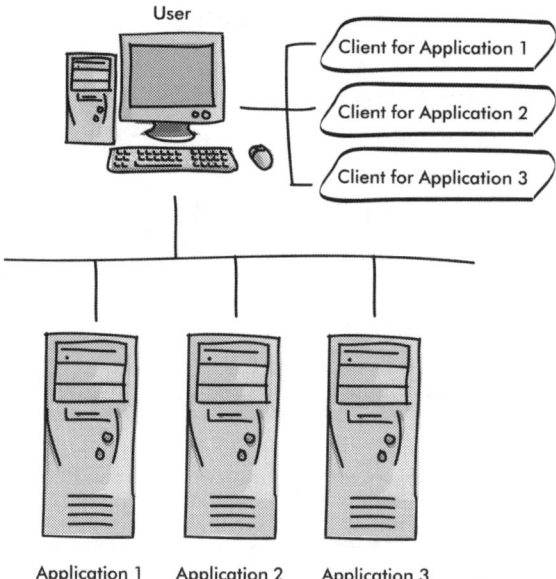

User

Client for Application 1

Client for Application 2

Client for Application 3

Application 1   Application 2   Application 3

Figure 1.3
The client-server model

The proprietary nature of HRISs and other business systems also usually meant that systems would not communicate with each other. This increasingly became recognised as a problem and so software designed to meet all the needs of organisations in one package, referred to as **enterprise resource planning** (ERP) systems (for example, SAP and PeopleSoft), started to appear on the market. However, although these were much more powerful packages, they remained proprietary systems and it was difficult for external systems to connect to them.

So computerisation, although it seemed like a revolution at the time, did not really change things greatly. There were now no hanging files to collect dust, but the records still did not do much. The Personnel Department remained a reactive part of the business, doing what was asked of it and contributing little to company profitability. When it did rouse itself from its slumbers it was to apply some new regulation or piece of legislation – hardly activities guaranteed to win friends and influence people.

This was largely because of two factors:

- this was how it had always been done, and

- the information stored was difficult to access and analyse

The e-HR revolution has the potential to change all this. So let us first try to answer the question posed as the title of this section - what is e-HR?

What is e-HR?	Put simply, e-HR is the strategic application of web-based technologies to HR-related systems, that along with other organisational changes will lead to more broadly-based access to HR information and wider opportunities for managing that information.

At this point we should just briefly mention another term that you may come across, **B2E**, which means 'business to employee' This term has evolved as a counterpart to the possibly more familiar B2B (business to business) and B2C (business to customer), which are used to describe different e-commerce relationships. In this book we shall use e-HR rather than the B2E alternative, although they essentially mean the same thing.

Why is e-HR important?

E-HR technologies have the potential to revolutionise processes carried out within businesses. Why? Take a look at Figure 1.4.

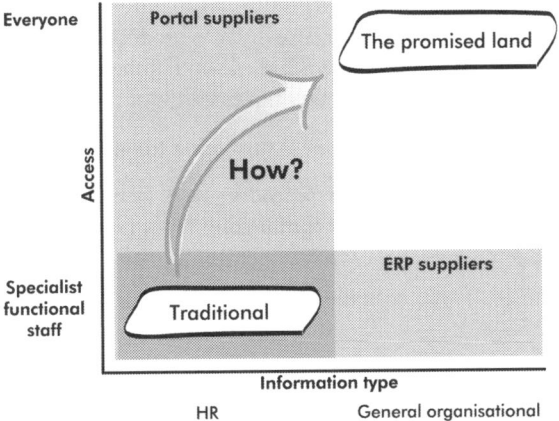

Figure 1.4
Providing information with wide access

Let us consider information in two dimensions - scope and access. Existing client-server systems are focused on particular parts of the business; for example, HR information tends to be people-focused whereas Payroll Department systems are payroll-focused. Client-server architectures limit access to people with the necessary client so we would place client-server HRISs in the bottom left-hand corner. This is in contrast to the browser-based Internet model, where a standard and widely available front end provides access to information: this is the portal approach, where the term 'portal' describes its function as a gateway to information.

Two dimensions means two ways to go, so we can develop systems that:

- integrate database access (the ERP route) and so widen the scope, or

- increase people's access to the database (the portal approach).

Or we can do both, and trip happily into the promised land of enterprise-wide access to all corporate information. So what would be the possibilities were we to reach this information nirvana?

- People across the organisation could directly access whatever information was relevant to their responsibility and seniority, giving managers the information they need and improving employees' work experience.

- The linking together of different sources of information and systems would enable totally new things to happen that people have never thought of before. It becomes very much easier to cross-reference information from different sources, making it possible to look for trends and relationships that would previously have been very difficult to identify, as illustrated in Figure 1.5. We can describe this as an emergent property - a property that only appears when different elements are combined.

    For example, single-celled organisms such as amoeba swim around happily, if somewhat aimlessly, on their own but, when combined, form sophisticated plants and animals with abilities that only exist because of the combination.

Web-enabled systems can do this, but how is this going to happen?

The answer is in either of two ways. ERP providers have integrated database applications and can now offer self-service, while the portal companies are now focusing on providing comprehensive front-end functionality that integrates across a wide number of different databases.

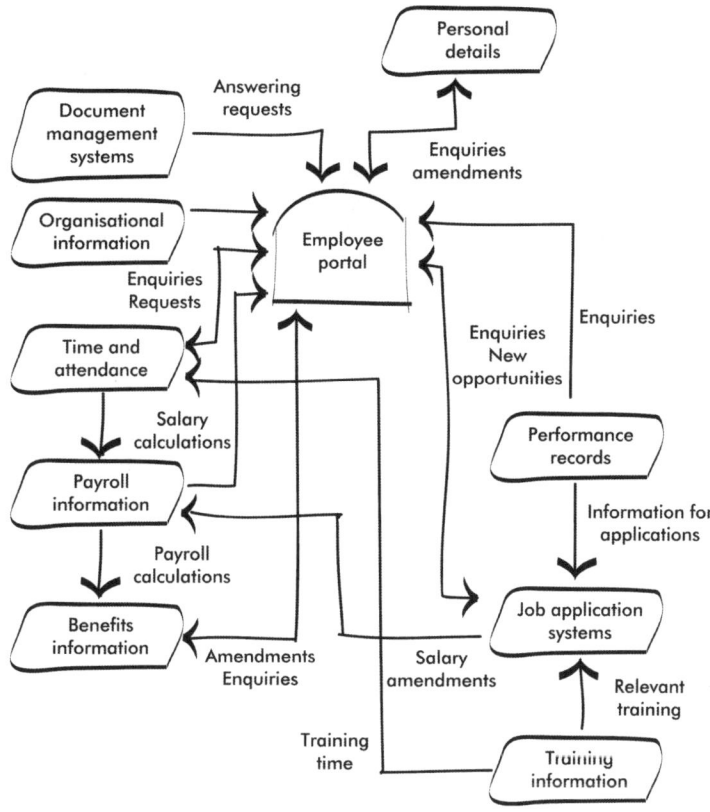

Figure 1.5
Connecting information systems across the organisation
This diagram illustrates how some of the separate sources of information stored across an organisation could be connected to allow enhanced functionality and new opportunities.

Improved access to information and the ability to connect different systems together are the fundamental reasons why e-HR can prove to be an effective way for an organisation to acquire competitive advantage. As an e-HR system grows and its tentacles pull in more and more separate databases you will find that the added value benefits begin to dwarf the cost savings. Synergy is indeed the keyword.

| **Synergy** | *The production by two or more agents, substances, etc., of a combined effect greater than the sum of their separate effects (Oxford English Dictionary)* |

Let us take a look at how e-HR approaches are being used.

What does e-HR mean in practice?

We can break down the possibilities into four distinct areas, as illustrated in Figure 1.6.

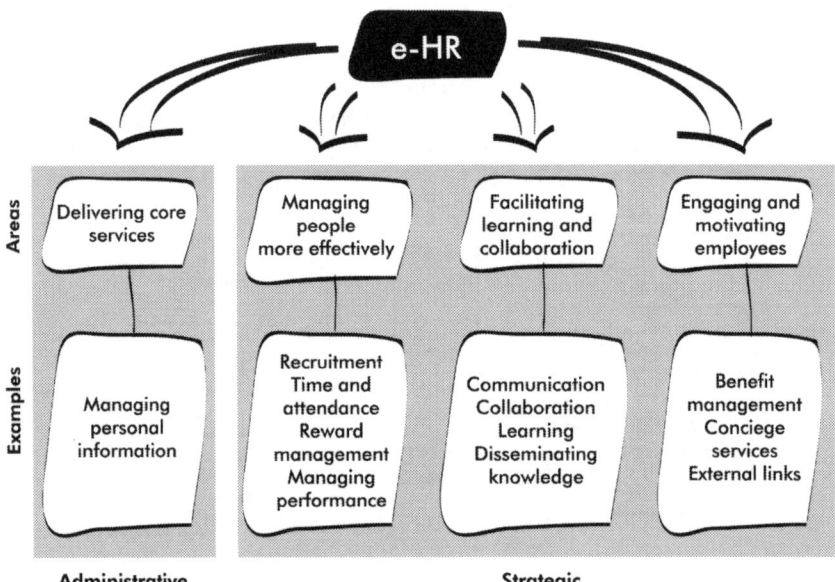

Figure 1.6
The four areas for e-HR

It is important to recognise that, although these activities may overlap in day-to-day business life, technical solutions may be quite distinct. For example, using e-HR to deliver HR services does not mean that you must also deliver training over the intranet or vice versa. Also within each area there is a range of potential applications, not all of which will be relevant to all organisations, and even the largest businesses may not feel the need to employ all the possibilities. ERP solutions tend to focus on core business processes, so while such a solution may meet most of your needs you may find yourself:

- not needing everything within the standard package, or

- looking to other suppliers for specialist 'point' applications.

 How you decide on what applications you need is the subject of Chapter 3, 'What kind of e-HR is right for your business?'

We can also distinguish between administrative and strategic applications. By administrative we mean applications that automate, and in many cases improve, existing routine processes. For example, connections between time and attendance, financial and e-mail systems makes it possible to automate and considerably speed up the collection of data for client billing purposes.

Strategic applications are those that allow a business to do things that it has never done before. For example, on-line collaborative applications make it possible for people working on different continents to see and talk to each other through their desktop computer while working jointly on a standard office application – perhaps a spreadsheet or a presentation graphics package. Improved access to information makes the devolution of responsibility to line managers much more practical. As time goes by, we shall see that these strategic applications of e-HR are those that offer the greatest potential for organisational development.

What are the benefits of e-HR?

HR Departments have traditionally been seen as reactive and a drain on a business rather than as critical to business success. However, in recent years there has been a growing recognition that organisations can acquire a competitive advantage over their competitors through the development of their human resources. They do this in a number of different ways:

- learning faster and applying this knowledge more quickly

- acquiring distinct abilities that cannot be imitated

- optimising relationships between different functions within the organisation

- improving customer service

- becoming more flexible and better able to respond to changes in the marketplace.

Internet and intranet technology offers a number of ways in which HR services can be managed and delivered. These can be summarised under six broad headings:

1. A more strategic approach to HR

2. Better support to management throughout the business

3. Greater potential for organisational collaboration and learning

4. Enhanced organisational prestige

5. Reduced administrative costs

6. A happier workforce.

Let us look at these in more detail.

A more strategic approach to HR

E-HR can help HR to take on a more strategic role by reducing the time needed for administration thereby freeing staff to take on the crucial strategic role, and by providing information for strategic decision-making. For example, HR staff previously involved in data processing could do some of the following:

- become involved in recruitment, such as investigating new ways of finding high-quality candidates or developing relationships with Internet recruitment agencies

- support training and development activities, through such things as helping to improve the quality of learning materials or using new systems to develop strategic information about the effectiveness of training

- develop new performance management information, such as developing profiles of high-performing individuals within the organisation or looking at organisational demographics with a view to improving succession planning

- identify potential new partners to become involved in e-HR-advertised third-party benefits

- help to improve communications activities.

The *Cedar 2001 Human Resources Self Service/Portal Survey*[2] reported that many organisations that had implemented, or were planning to implement, e-HR systems were incorporating non-HR specific applications that were, nonetheless, dependent on HR information – for example, purchase order approval, travel and expense management and time card approval systems. Being the guardians of such information places HR increasingly at the heart of organisational activity. The Cedar survey went on to suggest three different ways in which HR can provide a more strategic service:

- services focusing on such things as acquiring and retaining talent, improving the workplace environment, leadership development and defining corporate vision

- enhancing the technological image of the organisation

- providing quantitative information to help all employees with decision-making.

Let us think about the role which improving access to information has to play. Implementing systems that can pull together data from different sources and provide strategic information can help HR move towards a more proactive role. It becomes possible to provide information that will help identify parts of the business that are performing well or poorly and relate this to factors such as salary, competencies or training records.

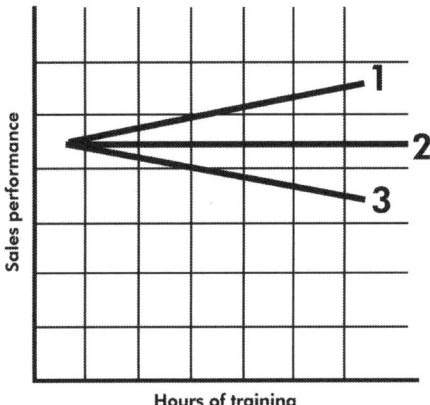

Figure 1.7
Just what effect does training have?
Most businesses fail to evaluate how training actually affects workplace performance: for example, does more training improve sales performance (line 1), make it worse (line 3) or have no effect at all (line 2)?

A recent study by Watson Wyatt[3] that investigated the relationship between human resource-related practices and shareholder value came up with some interesting conclusions:

- Organisations where high performers were better rewarded than average performers have a 0.8 per cent higher shareholder value.

- Organisations where poor performers were identified and supported so that their performance increased have a 0.7 per cent higher shareholder value.

- Organisations that identified and supported poor performers have a 0.7 per cent higher shareholder value

- Organisations which share their business plans and strategic goals with employees have a 0.6 per cent higher shareholder value.

- Organisations which share financial information, such as revenue or expenses per employee, with employees have a 0.5 per cent higher shareholder value.

Information is a crucial factor in each of these aspects of performance. Improved access to information therefore has a critical role to play in a successful business.

Jac Fitz-Enz[4] identifies a number of different pay-related measurements that an e-HR system can provide, such as:

- average merit increases due to meeting performance targets

- comparisons between salary averages for roles within the company and those for competitors

- differentials between high and low performers within the organisation.

Analysing information such as this can help you to identify why you are finding it difficult to attract high-quality staff or to see why staff turnover is too high.

Proactive use of information on such things as competencies can also help with employee motivation. What are the competencies of people in different departments and divisions? Are competency levels in certain regions higher than in others? How does this relate to performance? Linking performance to competency levels can help you identify management approaches or training initiatives that are proving successful or need to be improved.

Better support to management throughout the business

In recent years most organisations have been devolving aspects of HR management to line managers. Although the benefits of this have sometimes been unclear and line management may not welcome all aspects of devolution, HR's role in this change has been to help line managers achieve their objectives. This means providing line managers with the support and information they need to manage their staff effectively.

E-HR can facilitate this. It can give line managers improved functionality so that they can do their jobs more effectively and enables much more information to be available at line manager level so that informed decisions can be made quickly.

Providing more operational functionality

E-HR systems can provide line managers with systems that allow them to carry out their day-to-day tasks more efficiently and effectively. For example:

- E-recruitment systems can speed up the recruitment process and make it easier to find the right candidate for a position.

- The performance management process can be supported by on-line tools.

- Resources can be deployed more quickly.

- It is easier and quicker to take action on reward systems, such as allocating performance-related bonuses.

Providing better-quality information

Managers in organisations must have ready access to information that will help them make both short- and long-term decisions. Strictly speaking, information held in paper systems is often not information at all e.g. it is data, unstructured facts, which, to become useful must be extracted and organised – again, a routine administrative task.

Even information held in computer systems can be difficult for managers to extract – they may not have access to, or knowledge about, the relevant system. In order to get the information they need they may have to complete paper forms or make a telephone call to an HR system administrator, leading to more delays and more potential for misunderstanding.

The improved flow of information is not only upwards to managers. The downward flow to employees of information about the business is also improved. Just how are sales progressing? What was the result of that staff satisfaction survey last year?

Information and services available everywhere and all the time

Information becomes available on a just-in-time basis. Traditional methods of distributing information mean that people have a choice of two less-than-ideal strategies for retaining it: the squirrel strategy or the Mensa method. Squirrel strategists keep every piece of paper or e-mail that they are sent and might possibly be of use in the future. This means that they end up with huge amounts of increasingly out-of-date information that is so voluminous they cannot find anything. Mensa methodeers commit everything to memory, and then, unless they truly are super-brains, forget most things and retain an imperfect memory of the rest.

By means of web-enabling services and providing information on an intranet, e-HR systems provide an HR service all day, every day (including Christmas Day). You do not need to maintain an out-of-hours presence in a call centre and people do not have to rush along to the HR Department during their lunch hour to collect important pieces of information. And when people access information on the intranet, it is always up to date (as long as the webmasters are doing their job!).

Also, with the appropriate security measures and network infrastructure in place, managers can access the system from home or anywhere else in the world simply by establishing an Internet connection and navigating through logging-on procedures.

Intranet-based information is always there, up to date and easy to find, just when it is needed.

Integration of organisational systems

The reason why the Internet and browser-based applications have proved so successful is that they run across all platforms and provide easy ways of integrating all types of data. The same is true for intranet-based internal systems. Integration is why enterprise planning systems such as SAP and J.D. Edwards have proved so successful in managing operational functions, and now it is possible to link HR systems into these applications. Indeed, these suppliers are now offering e-HR systems of their own. Therefore instead of HR apparently hiding in the corner with its own specialised and mysterious systems, all organisational information can be linked together and delivered through the common browser interface.

Improved organisational monitoring

Commercial organisations may value e-HR because of its contribution to bottom-line profitability, but not-for-profit organisations, such as those in the public sector and charities, can also see benefits principally because it makes it much easier to monitor and quantify performance improvement. Indeed, this is a statutory requirement within local government.

E-recruitment: an example of improved services to management

As we shall see in Chapter 5, e-recruitment systems can connect vacancies having known competency requirements to employees already having those competencies. They can then be approached directly with details about vacancies, ensuring that the right people get to know about opportunities. Figure 1.8 illustrates the general principles.

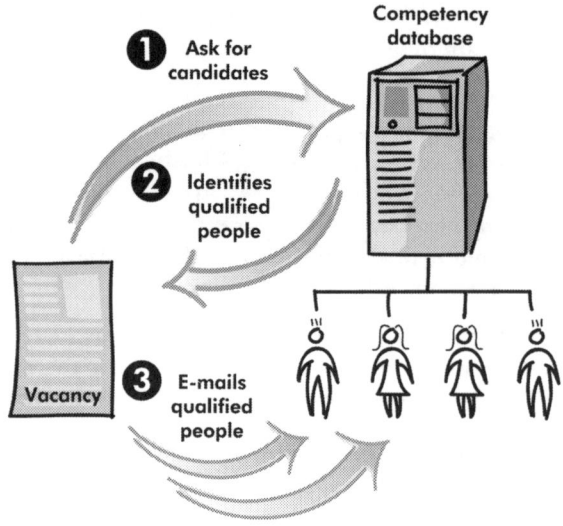

Figure 1.8
Using e-HR to help with recruitment

Similarly when an organisation decides that it needs to create new roles to address changes in the marketplace it can identify the competencies needed, and the e-HR system can see whether or not there are people with those competencies in the organisation.

To attract high-quality staff, organisations must make sure that they offer competitive salary and benefit packages. E-HR can make sure that such information is readily at hand. This makes it easy to keep an eye on how benefits packages compare with the marketplace so that high-quality staff can be retained. There are obvious advantages to being able to do this: replacing staff costs money through the expense of the recruitment process as well as the opportunity costs of people coasting through notice periods and new employees having to learn the job. Improving staff retention can cut these costs considerably. A virtuous circle of improved staff retention and salaries can get going (Figure 1.9).

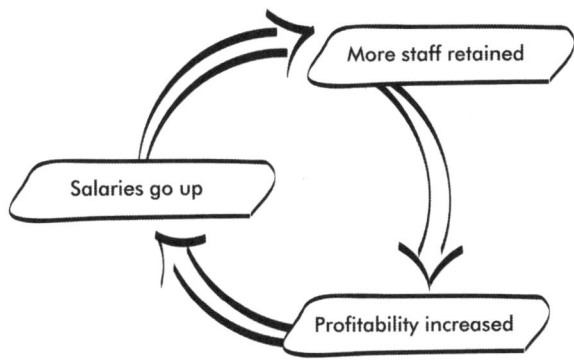

Figure 1.9
The virtuous circle of staff retention
Retaining more staff cuts recruitment costs so profitability increases. This allows the payment of higher salaries so staff are more motivated to stay.
And so it goes on ...

Greater potential for organisational collaboration and learning

Improving access to information does more than support the empowerment of people at lower levels in the organisation, it also increases the possibilities for learning. It does this in a number of ways:

- Learning opportunities can be delivered and managed more easily through e-learning.

- Business-related information can flow more easily, upwards, downwards and laterally.

- Opportunities for collaboration are increased as the technology makes it possible for people to arrange on-line meetings with the minimum of disturbance.

All of these make it more possible for businesses to truly become learning organisations.

Seamlessness of information

Although information may be stored in different places and use different methods or formats, modern technology makes it possible for it all to appear as if it comes from a single source. For example:

- Extensible Markup Language (XML) allows documents to be displayed on the intranet exactly as they were intended.

- Documents produced using a wide variety of word processing packages can be converted to Adobe Acrobat format, which can be viewed within a browser or downloaded to be printed off.

Enhanced organisational prestige

Some organisations may consider it as important to be seen as being at the cutting edge of technology. Investment in e-HR is a potentially high-profile way of doing this. It suggests a forward-looking company, making it more attractive to potential employees and investors alike.

Improving organisational prestige seems to be a particularly important factor for UK businesses. The Watson Wyatt e-HR survey of 2002[5] indicated that more than 40 per cent of UK companies saw e-HR as a way of proving their leading-edge credentials.

Reduced administrative costs

E-HR systems are often sold on the basis of their ability to reduce HR administration costs. Undoubtedly they have the potential to do this, but such savings will almost certainly be dwarfed by the other potential benefits. However, the relative ease with which such cost savings can be calculated means that they play an important part in developing a cost justification for an investment in e-HR.

It is also important to remember that other areas of the business may also see reductions in administrative costs. Let us look at this area of cost reduction in more detail.

Reducing HR-related costs

The traditional method of processing HR information involves a considerable amount of routine clerical work. Depending on the size of the organisation, a small army of people may be involved in transferring handwritten information to centralised computer systems or in putting pieces of paper in ever-growing personal files. The process is routine and repetitive, and is prone to all sorts of simple clerical errors.

These staff, although performing an important function, are not contributing to the organisation's profitability.

Thoughtfully implemented e-HR systems can reduce HR costs through reducing the need for routine administration and data inputting. However, downsizing and re-engineering carried out in the 1990s will have left most organisations with a minimum number of staff in non-production functions such as HR, so the savings from such automation will be relatively small compared to the benefits of an improved contribution to the business. However, it is important to remember that automation of HR administration means that there is no longer a directly proportional link between an organisation's head-count and the HR administrative staff needed. In other words, you will not need to recruit more staff for HR administrative purposes if your business expands.

Reducing costs through streamlining processes

One of the principal aims of e-HR implementation is to streamline processes and reduce the amount of routine administrative work carried out across the organisation in general and by the HR Department specifically. This can release staff for other more strategic responsibilities.

This makes us aware of the opportunity costs of administration: each minute spent filling out an internal form is a minute unavailable for advancing the business. Indeed, this aspect of cost reduction is what is generally used in cost-benefit analyses of e-HR implementation. Claims by suppliers that implementing e-HR can save hundreds of thousands of pounds per year are based on the opportunity cost of liberated time.

Cost savings can be significant[6] and do in fact provide some of the hard return on investment figures needed to convince sceptical Chief Executives. Many organisations are already reaping the benefits of these savings. For example:

- Oracle reported that in 1998 60 per cent of its HR effort was dedicated to administration. By 2000 an e-HR system had led to savings of $1.6 million for each 10, 000 of its employees, and it was now employing one HR staff member for each 2000 employees rather than one per 1000 previously.[7]

- Sears has reported investing $57 million in an e-HR system that is saving the company $16.5 million per year and they expect to have paid back the initial investment by 2004.[8]

- Ericsson claims to be saving $1 million per year through the introduction of a self-service HR system. 'Transactions costing $100 are now down to pennies' apparently, and it reports that processes are faster, more efficient and more organised.

In more general terms, the *Cedar 2001 Human Resources Self Service/Portal Survey*[9] reported that in 2001 96 per cent of North American organisations with employee self-service systems in place rated them as being 'successful' or 'somewhat successful'. The comparable figure for European organisations was 100 per cent! Other positive figures for North American companies quoted by the Cedar survey include:

- average costs of transactions reduced by 60 per cent

- cycle times reduced by 60 per cent

- HR administration head-count reduced by 70 per cent

- return on investment of 100 per cent in less than 22 months

- employee satisfaction increased by up to 50per cent

- enquiries to service centres reduced by up to 90 per cent.

'But,' I hear you say, 'these are all big companies that have invested millions. I don't have that sort of money.' That may be true, but it is important to realise that even small organisations can benefit from the e-HR revolution. And remember, Oracle, Sears and Ericsson are on the leading and bleeding edge of such technology. Their successes are reported for public consumption, but you can be fairly confident that, as pioneers, they will have made mistakes along the way. Organisations embracing e-HR from now on will have the benefit of their hard-won experience and can profit from the lower costs of off-the-shelf products rather than having to develop their own products, as the pioneers have done.

It certainly can be expensive to invest in sophisticated e-HR systems, but as the market matures and products become more standardised, costs will fall. Also, as we shall see later in this book, it is becoming increasingly easy and economic to rent access to an e-HR system from an application service provider (ASP).

A happier workforce

Happy employees are more likely to stay in their jobs than those who are dissatisfied. We all have a gut feeling that this is true, but is there any evidence to support it? Organisational Diagnostics, a US-based company specialising in organisational surveys reports that for every 2 per per cent improvement in employee satisfaction there can be a 1 per cent reduction in employee turnover[10]. So if we believe these figures, we can see that there is definitely value in providing services to employees that will increase their satisfaction.

Dave Ulrich says that the purpose of the HR Department in any organisation is to develop a 'High Performance Work System' (HPWS) by:

- linking selection and promotion decisions to established competency assessments

- having strategies that identify and find people needed to help the organisation respond to changes in its marketplace

- attracting, retaining and motivating high-quality employees.[11]

E-HR systems can help meet these needs. Self-service HR sends out a positive message to employees, "We trust you to look after your own information". People feel as if they are being treated as adults. The information also seems more confidential. They enter it themselves on to the system and do not need to hand personal information over to, quite possibly, junior employees for data processing.

Other on-line services can help improve the feel-good factor:

- On-line flex services allow people to take greater control over their benefits package, buying in to the services that they need at that particular stage in their life rather than putting up with a 'one size fits all' package.

- On-line total compensation statements make it easier to see how their employer provides for them in ways other than just take-home pay.

- External services, such as on-line shopping or concierge services can save people valuable time.

- Information is more personalised: individuals may feel less like cogs in a great machine.

What challenges will e-HR present?

Not another fad?

Proactivity implies innovation, and innovation implies trying out new things. Inevitably some of these new things will not work as well as we initially hoped, and, human nature being as it is, the failures will be discussed more and remembered better than the successes. The last few decades have seen businesses enthusiastically embrace a number of new ideas that have turned out to deliver less than they promised. For example, the change of name from Personnel to Human Resources (has anyone out there seen a difference?), business process re-engineering (now criticised even by its inventors for failing to address human aspects of organisations), and the importance of characteristics of 'excellence' within businesses (many of which have gone to the wall).

And now e-HR. Of course, only time will tell whether e-HR will live up to the hype that always surrounds big new ideas, but what we can probably expect is that the initial enthusiasm will be followed by a period of reflection on what went wrong, followed by a consolidation and increasing acceptance of its benefits. To some extent we can already see this happening. Many of the early adopters have seen where they could have done things better and their meditations are rippling through the rest of the business world.

As the agents for this new initiative, HR managers will have a key role in articulating to others (including their own staff) the challenges and benefits that e-HR will bring. Expectations must be managed: disillusionment often occurs because new initiatives were oversold and failed to live up to the hype.

Breaking down the barriers between HR and IT

IT staff within businesses have always seemed somewhat removed from everyone else. They probably have different offices and certainly talk in a different language. However, in recent years, integration between IT and production functions within businesses has improved as computer technology becomes ever more closely integrated within day-to-day business activities.

But, to a certain extent, HR and IT staff remain apart. After all, HR staff think of themselves as 'people-focused', certainly not like those people in the IT department who spend all of their working lives talking to their computers. From a career point of view, it has, in the past, been difficult to find work within HR that also calls for a high level of IT skills, but there are signs that this is changing. In a 1997 report for the Institute for Employment[12], Robinson comments that 'an embryonic career structure seems to be emerging for HR professionals who want to specialise in computerised systems'. The report goes on to say that HR practitioners recognise that improved HR systems can help them provide better-quality information and are consequently welcoming and enthusiastic.

The e-HR trend is accelerating this. Databases and systems will need to be maintained and updated and this can only be done by people with the right blend of HR and IT skills.

Raising the profile of HR or putting your head over the parapet?

Unlike previous generations of HRISs that stood alone and were only of interest to HR staff, e-HR systems are open to everyone and may be closely integrated with every aspect of the organisation's systems. In some cases HRISs have been bundled in as a low-cost addition to an ERP, so their purchase may have been unnoticed.

However, e-HR systems are not cheap. This means that the investment required to implement e-HR systems will very quickly come to the attention of senior managers who will expect full and complete justifications for the expenditure.

HR managers may not be experienced in doing this. They will need to have a clear grasp of the value chain and cost-benefit analyses that they have carried out. They will need to be able to talk confidently about opportunities presented and constraints imposed by network architecture.

HR Departments may also find that, for the first time, they are competing against other departments for strategic activities and investments. Acquiring the diplomatic skills needed to survive and prosper in a potentially competitive environment may prove challenging to people who have previously felt comfortable in a more traditional HR role.

HR staff becoming customer-focused

HR has always been seen as a reactive function – waiting for people to ask before doing anything. Successful implementation and operation of e-HR systems requires a change in mindset towards focus on the customer. Who are our customers? What do these customers want? What can we do for them?

HR departments will need to become much more proactive and more closely involved in the organisation's everyday profit-making activities.

HR staff needing to understand the business

The close integration between HR and the business that e-HR requires means that HR staff must have a close understanding of how the business works. The successful e-HR professional will need to understand how the different parts of the business work together and what HR can do to help this. Career moves from operations to HR and vice versa will need to become much more frequent.

E-HR systems make time savings possible for the HR function, but these can only be achieved if HR professionals understand the business and know what information is going to be needed so that they can provide it before it is asked for.

HR staff losing contact with people

Any automation process runs the risk of depersonalising what is happening. Inserting a computer system between employees and HR departments may cause HR staff to lose contact with the people whose interests they represent. Employees may feel that the organisation has become a little less human. These are real dangers and are issues that need to be taken into consideration during the planning and implementation process.

In reality, much of a traditional HR department's time is taken up by administration. Letting a computer system take over the task of managing data can free up time for HR staff to do what they probably enjoy the best – dealing with people.

Maintaining quality of service

A significant danger with any empowerment initiative is that service quality levels will fall. While people-related decision-making is dealt with within the four walls of the HR Department there is at least some feeling of being able to monitor and control what decisions are being made. However, providing systems to line managers that will enable them to carry out functions previously dealt with by HR can potentially give rise to quality control problems. For example:

- Will line managers stick to the requirements of your Equal Opportunities Policy? While recruitment is managed centrally it is relatively easy to make sure that the correct guidelines are followed, but with devolution this is not so easy.

- Can you guarantee that new employees are inducted effectively? Devolution of the induction process to line managers supported by an e-learning induction programme could just end up with a new employee being shown to their desk and computer.

You will need to make sure that the new expectations on line managers are clear and that what subsequently happens is monitored.

Keeping information secure

One of the key attractions of e-HR is the idea of self-service: – giving employees the responsibility to manage their own personal information. But as soon as responsibility for this is devolved from one tried and trusted person in HR to everyone in the organisation it becomes possible for the wrong person to access personal information. Information security is a legitimate concern: in fact the Cedar 2001 HR survey[13] reports that fears about security and privacy were the main obstacle to implementing e-HR solutions in Europe.

It is therefore very important that everyone follows simple security procedures, such as keeping passwords unpredictable and confidential, and that the organisation sets up security systems that make unauthorised access as difficult as possible.

 Security issues are covered in more detail in Chapter 8.

Ensuring access to the system

Although offices are becoming increasingly computer-based, many people in many different jobs do not have ready access to a networked computer. For such people the introduction of e-HR can seem like a barrier.

There are, however, ways around this.

- Existing methods can remain in place for people who cannot access a computer.

- Call centre support can provide people having limited access to a computer or restricted IT skills with a way of accessing the system. This may be an interim solution while organisational skills and infrastructures are augmented, or a permanent one.

- Kiosks can be installed in convenient areas such as canteens or on the shopfloor. P & O Nedlloyd report great success[14] in introducing an e-HR system despite many of their staff being crew on ferries without constant access to computers.

Ensuring access to people with disabilities

One of the ironies of e-HR is that, while it has been designed to improve access to information, the browser interface that it uses can, if not correctly designed, make it harder for people with disabilities to use the system. This is mainly because of the shift away from a text-based interface to one relying on graphics. This has a number of implications:

- Interfaces that rely on mouse-clicking rather than keyboard input make it difficult for people who cannot use a mouse – for example, people with physical disabilities who cannot move a mouse with the required degree of precision or click the mouse button.

- People with visual disabilities often rely on special screen-reading software that scans text on the screen and generates this as audio so that the computer literally reads the screen out to the user. Of course, this cannot happen if graphical icons replace words on screen.

While traditional office applications are often carefully designed to allow keyboard and mouse input (for example, it is quite possible to use Microsoft Word without a mouse, and expert users actually find the keyboard shortcuts provided speed up their work), web designers have acquired something of a reputation for being insensitive to users with disabilities. For example, screen-reading software sometimes reads just hyperlinked text and 'Click here for more information' becomes the meaningless 'here'.

However, the time is approaching when designing software so that people with disabilities can use it will not just be a matter of courtesy but a legal requirement. The Disability Discrimination Act requires that all services take reasonable steps to ensure accessibility for people with disabilities, and while case law has not yet defined e-HR systems as being services within the meaning of the Act, it is only a matter of time before it does so.

You should therefore make sure that the e-HR system you implement is accessible to all employees, regardless of their physical abilities. And it is relatively easy to do. For example, you can make the browser interface usable by:

- identifying all graphics that appear on screen with a meaningfully written label known as the 'Alt' tag, which appears if users choose not to have graphics display on screen

- using a sans-serif typeface such as Arial or Verdana for all on-screen displays

- using colour schemes that provide a high contrast between text and the background, and avoiding patterned backgrounds.

There are also various things you can do to make sure that a browser interface is as easy to use as possible for people with disabilities.

Check Bobby compliance

Bobby is a site managed by the Center for Applied Special Technology. It provides information on design guidelines for web sites and also allows you to test pages for compliance with the accepted standards.

Check compliance with W3C standards

W3C (the body responsible for setting World Wide Web standards) operates the Web Accessibility Initiative, which defines standards aimed at making sure that the Web is accessible to all. As Tim Berners-Lee, the Director of the W3C and acknowledged inventor of the World Wide Web, has said, 'The power of the Web is in its universality. Access by everyone regardless of disability is an essential aspect.'

Look through Microsoft's guidance

The Microsoft web site provides useful information about how to check pages for accessibility.

Useful accessibility-related web-sites	<ul><li>Bobby bobby.watchfire.com/bobby/html/en/index.jsp</li><li>W3C www.w3.org/WAI/</li><li>Microsoft www.microsoft.com/enable/</li></ul>

Changing the ethical position of the organisation

The study of ethics is concerned with standards of conduct and how these are perceived. In the context of HR and the organisation we are interested in how individual employees see their organisation as behaving. Buckley et al.[15] observed that organisations (in the United States at least, where their studies were carried out) are showing an increased interest in behaving ethically. This may be because they see levels of dissatisfaction and cynicism rising, particularly amongst certain demographic groups, such as ethnic minorities, the young and the less well-off. They also report that 63 per cent of Chief Executive Officers of Fortune 500 companies feel that strong ethics yield a strategic advantage for their businesses.

So how do ethics manifest themselves in human resources systems? Ethics is intimately tied up with notions of fairness and, quoting earlier research by Bies and Moag, they say that perceptions of fairness are based on the following six factors:

- Consistency: procedures should be consistent.

- Bias suppression: decisions should not be based on self-interest.

- Accuracy: decisions should be based on good information and informed opinion.

- Correctability: it should be possible to change decisions if warranted by additional information.

- Representativeness: decisions should take into account all the groups involved.

- Ethics: decisions should be in line with prevailing moral standards.

If we consider these six factors we can see that the removal or reduction of the human element in HR procedures as a result of introducing an e-HR system could be seen to have both positive and negative effects:

- positive, through the consistency of technology, the elimination of self-interest and the accuracy ensured by self-management of data.

- negative, through the possible but incorrect assumption that an automated process must always make the right and non-correctable decision and that a simplistic, machine-based decision cannot possibly take into account all the subtleties of a situation.

You therefore need to plan carefully how such systems are going to operate and how and when human intervention may be necessary. There are several areas where the issue of ethics is particularly important.

Recruitment and promotion

Recruitment and promotion processes must be seen to be fair. Automating internal recruitment and promotion procedures through the use of e-recruitment methods and linkages to appraisal records could be seen to:

- increase fairness by eliminating personal bias in shortlisting potential applicants, or

- reduce fairness by apparently hiding the selection process in a box

 E-recruitment is covered in detail in Chapter 5.

Performance management

The political aspects of performance management and appraisal have long been recognised. Individuals' competency ratings may reflect more their relationship with their manager than their actual performance in the job. Linking recruitment processes with performance appraisal data may make people feel excluded from promotion opportunities because they have a difficult relationship with their current line manager.

The trick here, therefore, is to recognise that automation of HR processes through the implementation of e-HR can potentially change the perceived ethicality of how an organisation deals with its employees but to continue to make the whole process as transparent as possible.

Employee monitoring

Some organisations are starting to offer employees the chance to buy services from external organisations through their portal. For example, you may be able to access on-line shopping at a supermarket or connect to a travel agency and enjoy preferential terms. The danger is that transactions conducted through these links could be monitored and, even if they are not monitored, employees may be suspicious that they are.

The ethical problem with this is that the employer could be seen to be intruding into a person's private life. Consider some possible scenarios. An employee is using the on-line supermarket link to order large quantities of whisky: does this mean that the person has a drink problem? If so, does the employer have any right to do anything with the information? Another employee may be regularly booking expensive foreign holidays that seem to be far more expensive than their salary would permit. If financial irregularities were to be discovered in parts of the business where this employee works, how might this information be used?

These are complex ethical issues that need to be considered carefully. At the very least, it should be made clear to employees if a monitoring policy is in place. It is also important to ask whether any such information should be recorded at all.

Differing cultural expectations

Organisations operating in different countries can experience considerable difficulties when trying to streamline processes through implementing an e-HR solution.

First, there are the soft, social challenges. Different cultures will react to the introduction of e-HR systems in different ways, some finding it less easy to accept than others. At a practical level this can happen through the problems of deciding what language to use. Will the organisation choose to use its official business language or will it use the local language for each country? While it may be acceptable for normal business activities to be carried out in, say, English, this may not be the case for the more sensitive areas of HR administration. Some organisations have found themselves having to compromise, with core functionality being in the business language and non-core functionality in a local language.

Second, there are the practical challenges. Each country may have its own particular way of doing things (literally a Spanish practice?) that cannot easily be changed. This may be due to national legislation or long-held traditions.

Increasing expectations on line management

Many changes made in business practices in recent years have resulted in increasing expectations on line management. The introduction of e-HR systems adds yet another twist to this tale. Line managers will be told that they now have access to a lot more information that will help them run their sections or departments more effectively. While this is attractive from a senior management perspective, line managers may view it with dread. More expectations, more responsibilities.

At the very least, introduction of these new opportunities (or responsibilities) will have to be sold carefully to line managers. Careful consideration will need to be given to training needs.

Getting the best out of e-HR

It is always easy to be carried away by success stories like those mentioned earlier in this chapter and those that e-HR systems suppliers are only too willing to tell you. But, in reality, many organisations that have invested in e-HR systems have not yet seen a positive return. A survey carried out by Watson Wyatt in 2002[14] revealed that many companies were not achieving the returns on investment that they had expected. However, the report went on to identify three factors that seemed to be common amongst those companies that were experiencing success.

Factor 1: a formal documented e-HR policy

Many organisations have introduced e-HR systems by using something here and something there and then adding a little something else along the way that seemed to be a good idea at the time. This approach does not work unless you are very lucky. The successful organisations were those that had carefully analysed where e-HR could best help the business and had then written this down in a formal strategy document that:

- outlined what systems that they would introduce and when they would do this

- had the full support of senior management and other stakeholders.

According to the Watson Wyatt survey, only 20 per cent of organisations responding to the survey had actually done this, but these reported a 28 per cent better cost efficiency for the HR Department than the other 80 per cent.

A strategic plan for implementing an e-HR system should contain a number of elements:

- what systems you are going to introduce and when

- what hardware and software will be needed

- what you will do to manage the organisational issues that will arise

- how the technological issues arising from the implementation will be managed and who will be responsible for them

- what the measures of success for the new systems will be and how this information will be used to guide and improve implementation.

Factor 2: A business case

Having a business case that explained exactly how implementing an e-HR system would benefit the business was also shown to be a crucial success factor. This observation would seem to fit the circumstances of the late 1990s when, in the period leading up to the dot.com bubble bursting, anything that had an 'e-' in front of it was assumed to be a guaranteed success. Many companies therefore ploughed ahead with investments in e-HR systems without establishing a business case. After the bursting of the bubble and with clouds gathering over the global economy in 2001 organisations started to realise the importance of only making investments once a business case had been established.

 How to go about developing a business case is covered in Chapter 3.

Factor 3: A best-fit solution

The third success factor was shown to be the implementation of solutions that really did support the key operations of the business. This can only be done by thinking carefully about how the business works and how HR can help improve its effectiveness. Organisations wanting to do this carry out a value chain analysis, which is described in more detail in Chapter 3.

Summarising ...

This chapter has explained some of the basic ideas underlying e-HR. Here is a summary of what the chapter has covered.

- E-HR refers to the application of web technologies to deliver HR services.

- E-HR can be used to provide administrative functions, such as personal information and absence management, as well as strategic functions such as performance management, e-learning and providing extra benefits to employees.

- E-HR can provide a number of benefits:

    - new opportunities for HR

    - better support to management throughout the business

    - greater potential for organisational collaboration and learning

    - enhanced organisational prestige

    - reduced administrative costs

    - a happier workforce.

- Introducing e-HR also presents a number of challenges:

    - Hoped-for returns may not be achieved.

    - Barriers between HR and IT will need to be broken down.

    - The profile of HR will be raised.

    - HR staff must become more customer-focused.

    - HR staff must develop a better understanding of the business.

- There is a danger of HR losing contact with people.

- Information security becomes a much more important issue.

- Everyone must have adequate access to the system.

- E-HR systems must not discriminate against people with disabilities.

- E-HR systems may introduce ethical problems as a result of changes in processes.

- It may be difficult to take transnational cultural differences into account.

- Getting the best out of e-HR requires a formal strategy, a business case and best-fit solutions.

Notes

1. PeopleSoft, (2001), 'The ABCs of Return on Investment', http://www.peoplesoft.com/corp/en/products/line/hrms/articles/hrms_roi.asp

2. *Cedar 2001 Human Resources Self Service/Portal Survey*, Cedar, http://usa.cedar.com/USA/whitepapers/

3. Watson Wyatt, (2001), *Human Capital Index: Human Capital as a Lead Indicator of Shareholder Value*, http://www.watsonwyatt.com/research/

4. Fitz-Enz, J. (2000), *The ROI of Human Capital: Measuring the Economic Value of Employee Performance*, New York: Amacom

5. Watson Wyatt, (2002), *B2E/eHR Survey Results 2002*, Watson Wyatt, http://www.watsonwyatt.com/research/resrender.asp?id=2000861&page=1

6. *Online Employee Services: Benchmark Findings*, extracted from *Innovative Practices in Human Resources*, quoted in www.human-resources.org/online-employee-systems.htm

7. Harrington, A., (2000) 'Self service HR', *CA Magazine*, November, **Vol. 104**, No. 1132.

8. Wiscombe, J., (2001) 'Using Technology to Cut Costs', *Workforce*, September 2001, **Vol. 80**, No. 9.

9. *Cedar 2001 Survey*, note 2 above.

10. PeopleSoft, (2002), Organisational Diagnostics report (unnamed), cited in 'Workforce Analytics Return on Investment', http://www.peoplesoft.com/servlet/SmartInquiry/WE00005299/email

11. Becker, B. E., Huselid, M. A., and Ulrich D., (2001), *The HR Scorecard: Linking People, Strategy, and Performance*, New London, CT: Harvard Business School Press.

12. Robinson, D., (1997), 'HR Information Systems: Stand and Deliver', www.employment-studies.co.uk/summary/335sum.html, extracted from report of same name, Institute for Employment Studies.

13. *Cedar 2001 Survey*, note 2 above.

14. Trapp, R., (2001), 'Of Mice and Men (E-human Resource Management)', *People Management*, June, **Vol. 7**, No. 13.

15. Buckley, R et al, (2001) 'Ethical issues in human resources systems', *Human Resource Management Review*, **Vol** 11, pages 11-29.

16. Watson Wyatt, (2002), 'eHR: Getting Results Along the Journey, http://www.watsonwyatt.com/research/resrender.asp?id=W-524&page=1

chapter 2

How does intranet technology work?

In Chapter 1 we referred to the need for HR staff to become more comfortable with IT. The aim of this chapter, therefore, is to provide an explanation of the technology underlying e-HR systems. As with all explanations of technology it is hard to know just how far to go with an explanation, so those readers who feel that they would like more information are pointed in the direction of the many books available that discuss networking, intranets and the Internet in more detail.

This chapter is therefore aimed at readers with a limited understanding of how intranet technology works. Readers who feel comfortable with the subject are invited to skip the chapter and move on.

Networks and intranets

In order for data to pass between computers within a network, each computer must package the data that it is sending in a way that other computers in the network can understand, much as human beings who wish to communicate must find a common language. This is achieved by the use of a **network protocol**. There are a number of different protocols in use, and which ones any particular network uses depends on a variety of factors, such as the operating systems employed within that specific network. Networks usually operate several different protocols at the same time, again just as a group of people may find they need to use several different languages in order for everyone to understand what is being talked about.

One such protocol is **TCP/IP**, which stands for Transmission Control Protocol/Internet Protocol. This is the protocol used by computers communicating within the Internet, and its adoption within internal networks has led to the creation of **intranets**. Intranets and the Internet are therefore functionally identical, the only difference being that an intranet is a network internal to an organisation while the Internet links computers all over the world using ordinary telephone lines. As e-HR systems are generally operated within organisations on intranets (although some users may connect via the Internet) we shall use the term intranet in this book to describe the network being used.

Figure 2.1 shows the essential components of an intranet.

The heart of the network is the server, although in larger networks there may be many servers. Individual computers are connected to these servers by network cables. Note that these cables will be the same ones that have been used by other networking applications long before an intranet was established. Setting up an organisational intranet does not therefore mean that a new network has to be installed: it is simply a new way of using an existing network. Older-established networks may not actually be using the TCP/IP protocol, but implementing it is not difficult.

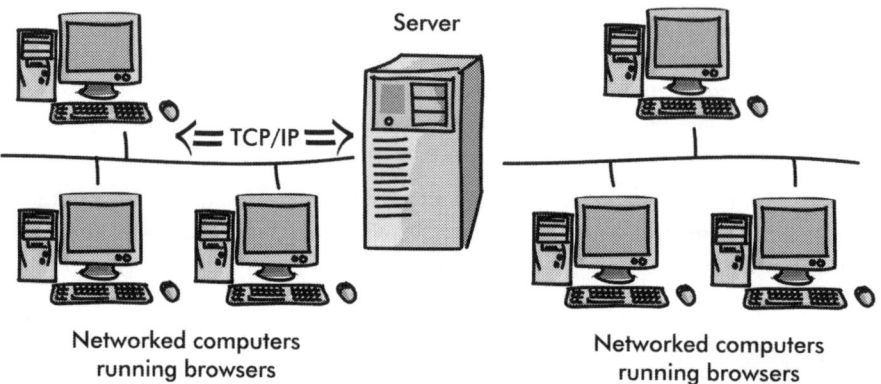

Figure 2.1
Essential components of an intranet

Anyone on the network who wants to access the intranet must have a **browser** installed on their computer. This is an application specially designed for navigating intranets and the Internet. The market leaders here are Microsoft Internet Explorer, mainly because it is an integral part of all modern versions of Windows operating systems, and Netscape Navigator. Apart from minor differences between how these display information on-screen and more significant differences in facilities provided to the user, they are more or less interchangeable. However, to minimise problems caused by the inconsistencies and to simplify maintenance issues most organisations standardise on one or the other and ask suppliers to optimise systems for that particular browser.

Within the browser will be stored:

- the name of the server to look for when it is opened, and

- the filename of a particular page to ask the server to send.

This is what people usually refer to as the browser's homepage. Let us assume that the browser automatically looks for 'http://intranet.acme.com/homepage' when it is opened. A string such as this is known as a **URL**, or Universal Resource Locator, or often just as a 'web address'. A URL contains three elements:

- a protocol identifying the type of information, in this case 'http'. (HTTP stands for **Hypertext Transfer Protocol**, which is a code sent out by a computer that wants to make contact with a web server holding web pages; by contrast, a computer that is looking to copy files from another computer would send out its request using the File Transfer Protocol, or FTP).

- the name of the server, in this case 'intranet.acme.com'.

- the specific filename needed, in this case 'homepage'.

The user opens their browser. This first checks that the computer is connected to a network and, if so, will then look for a web page (because of the 'http') on the browser's homepage server ('intranet.acme.com') called 'homepage'.

The homepage server will be running special web server software that looks for requests for data using HTTP coming from the network. Examples of web server software are Microsoft Internet Information Server or Netscape Communications Server.

Once the browser has found the server it sends a message using HTTP saying that it wants to see the contents of the homepage file, '/homepage'. The server sends the file to the computer, packaging up the data and sending it using TCP/IP. The browser translates it into a readable format using HTTP so that it can display the contents on the screen.

The user then looks at other pages by typing a new URL into the browser or by clicking on a **hyperlink** within the content of the page that automatically sends a URL to the relevant server. In this way the user can move from page to page.

What a web page contains and how it looks on-screen is specified by the language used to create the page, **HTML**. HTML stands for Hypertext Markup Language, which is a programming language originally developed to enable the display of text in a browser. Although it has developed in sophistication over the years, it remains somewhat limited in what it can do and so considerable effort has been made to develop other languages that can work alongside HTML to increase the functionality of web pages. This includes such languages as Java and JavaScript which allow the browser to instruct the computer to carry out operations, rather than passively display information.

Another new language of increasing importance that works alongside HTML, and which will in due course replace it, is **XML** (Extensible Markup Language). This actually comes from the same origins as HTML but has been designed to be much more flexible. Strictly speaking, it is not a programming language at all, but more what programmers call a metalanguage. It is used to develop a 'style sheet', a block of code that is attached to a file that enables the browser to display the information in the file exactly as it would be in its native application. Browsers will therefore be able to display information created using word processors, spreadsheets or databases just as it was intended to be displayed. This clearly opens up a huge range of possibilities for integrating organisation-wide information. If you want to find out more about XML you will find an ever-growing number of books written specifically on this subject.

XML stylesheets can be designed to meet the needs of specialist applications. A number of these are appearing, including some designed to make HR information available. These are being referred to as HR-XML.

 If you want to find out more about the development of HR-XML, you can look at the work of the HR-XML Consortium:

- www.hr-xml.org/channels/home.htm

How intranets have developed in complexity

The previous section has described the principles of a simple intranet. You will find that modern intranets, although relying on the same underlying technologies of HTTP, TCP/IP and HTML, are much more complex, so let us now take a look at how this development has occurred. This will help you understand how the basic ideas behind e-HR have developed.

First-generation intranets

These are simple intranets designed for the user simply to look at. The user cannot enter any information and the content stays the same until someone edits the file on the server. Pages such as this are very common on sites developed by people with little technical knowledge or time. Pages in such sites are usually described as 'static', as the information on each page is fixed and does not change in any way.

Their chief disadvantage is that such pages rarely change and so, from a user's point of view, there is often little point in going back and reading them.

This should be the stage at which HR Departments start to think about how they should structure their intranet site. The key page is the homepage, the first page that people will see when they look for HR on the intranet. It is key because if people do not feel attracted by what they see, the chances are that they will not look any further. Figure 2.2 shows how a simple HR site could be structured.

The home page contains high-level information and is essentially a menu showing where more detailed information is to be found. So, for example, a user wanting information on health and safety training would click on a hyperlink within the home-page that would take them to the 'Learning and development opportunities' page. From there another link could take them to a page containing specific information on health and safety training.

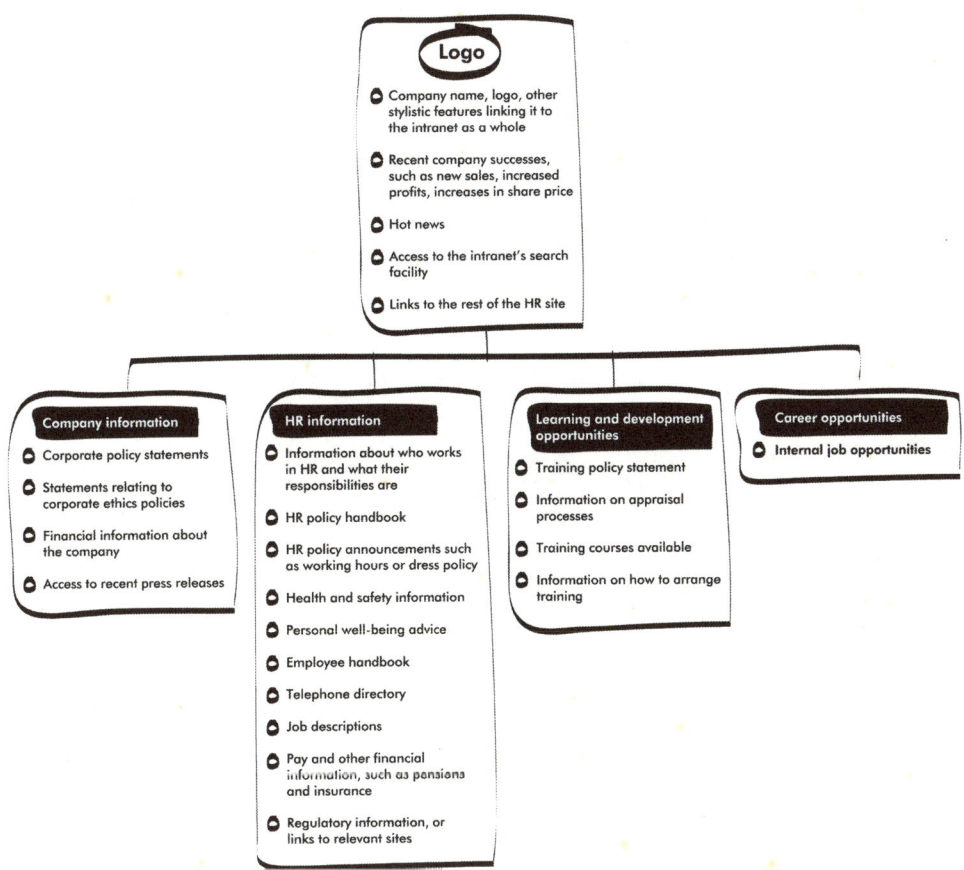

Figure 2.2
Typical basic HR site

Second-generation intranets

Second-generation intranets, like first-generation intranets, contain static pages, but they do allow the user to carry out limited activities. Such sites will usually contain the same sort of information as described above. For example, the page may contain a holiday request form and the user can print this out, write their information on the form and post it to the HR department. Alternatively, they may click on a hyperlink that allows them to download a word processor document that they can complete and e-mail to HR.

Development of such pages requires some extra technical knowledge, but they are well within the bounds of possibility for a reasonably computer-literate person with access to a modern web design package such as Microsoft FrontPage or Macromedia Dreamweaver.

Watson Wyatt's e-HR survey of 2002[1] reported that 74 per cent of businesses were still using such static intranets for HR services. However, looked set to be changing quickly: 75 per cent of their respondents were planning to move to the next generation in intranet development by 2004. Let us now take a look at what such technology implies.

Figure 2.3
Second-generation intranet

Third-generation intranets

The step up to a third-generation site is very significant. Rather than being pages always containing the same, fixed content, they are now designed to extract information from and post information to a database. For example, an area on a web page in a first- or second-generation site would contain fixed text. However, in a third-generation site the area will load content from a database and display this.

There are three reasons why the small step from second to third generation is actually a giant leap:

- It becomes much easier to change the content of web pages, as all you have to do is change the information in the database. You do not need to have specialist web programming skills.

- Users can now enter information directly into a central database that can be accessed by other people. This cuts out a level of processing.

Because the information on the page comes from a database, it can display information fed into the database from other sources.

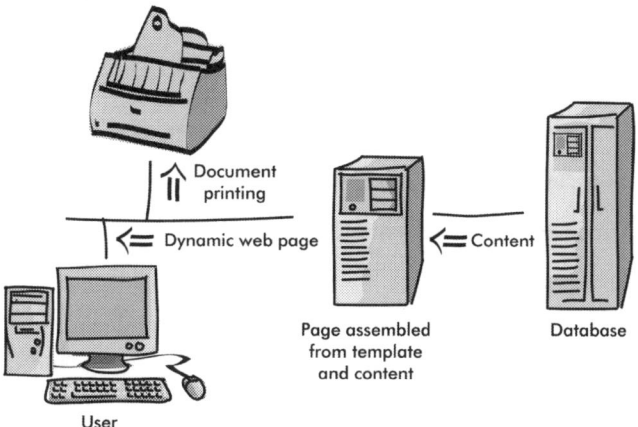

Figure 2.4
Third-generation intranet

The disadvantage with this level of sophistication is that it now requires high-level programming skills and special databases. First- and second- generation intranets use servers that simply retrieve files requested by browsers and send the data back, but third-generation servers must send instructions to databases asking for specific information, retrieve this and send it on to the browser.

There are various ways in which this can be done. The original way was by using conventional programming languages to write special scripts known as Common Gateway Interface (CGI) scripts. However this method is generally being replaced by other techniques that are more efficient and easier to program, such as Microsoft's Active Server Pages (ASPs, not to be confused with Application Service Provider, which is something completely different) and PHP, a language specially developed to link HTML pages with databases.

While it would be quite feasible for an enthusiastic HR person to put together first- and second- generation pages, third generation pages require significant involvement of the IT department or outside suppliers.

As well as the difficulties created by wanting the browser and database to talk to each other, security now becomes an issue. If users can change the data held on central databases, you must make sure that the users are who they say they are!

The scope of such intranets is potentially much broader than for first- and second-generation intranets. Users can now carry out many more HR-related functions using the intranet, for example:

- enrolling on training courses
- updating personal information

- applying for leave on-line.

The ready availability of on-line information means that there may now be a separate section available to managers, where they can interrogate the system for statistical information. For example, they may want to look for information on:

- absenteeism in their department

- performance appraisal information for their staff

- salary costs.

It is only when an HR intranet reaches this level of sophistication that it can start to help the HR Department take on a more strategic role within the organisation.

Fourth-generation intranets

Fourth-generation pages currently represent the highest level of sophistication. Such systems recognise the user on the basis of their logging in details and then present information on the page that is relevant to that particular person. People with managerial responsibility would therefore receive different or additional information and be offered more functionality than people with no managerial responsibility. Staff working in a London office could be provided with different information from those working in, say, Edinburgh.

Such systems are often described as **role-based** or as employee **portals**. Portals are increasingly being used to provide 'the prime electronic point of contact between an organisation and its customers, partners, suppliers and employees'.[2] They do this by providing a single interface through which authorised people can access information stored in the multitude of databases that modern organisations rely on.

As discussed in Chapter 1, older, legacy technology relies on the client-server model, where users have to have special client software on their computer if they are to be able to access data stored in the server, which means that such data is only available to a select few. Not only that, each system requires a separate sign on procedure so that users may have to enter several different user names and passwords. Because the systems are discrete and may not interconnect, users may have to manually record data from one system on the back of a convenient cigarette packet and then enter it again into another system in order to extract the precise information they require.

It is important to note that sometimes portals are not actually delivered through a standard browser. They may be designed to look very much like a standard browser, but they still use client-server technology designed so that the software needed on the user's computer is as small as possible. For this reason they are sometimes known as **thin-client** systems, although in time it is quite possible that such applications may disappear to be replaced by pure browser systems.

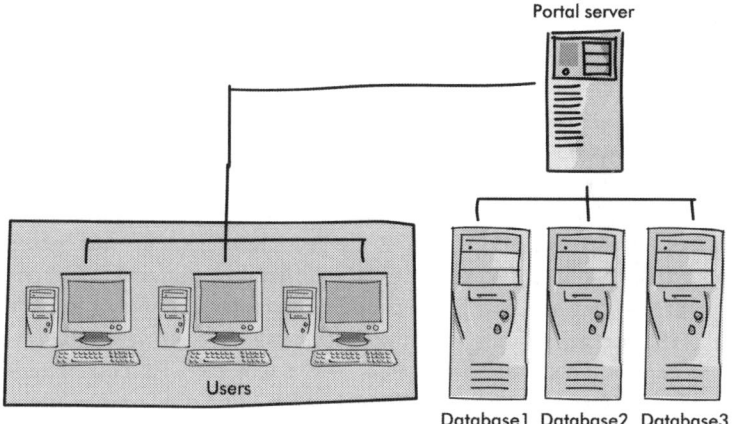

Portal server

Users

Database1 Database2 Database3

Figure 2.5
Portal system

The term 'thin-client' is used somewhat liberally in this context. It is really a term used to describe a generic hardware configuration where a server does all the data processing and a user's computer merely displays the output. However, in the e-HR context, it is also used to describe both a browser and a specific application client. So when a computer salesperson refers to their system as using a 'thin-client' approach, it may be worthwhile clarifying exactly what they mean by this.

Portals are tools for employees and managers allowing access to multiple databases, making such things as monitoring performance, resource deployment and collaboration much easier. With a portal, the user logs in once, the system recognises who they are and what system rights they have and opens connections to whatever database they need. They can pull data from different databases simultaneously, making it possible to instantly generate information that would have previously taken hours.

Human resources information is only part of this. Depending on the extent to which the portal has been woven into the fabric of the organisation, it may be possible to call on data relating to sales, stock levels or share price, for example. HR managers can then query the system to see if there is any correlation between the competency levels in a department and sales performance, or between training hours undertaken and absenteeism.

With the level of programming complexity that such systems require, they move beyond the realms of most internal IT departments and are generally purchased from specialist external suppliers. They require significant investment although it is possible to arrange for external companies to manage data on your behalf. Described as Application Service Providers (ASPs) they install the e-HR system on their network and clients transfer data via public telephone networks or leased line systems as necessary. This can prove to be a much cheaper and easier solution.

 ASPs are discussed in more detail in Chapter 8.

Because fourth-generation intranets seek to integrate information from a wide variety of sources it has become increasingly important to find ways in which different types of information can be displayed through a common platform. In the early years of the Internet and intranets this was done by HTML but, as the years have gone by, this has become less and less standard, so that now, for example, HTML that runs perfectly on Microsoft's Internet Explorer may not necessarily run properly on Netscape's Navigator. The original designers of HTML also never imagined how today's users would want to use it to display information, so its functionality is quite limited. This is why XML (discussed earlier), as a language that allows information from different sources to be displayed as intended, is becoming of increasing importance.

Summarising ...

- Intranets and the Internet use the same technologies of HTTP, TCP/IP and HTML.

- New technologies such as Java and XML are being developed to make web pages more functional and allow them to display information more effectively.

- First-generation intranets use static web pages and provide no functionality to the user.

- Second-generation intranets also use static web pages but provide some simple functionality, such as the ability to download documents.

- Third-generation intranets rely on dynamic web pages where the content of pages is pulled from a database and displayed to users within a template. Users can also send information to the database.

- Fourth-generation intranets recognise who is accessing a page and modify the content appropriately as well as providing full third-generation functionality.

Notes

1. Watson Wyatt, (2002), *B2E/eHR Survey Results 2002*, Watson Wyatt, http://www.watsonwyatt.com/research/resrender.asp?id=2000861&page=1

2. Howlett, D and Rodgers, K, (2002), 'Delivering Value Back to the Business', available from: www.portalsforprofit.co.uk.

chapter 3

What kind of e-HR is right for your business?

The aim of this chapter is to show you how you can identify where e-HR could be of most benefit to your business. This is a very important thing to do, as it can be very easy to listen to the 21st century version of the snake oil salesperson and invest in an e-HR system that does not provide you with the returns that you expected. The chapter looks in general terms at the function of HR within any business and looks at how these HR-related processes can be improved by the introduction of an e-HR system. You will find that each of the functions discussed is covered in greater detail in subsequent chapters.

A process for planning an e-HR system

If you have read the glossy brochures produced by HR software companies you will have come to realise that such systems can provide many different services. You will be unlikely (and probably unwise) to decide to buy everything your supplier can provide, so you will find yourself having to make decisions: what e-HR solutions will be of most value to your business?

There are two ways you can go about making this decision. One way is to do what you have always done and use e-HR to deliver the services you have always provided in the past. But are these the right services? Are these the services where e-HR can really make a difference to the business? If you can confidently say 'yes' to these questions and provide the evidence that they are the services to offer, excellent. If you cannot do this, then you must go back to the basics of what your business is about and decide where e-HR really can add value.

One report[1] suggests that, despite a 40 per cent increase in IT investment in HR services since 1998, HR costs for the average company have actually risen by 16 per cent. This was attributed to organisations often failing to consider how technology could be used to its fullest extent to streamline and automate processes: businesses merely used IT to automate what they had always done, and if that was a sow's ear to start off with …

In the following pages, we look at how to put together a plan that will justify an investment in e-HR. The process is summarised in Figure 3.1. Each step in the process you must follow is explained in more detail in the following sections of this chapter, but to summarise:

1. Where are you now? Think here about the big picture for HR service delivery and management in your organisation.

2. Analyse what goes on in your business and see where HR can add value. You do this by carrying out a value chain analysis of what your business does.

3. Identify what constraints you must work under:

    *   What is your budget?

    *   What are your technical constraints?

    *   Are any business-critical systems involved?

- What are the cultural issues?

4. Look at what you have found out about what your business wants and what your infrastructure can allow it to have and make your decisions about what systems will actually work and will offer the most benefit to the business. This will allow you to put together your first draft e-HR blueprint.

5. Prepare a business case to justify what you are proposing. Without this analysis you will not be able to win the investment necessary. Eliminate any aspects that you cannot justify financially and finalise the content of your blueprint.

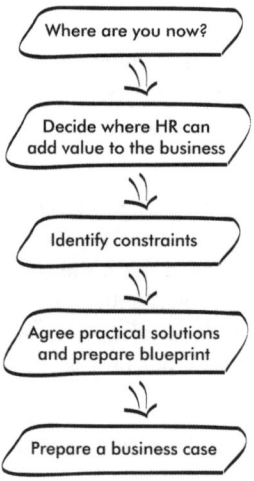

Figure 3.1
The process for deciding on an e-HR solution

Where are you now?

Before getting down to detail you need to think about how your HR service delivery and management function fits into the big picture. Ask yourself questions such as:

- What is the status of your HR Department?

- What successes (or failures) has it had in recent times?

- What influence does it have in the organisation?

- Who are other people in the organisation who must be won over?

- What is the organisation's philosophy and what implications does that have for an e-HR solution?

- Where is the business going and what implications does this have for HR?

It is important to think about questions such as this before going any further because embarking on an e-HR route may be a journey into unexplored territory. On the way, you will have to win and manage big budgets, deal with the mysteries of the IT Department and make sure that what you propose fits into the business's overall strategies. Be prepared.

Decide where you can add value using e-HR

Once you have painted the big picture, you can start to look at the detail. As discussed in Chapter 1, implementing e-HR means that HR staff must become much more proactive in finding out who their internal customers are and what they want. Only by doing this can you draw up a list of priorities.

A useful way to do this is to think about the concept of the value chain, as developed by Michael Porter.[2] He defined the value chain as '... a collection of activities that are performed to design, produce, market, deliver and support [the business's] product.' Activities are physically distinct operations that use such things as material inputs, human resources, technology and information to create material outputs and information.

He went on to identify a number of different types of value activity and to distinguish between **primary** activities (those specifically concerned with the actual purpose of the business) and **support** activities (those activities that run across the primary activities and enable them to happen). He represented these activities in a manner similar to Figure 3.2.

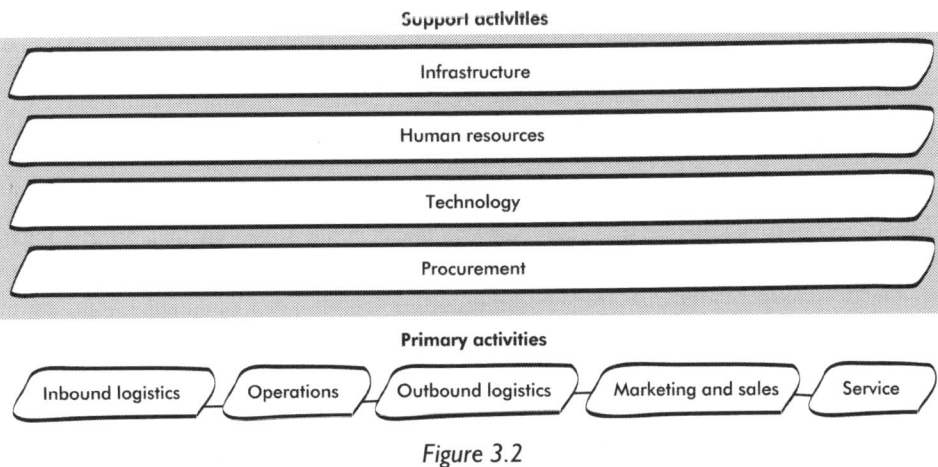

Figure 3.2
A generic value chain

In general terms a value chain summarises the process by which an organisation adds value to inputs and then provides them as outputs to customers. So a supermarket buys in foodstuffs (inbound logistics), distributes them and merchandises them in its branches (operations) and provides a means for customers to buy the foodstuffs (outbound logistics). Marketing and sales encourages customers to visit the branches and service looks after customers' queries. Clearly the balance between the different primary activities will vary from one type of business to another, but in all cases you will be able to identify the five different activities.

HR is a support activity: it runs across all five primary activities, providing a range of services to the people responsible for the primary activities. As such, it could be seen to act like a lubricant for the chain, making sure that the links move together efficiently and that each link in the chain is able to add the value that is necessary.

Using the value chain concept

When deciding how e-HR can best benefit your business it is important to think about what lubricating activities HR carries out. Once you have identified these processes you can start to think about:

- how much they are actually costing the organisation so that by breaking down the costing process you can see where savings can be made

- how the technology associated with e-HR has the potential to improve or add value to the process.

To help you decide what areas to look at in more detail, ask yourself questions such as these:

- In what areas of the business do employees need more motivation?

- Are any managers asking for more help with managing their staff?

- Do you have any evidence, or are you being told, that the HR function is costing too much?

- Are there any areas of the business where more training is required?

- How effectively does information flow around the business?

Answers to questions such as these will help you decide what areas may be a priority for e-HR applications. You can then start to probe more deeply into these areas to see where e-HR may be able to add value or reduce costs.

Be aware that you will be able to identify financial benefits under three headings (see Figure 3.3):

1. **Direct tangible**, essentially reducing costs – for example, eliminating data processing activities and paper from production, distribution and storage.

2. **Indirect tangible**, or improving productivity, where time spent by staff on routine administrative tasks is freed up for profit-generating work.

3. **Intangible**, or adding strategic value, where the improved access and availability of information enables new things to be done.

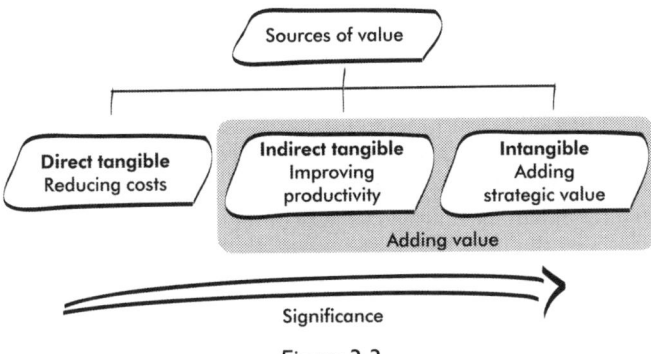

Figure 3.3
Financial benefits due to e-HR

We can consider the second two items under a more general heading of adding value. You will find that adding strategic value is the most significant of these, although it is also the hardest to quantify. Let us look at these in more detail.

Direct tangible benefits

Direct tangible benefits are those cost savings that arise immediately from changes in HR procedures, and these are probably the most obvious areas to consider. Examples will include such changes as:

- savings in administrative time

- reduced printing, distribution and storage costs.

You will be making savings on salary costs if staff are made redundant as a result of introducing an e-HR system. However, you must also take into account the costs of redundancy, such as redundancy payments, counselling and so on.

However, for most organisations the savings made from this source are likely to be relatively small. Even large organisations may only have perhaps 20 or so people working in HR and previous downsizing activities will often mean that the numbers currently employed are at a minimum. With organisations spread over different sites or even countries you may already have reached a staffing level below which you would not be able to carry out such things as statutory obligations. The scope for making significant savings from this route is therefore limited for most businesses.

Cost savings in such things as printing, distribution and storage will also be measurable but probably not huge, especially when compared with the costs of implementing an e-HR solution. Also remember that savings on such things as storage costs may mean that extra storage space is available for other business activities.

Indirect tangible benefits

Indirect cost savings are those that arise from improving staff productivity by changing business procedures. Here are some examples of where this can happen:

- Because staff are not spending time carrying out routine and administrative tasks they have more time available for their productive responsibilities, which should mean that their output increases.

- There will be specific benefits associated with each particular type of e-HR implemented. For example, an e-recruitment system may mean that you can find a suitable candidate for managing a new business project much more quickly than you could, had you used traditional methods. With this new project manager in place more quickly, the project will be up and running and generating profits earlier. There will also probably be cost savings for the business function concerned, such as in administrative time, preparation of adverts and so on, although these are likely to be small compared to the benefits.

- You will also see indirect tangible benefits in the increased productivity of HR staff who were formerly employed in data processing.

Intangible benefits

Intangible benefits are those that come from doing new things that were not previously possible. Often with such benefits you can see that benefits and savings will occur but it is impossible to state a figure. For example, you think that the new system will improve communication and collaboration between some departments and this will improve the performance of the business, but by how much?

There are two points to make here. Firstly, the soft benefits that you claim must be consistent with the organisation's strategy. Closer integration with the business must mean that everything you do is in line with the direction the business is moving in. Secondly, rather than wasting time trying to come up with figures quantifying the benefits, you may find it more useful to think about the competitive advantage offered by the new systems. How will improved communication and collaboration between departments position your business against your competitors?

Working out the benefits

Derived from a structure proposed by Armstrong,[3] Table 3.1 provides a summary of many HR functions and processes for which e-HR may have some relevance. It also shows what costs are associated with these processes and where e-HR has the potential to add value to the business.

Table 3.1

HR functions and the potential for reducing costs and adding value

Function	Processes	Associated costs	Potential for adding value
Organisation	Administration of personal information	Production, storage and distribution of paper forms	Elimination of errors
		Administrative time in processing paper forms	
	Promoting collaboration	Travelling time, expenses and associated opportunity costs	Flexible, world-wide collaboration
Knowledge management	Disseminating knowledge		Easier access to internal information
Resourcing	Resource planning	Opportunity costs of absences in key posts due to retirement, other natural wastage	Proactive planning for training and recruitment needed
	Recruitment	Advertising	Identification of potential candidates
		Agency fees	
		Interviewing costs	Pre-interview on-line testing, improving average quality of interviewees
			New jobholders in post more quickly
	Time and attendance	Administrative time	Real-time analysis of absence patterns
Performance management	Managing training	Trainer time	Greater flexibility for providing training
		Cost of printing and distributing training materials	Access to wider range of materials
		Administrative time in maintaining records	Streamlined process for managing training and individuals' learning records
	Managing appraisal programmes		Centralised storage and easier access
			Potential for linking to training opportunities

			and internal recruitment procedures
Reward management	Managing payroll processes	Printing and distribution costs Administrative time dealing with enquiries Administrative time transferring information between different systems	Faster links between performance and reward, leading to improve motivation
	Managing benefit systems	Printing, storage and distribution of paper information Administrative time updating and distributing information, processing benefits	Greater flexibility in managing benefits
Employee relations	Providing information	Administrative time	Information to those who need it when they need it
	Conducting surveys	Developing and distributing questionnaires Administrative time dealing with responses	Streamlined distribution processes Automated calculation of responses

By getting to know your business better you will develop an understanding of what areas falling within the HR remit are preventing the primary activities from working to their full potential. You should then try to quantify the costs of these issues and see how, by streamlining and automating the process through an e-HR application, you could improve their efficiency and cut costs.

Let us look at some of these areas and see how we can quantify how e-HR can reduce costs or add value to the business. These areas are all discussed in more detail in subsequent chapters, so here we shall confine ourselves to a brief description of how costs could be reduced or value added.

Administration of personal information

Personal information relating to employees is typically held within paper records or client-server HR information systems. Changes to this information rely on employees informing the HR Department of new information, often using paper forms, and this is then clerically entered into the official records. We therefore need to consider the costs of both this traditional process and the e-HR alternative.

Costs associated with changes in procedures are often calculated using a technique known as **activity-based costing** (ABC). Using this method you break down each step involved in a process and record the time that each step requires. Then, knowing the hourly cost for the employee carrying out the step, you can calculate the total cost of the procedure.

Table 3.2 shows an example of the costs incurred whenever an employee needs to make a change to their basic personal details, such as a change of address.

Table 3.2
Activity-based costing for recording
change of address using traditional methods

Step	Who	Step	Process time (mins)	Elapsed time (days)	Labour costs (£)
1	Employee	Completes change of address form	5	1	0.92
2	Employee	Employee submits form to HR Department	3	2	0.55
3	Administrator	HR administrator updates HR system	5	2	0.78
				Total process costs	2.26

Using labour costs taken from the Office of Statistics New Earnings Survey 2001[4] for public sector clerical and managerial grades[5], this shows that, based on these estimated times for completing each task, the whole process costs £2.26 each time it is done. Note that we have not considered the cost of producing, and distributing and transmitting the paper change of address forms. In a full analysis, you would need to take these costs into account as well.

Now look at the alternative where the process has been automated using a self-service HR system.

Table 3.3
Activity-based costing for recording change of address using e-HR

Step	Who	Step	Process time (mins)	Elapsed time (days)	Labour costs (£)
I	Employee	Completes change of address form on-line	3	I	0.55
				Total process costs	0.55

You can see that there is a considerable saving. The employee spends less time on the process because they can easily find the change of address form on-line. Administrative costs for transferring information from the paper form on to the system are cut out completely. And because the system is updated immediately by the employee, there is no elapsed time during which correspondence could be sent to the old address and the possibility of transcription error is eliminated.

The saving for this transaction is £1.71. Of course, this is for one transaction by a single employee so you must now consider how many employees will be carrying out this transaction and how often they will do it. For example, if you had 500 employees and on average they change some part of their personal details five times a year, the total savings would be £4275 each year.

Repeat this analysis for every aspect of HR administration that you carry out and that could be automated by e-HR and you will start to see a sizeable saving.

Also reflect on the added value created by having accurate information.

Promoting collaboration

Collaboration costs time and money. People look for ways to avoid going to meetings because of the time that they will take to get to the venue, and training programmes are cut or offered in inappropriate formats because of the cost of delivering classroom-based events. Of course, there are always two sides to such cost-cutting decisions. Cutting down on meetings during a product development project may mean that vital information is not imparted and sub-optimal delivery of training may mean that people's performances lack the quality they should have.

Let us think about the range of costs associated with a meeting to which people must travel:

- travel costs for each participant (mileage, flights or train fares and taxis)
- overnight accommodation if necessary
- hire of facilities for meeting
- subsistence costs, such as lunch or evening meals

- loss of productivity while travelling.

Try working out the costs for meetings held within your organisation and you will see just how expensive meetings can actually be. An on-line collaborative tool can eliminate all of these costs. If you multiply the costs per meeting by the number of meetings you expect each year and then compare this with the cost of buying or renting a collaborative software package you should see a very attractive return on your investment.

And, of course, by making collaboration more attractive from a cost point of view, more collaboration can take place, improving the effectiveness of the organisation.

 On-line collaborative tools and how they can be used are covered in more detail in Chapter 6.

Disseminating knowledge

More and more people are being described as 'knowledge workers', their effectiveness depending on what they know and how they use that knowledge. The principles of synergy tell us that the whole is greater than the sum of its parts, but bringing all of the individual elements of an organisation's knowledge together into a coherent whole has traditionally proved extremely difficult. There are the practical difficulties of spreading knowledge and information or making it easily accessible, and perhaps more importantly, the cultural challenges associated with encouraging people to share what they know: after all, knowledge is power.

Although intranet technology cannot do very much about the cultural challenges, it can provide a means by which knowledge and information can be disseminated more effectively. Many knowledge-based organisations are starting to find ways by which their employees can share what they know, and they are reaping the benefits in terms of an increased competitive advantage.

 Knowledge management and the technologies available are discussed in Chapter 6.

Resource planning

'People are our greatest asset'. E-HR allows you to walk that talk more effectively. While it is very easy to compile an inventory of an organisation's equipment and machinery and see how this fits in with the business strategy, it can be very difficult to do the same thing for the people assets. HR Departments may jealously guard such information, perhaps for valid reasons of confidentiality, but the problems of gathering such information at a departmental level means that it can be difficult to decide how well-equipped, from the people point of view, the business is for a new venture.

This has its costs. A business may start a new venture and then discover that it does not have enough people with the necessary skills, or conversely it may decide against seizing a new opportunity because it is not confident that it has the necessary people. Some organisations face demographic issues as large percentages of the most skilled and highly-qualified people moving towards retirement age, but the evidence for this is only anecdotal.

E-HR systems can provide tools that make it much easier to collect, store and make available information about skills and knowledge available within the organisation. This can allow departments to make quicker and better-informed decisions about new ventures.

Recruitment

There are various aspects of the recruitment process that we can analyse and attempt to cost. Firstly, let us look at the cost of finding a new employee, what Fitz-Enz[6] calls the **cost per hire**. He calculates this from the following:

$$\text{Cost per hire} = \frac{AC + AF + RB + TC + RE + RC + NC}{H} + 10\%$$

where:

AC = advertising costs
AF = agency fees
RB = referral bonus
TC = travel costs
RE = relocation
RC = recruiter costs
NC = unsolicited no-cost CVs
H = number of people recruited

You should be able to identify all this information from your previous recruiting activities, so that you can calculate how much you are currently spending on the process of recruiting a single employee.

How might e-HR be able to help? One obvious area is in advertising. If you are advertising externally through such things as national newspapers, these costs are likely to be considerable, especially if you are only recruiting a small number of people through the advertisements. Even for internal recruitment, there will be advertising costs, principally the time required to produce the advertisements and the distribution costs. Contrast this with the costs through an intranet or Internet solution. You post details of the positions on your intranet and Internet web site, use proactive methods to make sure that qualified people know about the vacancies and you should find that the advertising costs are greatly reduced.

As well as allowing you to reduce costs, an e-HR-based approach to recruitment (referred to here as **e-recruitment**) offers potential for adding value to the recruitment process. For example, let us think about a measure of the speed of the recruitment process, the **time to fill**.

$$\text{Time to fill} = \text{Date person starts job} - \text{Date vacancy identified}$$

Essentially, by speeding up the process by which potential applicants find out about the post and apply for it, considerable savings in the time to fill can be made, perhaps of the order of several weeks or even a few months (see Figure 3.4). So how does this add value to the business? Clearly while a post is vacant nobody is doing the necessary work. Other people may have to cover for this or, if the post is a new one, it will not be generating income for the business. Therefore any saving in time to fill is adding value.

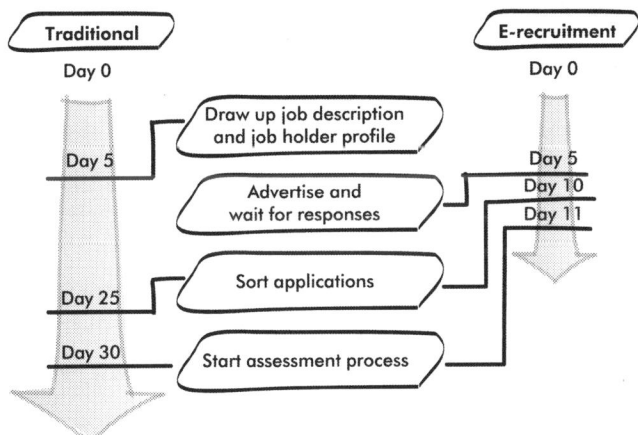

Figure 3.4
Speeding up the recruitment process
E-recruitment saves time by targeting likely applicants and speeding up the advertising process, as well as making applying and sorting applications easier.

 There is an example of how e-recruitment compares with traditional methods in Chapter 5.

You can also use the cost per hire figure when investigating the cost of staff turnover. Turnover is very much affected by employee motivation, so if you find that turnover is excessively expensive you may want to consider e-HR applications that can help with motivation.

So what is the cost of staff turnover? There are three major costs associated with replacing any member of staff:

- the cost per hire (which is described above)

- the costs of training a new member of staff (say 15 per cent of salary)

- the opportunity cost of lost production covering the time between the departure of the old member of staff and the new employee working effectively (perhaps two months paying the new employee a salary which, in business terms, they are not justifying)

Work out what the cost of having to replace one person is and then see how much money you could save by reducing your turnover rate by just 1 per cent.

Time and attendance

Keeping a record of where employees are and what they are doing is a vital activity for all businesses for a variety of different purposes. Hours of work must be recorded for payroll purposes, billable hours must be converted into sales invoices and absences must be tracked, to provide just three examples.

Let us think about absence management. Existing HR information systems can certainly record information about absences but they have certain drawbacks:

- There is a time delay between the recording of the absence in the employee's department.

- Information on absence is not readily available to line managers.

- There may be costs incurred in transferring data from different time recording systems.

Because information on absences that is entered at a departmental level is immediately available to an absence management system for analysis, absence patterns can be displayed in real time and to a line manager's desktop. They can therefore track emerging absence patterns and quickly take action to deal with them.

Value is also created by making time and attendance data available to other systems – for example, for invoicing or project management purposes.

Absence also has its costs. If the average salary in your business is, say, £20 000 and people work for an average of 47 weeks per year, you are effectively paying them about £85 each day (not including other costs of employment). Multiply this figure by the number of employees and the average number of days' absence each year and you will have a rough idea about the cost of absence. How much could you save if improved availability of absence information could cut this absence rate by just 1 per cent?

 You will find more information about e-HR approaches to time and attendance in Chapter 5.

Managing training

E-HR offers many different ways for improving the cost-effectiveness of training.

Firstly it offers a new means for delivering learning opportunities. A huge amount of hype has surrounded e-learning in recent times, which tends to obscure the fact that it is, to some extent, a new way of bottling old wine, although it is a very attractive bottle. Training can be delivered to every employee's desktop, and not just what has previously been called computer-based or multimedia training. Learners can communicate with trainers or other experts using e-mail. Collaborative software allows people sitting at their desks to participate in classroom-type events, communicating by voice or through their keyboard with other learners and a trainer, all of whom they may be able to see through video streamed to their computer.

You should be able to find figures for how much your training currently costs. How this is made up will depend on what sort of training you deliver. Workshop training has relatively low development costs but incurs expense every time an event is run, due to the trainer's costs, travel, accommodation and subsistence costs for all involved, as well as the opportunity cost for time away from the job. Distance learning has much higher development costs but is relatively cheap to run if it can be delivered to a large number of people.

E-learning has a similar cost breakdown to ordinary distance learning, but it can be much more expensive to develop. Depending on the sophistication of the materials it can cost anywhere between £5000 and £30 000 for an hour of learning material.

Learning Management Systems (LMSs) can record the results of such training and provide a means by which people can look for and book places in training programmes. Such systems can link in with capability or competency databases so that people looking to improve their skills in a particular area can easily identify training that will help them to achieve that. However, it is important to remember that not all LMSs are web-enabled, especially older versions. These may not be integrated with other business systems, nor will it be possible to do so.

While it is very difficult to calculate the value added by improved training, it is relatively simple to calculate the costs of training administration. Examine your budgets and see how much you spend on this each year. How much could you save if an LMS could reduce this by just 1 per cent?

Systems such as these can reduce costs through simplifying administrative procedures but, more importantly, can add value by making training and easier to find and more immediately available. This means that people can acquire necessary skills much more quickly (the just-in-time principle) allowing organisations to react to external events much more quickly.

 You will find more information about e-learning in Chapter 6.

Managing appraisal programmes

Appraisal programmes come in a wide range of shapes and sizes but the purpose of all is to find ways by which individuals can help the performance of the organisation within which they work. Although the mechanics of the appraisal process are different for every organisation, a common factor is the need to collect and record information. People may be assessed against required competencies or capabilities, and their levels in these assessments must be recorded. Goals may be set for the coming year and people will need to record these in such a way that they can review their progress towards achieving them with their line manager.

What often makes performance management systems frustrating is the poor accessibility of the information. As discussed above, summaries of the capabilities of people within a department may not be available and there may not be direct links between the capability database and the list of training opportunities within the organisation. Performance management can also seem to be a bureaucratic process, with a lot of time spent on administering paperwork.

In addition to providing a means of simplifying and reducing the costs of administering appraisal processes, e-HR systems can allow the appraisal process to feed into a system that lives and breathes, drawing information in from some sources and feeding it out to others. Individuals can more easily see what learning opportunities can help them and line managers can obtain a much better picture of what their team's abilities are and what might be needed.

There are therefore potential benefits to be gained in improved motivation and easier access to information that will help improve performance.

Managing payroll processes

Every month the Payroll Department must produce and distribute payslips for all staff. This is a highly routine procedure, involving much printing, which, for confidentiality purposes, often requires relatively expensive forms or envelope stuffing. The payslips must then be distributed.

If people have access to an e-HR system this can be eliminated. Pay information is held in a database and is only accessed by employees when they want it. The system can automatically generate an e-mail that is sent to each employee. This provides a link that, when clicked, will display within their browser all the information that would normally be on a printed payslip. If the employee wants a printed version, they can print it out. If they lose an old payslip, no problem, log on and print out a new one. Previously they would have had to ring the Payroll Department and explain to an administrator what they wanted. The administrator would then have printed off a replacement payslip and put it into the post. This process would therefore take several days from beginning to end and cost administrative time.

The system can therefore reduce the administrative costs associated with monthly salaries and simultaneously provide an improved service to employees.

We earlier looked at time and attendance systems. Data within these is often used for calculating payrolls, but lack of integration between systems can lead to errors in transferring data. For example, if a business uses paper timesheets that are sent to the Payroll Department where an administrator transcribes figures into the payroll system, errors will happen from time to time. You can use an activity-based costing approach to estimate how much this might be costing the business. For example, in a business with 1000 monthly-paid employees, imagine that the average number of payslip corrections each month is 0.5 per cent. That means that there are 60 corrections each year. If each correction requires, say, 10 minutes of a payroll administrator's time and 10 minutes for a manager, then using the previously quoted figure of £9 40 for the administrator and £17.64 for the manager (using figures from the same source) gives us an annual cost of £2704.

Managing benefit systems

Payroll and benefits administration departments contribute to the value chain by making sure that people are correctly recompensed for playing their part in the operation of the business. The best way for them to add value is therefore to make sure that everything works smoothly and error-free, and that costs are kept as low as possible.

Automation of the system through e-HR should help to make sure that errors are reduced. The fewer times data is transferred from one system to another the better: traditional paper-computer hybrid systems mean that there is always the chance of errors being introduced as the administrator types information into a computer from a paper form completed by the employee.

Eliminating the number of administrative tasks needed to complete transactions can reduce costs. Look at the simple analysis in Table 3.4 for an employee applying for annual leave using traditional methods. This uses labour costs taken from the Office of Statistics *New Earnings Survey* 2001 for public sector clerical and managerial grades.

Table 3.4
Activity-based costing for applying for
annual leave using traditional methods

Step	Who	Step	Process time (mins)	Elapsed time (days)	Labour costs (£)
1	Employee	Completes leave request form	5	1	0.92
2	Line manager	Verifies that dates are acceptable	5	2	1.47
3	Line manager	Signs form and returns	2	3	0.59
4	Employee	Employee submits form to HR Department	5	4	0.92
5	Administrator	HR administrator updates HR system	3	5	0.47
		Total process costs			4.38

Note that this analysis ignores the costs of such things as production, storage and distribution of paperwork and internal postage. Although smaller than the costs of labour, they are not insignificant and should be taken into consideration.

Table 3.5
Activity-based costing for applying for annual leave using e-HR methods

Step	Who	Step	Process time (mins)	Elapsed time (days)	Labour costs (£)
1	Employee	Completes leave request form on-line	3	1	0.55
2	Line manager	Verifies that dates are acceptable	3	1	0.88
3	Line manager	Signs form and returns, acknowledgement sent to HR	1	1	0.29
		Total process costs			1.73

We now do the same thing for the process after it has been automated. In Table 3.5 you can see that the administrative steps have been eliminated and that the employee and the manager's time are also reduced. This is because:

- the employee goes straight to the leave request form on the e-HR portal and does not have to look for paper forms

- the manager can be given information about how this application interacts with other planned leave along with the e-mailed application and does not have to get up to take a look at the holiday planner on the wall (hoping that it is actually up to date!).

The table shows the cost of the new procedure, and you can see that there is a saving of £2.65 per transaction. Of course, this is for one leave application by a single employee so, again considering 500 employees who on average all ask for to take time off five times a year, the total savings would be £6625 each year.

Harder to quantify but just as important are the opportunity costs. Time spent by managers in processing administrative functions is time lost to carrying out the income-generating work for which they are, of course, actually employed. Administrative staff who drop out of the process completely could possibly be more profitably employed in other more strategic functions.

Providing information

Passing on information to employees has always been an important function of HR. A considerable amount of time and effort is often expended in printing, storing and distributing newsletters, magazines, leaflets and notices. But it is often difficult to know just how effective these processes are. How many in-house newsletters hit the wastepaper bin without even being read? How many people read the notices on the noticeboards? Where is that procedures manual when you need it? Why is the telephone directory always out of date?

Intranet technology can provide a useful replacement or supplement to these traditional methods of distributing information. With an e-HR portal on the intranet a company can provide access to policies and procedures manuals. Information of a more transient nature can be delivered by e-mail, perhaps to everyone within the organisation or perhaps just to people who have registered an interest in that particular subject.

Such electronic means of distributing information provide a way to reduce costs and, more importantly, add value by ensuring that information is up to date and always available.

Identify the constraints you must work within

So far, your plan is just a wish list – what you would like to do given a free hand. But of course, life is not like that: you have to take into account the world about you and the constraints that it imposes. We can identify four main areas where there will be constraints on a new system, budgets, technical compatibility, business-critical and cultural issues.

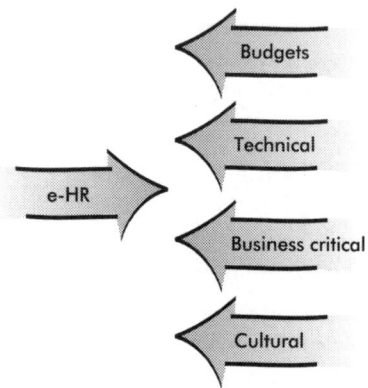

Figure 3.5
Constraints to e-HR implementation

Budgetary constraints

Basically, can you afford it? E-HR systems can be extremely expensive and you need to know what your budget will allow you to do. If capital outlay is a problem, you could consider renting a system from an Application Service Provider (ASP).

 ASPs are discussed in more detail in Chapter 8.

You may also find yourself competing with other HR initiatives. If this is happening, you should consider whether:

- the e-HR system you are proposing can complement these other initiatives

- your business case is convincing enough.

Technical compatibility

How easily will the system fit into your existing hardware and software environment? From a hardware perspective, does your network have the necessary bandwidth to allow the functionality that you would like? Do your existing servers have the necessary storage space?

If you are currently using a traditional HR information system will it be possible for the new system to access existing data?

While this constraint applies to all organisations, large or small, it is frequently more of an issue for smaller ones, as studies show that expenditure on hardware for e-HR implementation projects occupies a greater percentage of the budget for smaller businesses than for large ones[7].

You must also take into account the level of technical skills available in your business. Do you have the people necessary to implement and maintain an e-HR system? If not, you may again be interested in following the ASP route to e-HR.

Business-critical functions

Does anything that you propose to do have an impact on processes and procedures that are critical to the operation of the business? If so, it may be harder to get approval to go ahead with those aspects. On the other hand, if business-critical systems are involved it may make it more urgent to implement an e-HR enhancement.

An example of this type of issue is security. E-HR systems provide users with access to sensitive corporate information so it is vital to make sure that:

- personal information is only accessed by the right person

- people are not able to access more information than they need to.

 Security is discussed in Chapter 8.

Cultural constraints

Cultural barriers to e-HR manifest themselves in a number of different ways:

- Is the organisation ready for change? There may be a general feeling that the HR function works perfectly well as it is, thank you, and that there is no need to make changes on the scale that e-HR might imply. In situations like this an effective strategy is often to try to shake this complacency and to make people less satisfied with what is happening.

- Are people ready for the change in control? There may be a managerial culture that will resist the loss in control of some functions or be unwilling to accept the extra responsibilities that may result.

- Do people understand what e-HR means? People may find it difficult to understand what e-HR is and what implications it has. You may find yourself having to run an education programme.

You may want to implement e-HR solutions that you know will be readily understood and accepted. For example, when Cisco Systems was planning its e-HR system, Metro, one of the first applications they chose was the travel planning and expenses reporting system[8]. This was because these were applications used by people at all levels throughout the organisation. Getting this wide range of people to appreciate the benefits offered by a streamlined, automated system made it much easier to gain acceptance for later developments to the system.

Pulling a blueprint together

When you have thought about how e-HR can help your business and within what constraints it must operate, you have what we might call a set of achievable requirements. There are several things you must do next:

- Identify the kinds of applications to be introduced.

- Develop a clear understanding about what the technology can do. Look at different suppliers' products and ask lots of questions until you feel confident about the possibilities and limitations.

- Understand what the business process is trying to achieve. When you know what the success criteria are, you can think about ways of achieving these, and these ways may not be the same as those currently in use. Just automating the existing process may not be the best approach: think about what process changes may be needed.

- Consider what impact these new processes will have on people. What will they have to do differently? What implications will this have? What organisational changes may be required?

You will also need to think about the future:

- How is your organisation going to change over the next few years?

- Do you see expansion or contraction?

- What parts of the business are going to change? Are there new regulations or items of legislation appearing that will have an impact on what you do? If so, how will these affect the HR function?

Your blueprint is a statement of the complete solution options you propose, embracing the technology, process and people dimensions of the change. You then prioritise these options by working through the business case for the change (which is covered later in this chapter).

Later on you will also need to ask questions such as:

- How will we get staff to adopt the new technology?

- Who should we buy it from?

- Do we want best of breed or a pre-integrated suite of solutions?

- Should we buy, rent or outsource?

 Implementation strategies are discussed in more detail in Chapter 8.

Preparing a business case for an e-HR solution

Once you have decided what e-HR solutions will work for your organisation, you must prepare a justification for the necessary expenditure. This is often based around a financial analysis of costs and benefits, such as the internal rate of return or return on investment, but it is important not to focus exclusively on financial matters.

Such analyses are becoming increasingly important. Although in 1999 the Midas touch attributed to anything with the 'e-' prefix may have meant that justifying the investment in an e-HR solution was easy, the collapse of the dot.com bubble has meant that organisations are now extremely wary about such technological adventures. As Cedar put it 'organisations now realise that 'e-" initiatives - like any enterprise application - require solid business planning and credible ROI and that they must deliver business value.'[9]

Fitzgerald[10] proposed that justifications for new IT systems are often based on beliefs in benefits, rather than on reality, and that the history of systems implementation projects shows no relationship between the success of the implementation and the level of investment made. He stressed the importance of carrying out a 'multidimensional evaluation' based on eight steps.

1.   Identify the costs involved

Identify the costs for the implementation, including hidden and indirect costs such as training. You will have to take into account both start-up and ongoing costs, which will include the following items[11].

- **Start-up capital costs:** the costs for fixed assets required – in other words those assets that you expect to last for several years, such as software, hardware (both servers and user computers) and network equipment.

- **Other start-up costs:** those costs needed for start-up but which will be written off within the first year, such as design and development, training and marketing.

- **Ongoing capital costs:** recurring upgrading costs for the software and hardware, which may be between 15 and 25 per cent of the start-up capital costs.

- **Other ongoing costs:** the often-underestimated costs needed to keep the e-HR service operational, for example:

- – improving and maintaining e-HR services

- – salaries of staff responsible for e-HR system

- – ongoing training and marketing.

2. Define how the solution contributes to the organisation's strategy

Fitzgerald identifies this as a very important contributor to the success of an implementation. Does the proposed system contribute to the strategy or is it incompatible? Also, what will be the effect on strategy if the system is not implemented?

3. Analyse the benefits

In the previous section you looked at how e-HR could in general cut costs and add value. Here you analyse the specific benefits of this solution.

Consider both the tangible and intangible benefits. When presenting your cost-benefit analysis be very clear about the assumptions you are making when calculating tangible benefits. Remember that making savings in one place may create costs in another.

4. Identify likely secondary effects

Introducing changes to the way things are done always has secondary (and possibly unforeseen) effects. For example:

- • Simplifying one procedure may make another procedure more difficult and therefore more expensive.

- • Existing IT systems may be affected and changes will need to be made to them.

- • The new system may generate new information that must be dealt with. This may mean that you need to recruit better-qualified staff or retrain existing staff.

5. Put a value on future flexibility

Think about what the future may bring. Will the solution still be useful if the business environment changes? How will the system fit into existing management structures? Is the system scalable to meet projected future demand? Can you estimate the qualitative value of being flexible so that you can handle whatever comes along?

6. Review your constraints

Are there any factors that would make it difficult or impossible to implement the system, such as budgets, technical issues, business critical systems and organisational culture?

7.   Balance risk and return

However well you carry out your cost-benefit analysis and manage the implementation, there will be risks. Even if you implemented the system satisfactorily, secondary effects may present risks. For that reason be very clear about whether the return from implementing the new system outweighs the potential risks involved.

Also consider the risks of not implementing e-HR. What could happen within the organisation if the status quo is maintained? These risks can run from the mundane (personnel records are inaccurate) through to the strategic (the planned global initiative may stall because of the difficulties of inter-country co-operation).

A major risk you will have to justify is the level of investment needed. Let us look here briefly at some of the ways in which you will need to present the information you have calculated about investment and benefits.

The balance between financial risk and return is expressed in objective terms by a number of standard accountancy measures. These include the return on investment (ROI), the net present value (NPV), the internal rate of return (IRR) and the payback period. Let us look at what each of these means.

Return on investment

This is a measure of the profitability of the investment, and is calculated by:

$$ROI = \frac{Savings - Investment}{Investment} \times 100\%$$

Calculating Return on Investment

For example, if you have calculated that your implementation will yield savings of £600 000 for an investment of £500 000, the ROI will be 20 per cent. It is an important figure as it shows what the expected profitability of the investment is and is easy to calculate, but it does not say anything about time scales, how soon the savings can be expected. For that reason any business case must contain other measures.

Net present value

Most decisions about capital investments are made on the basis of the NPV of the project. NPV calculations take into account the fact that a bird in the hand is worth two in the bush, or in financial terms, £10 earned this week is worth more than £10 earned next week. When accountants look at future earnings they discount their value by a percentage that depends on such things as interest rates and inflation. To calculate an NPV you therefore:

- project the savings you can expect each year over the lifetime of the project

- reduce the value of each year's savings according to the discount rate you are using

- add up the savings and subtract the initial investment to give you the NPV

If the NPV is greater than zero, the project will be profitable.

Look at the simple example in Figure 3.6.

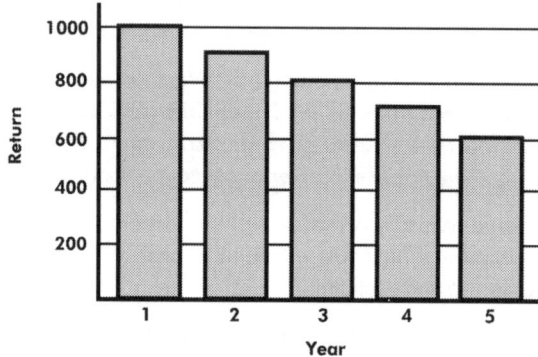

Figure 3.6
Calculating NPV

An investment of £4500 is projected to give returns of £1000 per year for five years. If you discount the returns at a simple rate of 10 per cent per year, this £1000 is worth £900 in Year 2, £800 in Year 3 and so on. The total return on the project would be £4000 over its lifetime and the NPV would be –£500. This project would therefore not be profitable. Notice, however, that the same project would give a return on investment figure of 11 per cent, which might seem attractive, were that the only figure calculated.

In practice the calculations can be quite complex and most accountants will have spreadsheets set up to perform the calculation. Alternatively you can take a look around the Internet where you will find a number of on-line NPV calculators.

Internal rate of return

The IRR of a project is related to its NPV. Look at the example in Figure 3.6. If we discount at 10 per cent a year the NPV is –£500 but if we had discounted at 0 per cent it would be +£500. There is therefore a discount rate that would give an NPV of zero (in this case 5 per cent). The discount rate where this happens is the internal rate of return.

Now, organisations will always have a **required rate of return** (RRR) that they expect for any particular type of capital investment project. If the IRR is greater than the RRR, the project will be profitable. Again, calculations of IRR can be complex and are best performed using spreadsheets that someone has designed specifically for the purpose.

IRR is usually seen as a less reliable method for evaluating a project than the NPV for two main reasons:

- If the benefits arising from the project vary from positive to negative during the project's lifetime, there will be several values of IRR, making comparisons against RRR more difficult.

- The calculations tend to favour projects that deliver large, early returns even though over the lifetime of the project the NPV is low.

Cost of capital

The cost of capital to a business is a measure of what the business will be giving up by investing in this project rather than investing it in other ways. This will therefore depend on such factors as bank interest rates. Businesses usually have a standard cost of capital figure that they use for making investment decisions.

Payback period

This is a simple statement of how long it will take for a business to recoup its initial investment. For example, if a business makes an investment of £90 000 and expects savings of £30 000 per annum the payback period is three years. The savings after this time are then pure profit.

| **Try these sites for on-line ROI and NPV calculations** | - www.datadynamica.com/IRR.asp |
| | - i98davsc.island.liu.se/ |

8.   Test the idea

Before committing yourself to a full-blown system try implementing one part of the system in a discreet area of the business. See how the implementation and operation proceed and take away lessons from this. Incorporate what you learn into your final cost-benefit analysis.

You may decide to pilot e-HR with a limited-scale application, in which case you should prepare a business case for the pilot, then, after implementation, evaluate its success and use this information to shape a business case for a full-scale implementation.

An example of a cost-benefit analysis

Let us take a look at what a real cost-benefit analysis for an e-HR system looks like.

Ericsson Inc. started the progressive introduction of an e-HR system in January 2000[11]. As a major force in the fast-moving telecommunications industry it needed to have human resources systems that allowed it to react quickly to changes in its marketplace. Also, from an image point of view, a technology-based business also needs to be seen to be using technology effectively. It introduced the system in stages starting with an automated compensation system followed by an on-line flexible benefit planning system and subsequently a pension administration system.

Ericsson estimates that the introduction of the system saved the company more than $1 million in its first year and that it has added more than $1 million in organisational value each year since then. On top of these benefits are those resulting from its being able to attract and retain talented staff. The Director of Benefits and HR for Ericsson, Chris Gonser, is quoted as saying 'We've not only cut costs, we've become more efficient, faster and more organised. Our services help with attracting and recruiting talent. We are providing more information more accurately. It's been very, very successful. People's appreciation has been overwhelming.'

This is part of the analysis that Ericsson Inc. carried out when they were considering the implementation of a system.

Table 3.6
An example of a cost-benefit analysis

Cost-benefit analysis assumptions	Impact valuation (estimation)	Annualised cost savings
Focus on employee attraction and retention	Unable to quantify	
Develop and provide tools to effectively and efficiently support Ericsson's business objectives	Unable to quantify	
Part of positioning as Ericsson Employer of Choice	Unable to quantify	
Technology-based solutions for a technology-focused organisation	Unable to quantify	
Integrated tools that support Human Resources division and initiatives	Unable to quantify	
Eliminate need for record matching software	3300 employees (35 minutes at average $55 800 annual pay)	$51,643.83
Eliminate ongoing support needed for record matching software	Internal and/or outsourced considerations for maintenance and ongoing support (1 full-time equivalent at $55 800 for 350 hours)	$9389.42
Streamline communications and centralise resources for consistent communications	Unable to quantify	
Timely and accurate benefits data and election data	11 400 employees (25 minutes at $55 800)	$127 427.88
Minimise print production and mailing requirements	Allows reduction from 30p to 03p communication piece (approximate costs: 30 pages, $30 000; 3 pages, $9000)	$21 000
Eliminate printing of on-line materials	On-line Open Enrolment Guide	$20 000

You can see that Ericsson considered both tangible and intangible benefits. The tangible benefits are relatively easy to quantify. For example:

- Duplication of record-keeping meant that clerical errors sometimes made it look as if there were two employees when there was in fact just the one. This meant that they had to use software that could compare records and identify spurious members of staff. Self-administered records meant that employees themselves could correct errors, which allowed Ericsson to cut the costs involved in purchasing and maintaining the record comparison software.

- Documents that previously were printed could now be made available on-line, eliminating the costs for storage and distribution, as well as ensuring that information was always up to date.

However, the analysis commented that the intangible benefits were probably much more significant. How do you quantify the benefits of attracting and retaining good staff? One talented person who is persuaded to join Ericsson rather than a rival because its recruitment processes suggested that it was a dynamic company that valued its employees could potentially add hundreds of thousands of dollars to the bottom line, dwarfing the benefits made by cutting out printing costs!

It is therefore very important that when you carry out a cost-benefit analysis that you consider what type of organisation you want to be and consider how an e-HR system could help you to achieve this.

Summarising …

This chapter has looked at how to decide where e-HR can fit into your organisation.

Here is a summary of the process.

- Decide where you are now. What is the relationship between your HR Department and the rest of the business?

- How can HR add value to the business? Consider the different functions covered by HR and see where e-HR could cut costs and add value. Which areas offer the greatest potential value? These are the areas you should focus on initially.

- Consider the constraints that would make implementation difficult. Think what strategies you would need to employ to overcome these.

- Draw up your blueprint for e-HR. What technology, process and organisational changes are proposed to deliver the desired solution?

- Prepare your business case, justifying the different types of investment needed.

Notes

1. Wiscombe, J., (2001), 'Using Technology to Cut Costs', *Workforce*, September 2001, **Vol. 80**, No 9.

2. Porter, M. E. (1998), *Competitive Advantage: Creating and Sustaining Superior Performance*, New York: Simon & Schuster.

3. Armstrong, M., (2001), A Handbook of Human Resource Management', London: Kogan Page.

4. Office of Statistics, (2001), 'New Earnings Survey 2001', check reference and link

5. The figures used in this example are for salary costs, in this case £11.04 per hour for the employee and £9.40 for an administrator. These do not take into account other employers' costs such as provision of benefits and overheads. The actual costs would therefore be somewhat greater were full costs to be used in the calculations.

6. Fitz-Enz, J., (2002), *How to Measure Human Resources Management*, New York: McGraw-Hill

7. *Cedar 2001 Human Resources Self Service/Portal Survey*, Cedar.

8. Cisco Employee Connection: Exploring the Frontiers of Intranet Technology', http://www.cisco.com/warp/public/756/gnb_gen/intra_wp.htm

9. *Cedar 2001 Survey*, note 7 above.

10. Fitzgerald, G., (1998), 'Evaluating IS Projects: A Multidimensional Approach', *Journal of Information Technology*, **Vol. 13**, No. 1.

11. *Cedar 2001 Survey*, note 7 above.

12. PeopleSoft (2001), 'The ABCs of Return on Investment', www.peoplesoft.com

chapter 4

Delivering core HR services

This chapter looks at what are perhaps the most obvious applications of e-HR in that they represent traditional functions of the Human Resources Department, managing staff information and compensation and benefit administration. Because this involved the storage of large amounts of information it has also been an area where computers have been used for some years. What is exciting about intranet-based HRISs is the opportunity they present for allowing the information stored to be used in a much more efficient way than has previously been possible.

Note that HR is also heavily involved in recruitment administration, but this is covered in Chapter 5.

Portals that provide access to HR administration are often used as gateways to other HR services and functions, such as e-learning, performance management and employee benefits schemes. It is therefore important that they are implemented and designed carefully. How to make sure this happens is discussed in more detail later in this chapter.

Managing information about employees

Do you remember the good old days of the Personnel Department? Endless rows of filing cabinets storing personal details about everyone in the organisation, people transferring handwritten information into files that grew ever larger – and ever more out of date. The chilly winds of downsizing and re-engineering started to put an end to that in the closing years of the last century. Personnel Departments became Human Resources Departments, in a public acknowledgement that 'people are our greatest asset'.

However, changing the name of the function will only becomes significant if Human Resources Departments can be seen to have shaken off the perception that they are just data processors. Of course, the big question is how to do this? One way is to reduce the amount of data processing done so that HR staff are free to do more strategic work. This can be achieved by letting employees do the data entry themselves using self-service HR systems.

What is self-service HR?

When you go to a self-service restaurant you help yourself to the food that you want. You do not rely on a waiter who may take a long time to serve you, and when they do, do it with less than perfect civility! It is the same with self-service HR: individuals perform the HR functions they need by themselves. So how might this work?

Think about what personnel-type tasks a typical employee might need to do. First of all, consider an employee changing their address. In a traditional system they would send an internal memo to the HR Department with details of the change of address, or possibly find a 'Change of address' form and send this. An HR administrator would then transfer this information into the existing HR information system. Clearly this takes time. The paper takes some time to travel from the employee to the HR Department, although an e-mail system would speed this up considerably. Secondly, it is quite possible for the administrator to transcribe the new address incorrectly, an error which might go undetected for some time.

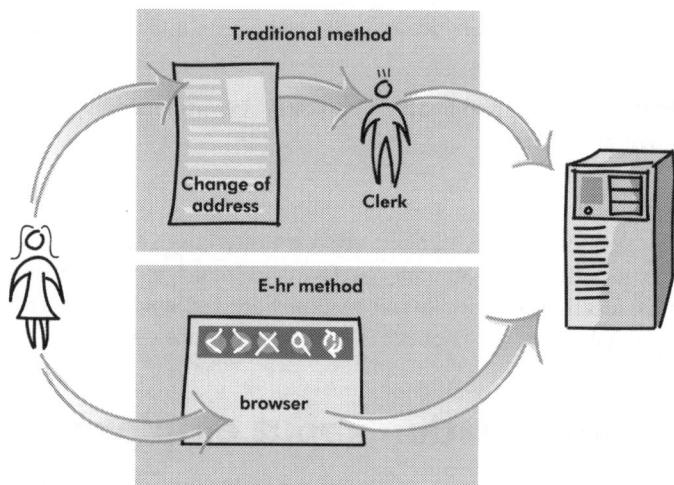

Figure 4.1
Comparing traditional methods with e-HR

With an e-HR system the process is simplicity itself. The employee accesses the 'Personal details' page from the HR portal and enters the new address details themselves. It is done quickly and efficiently, as the employee should be able to confirm that they have entered the details correctly.

Now think about the traditional way for an employee to put in a leave request. They may first of all discuss the dates they want with their line manager and then complete a 'Leave request' form. They then send this through the internal post to the HR Department, where an administrator transfers information about the application to the existing system, possibly a client-server HR information system. This would confirm whether the employee is entitled to this leave and if so, records it as having been granted. The administrator may then return a copy to the employee confirming that the leave has been granted, or possibly they could send l an e-mail. This process takes a considerable amount of time and effort.

Now look at how an automated e-HR system would deal with this. This is illustrated in Figure 4.2. The employee makes the request through the HR portal, possibly having discussed the dates already with their line manager. The system automatically forwards the request to the line manager by e-mail and the manager replies accordingly. If they have approved the request, confirmation is automatically sent to the employee, HR records are updated and information about the leave being taken is sent to any other Department with an interest, for example, the Payroll Department.

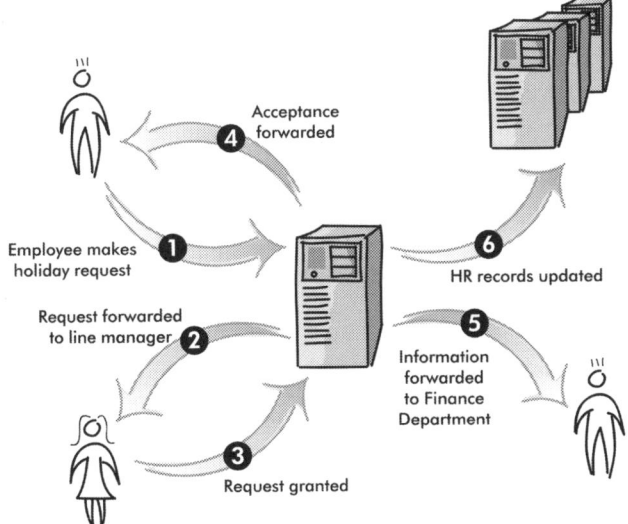

Figure 4.2
Applying for leave with a self-service system

Think about processes within your own organisation that could be automated in this way. What is the chain of events that is triggered when, for example, someone resigns? How much administrative time could be saved if this were automated?

What are the benefits of self-service HR?

Data held is more accurate

By making employees responsible for entering their own information, the accuracy of information held centrally should improve considerably. Transferring information manually from handwritten forms into databases is a common source of error, and as the information is then only used within the HR function the errors remain undetected. There is, in fact, a specialised software market for applications that analyse databases looking for near-duplications: with an e-HR solution you can cross off your shopping list the costs for buying and operating such systems.

HR administration costs are reduced

Transferring information from paper to a database is an activity that does not contribute to the business: in fact it is a drain.

As people are no longer needed to carry out routine administrative tasks such as data inputting, they can devote their energies to extracting data and converting it into useful information instead. E-HR systems have the potential to generate large amounts of potentially useful information – information that can contribute to the profitability of the organisation – but it will require hands to generate and publicise it. HR may no longer be seen as a drain but as a profit centre in its own right.

Paper shuffling costs are reduced

Using paper within administrative functions creates all sorts of potential difficulties:

- Where do you store this amount of paper?

- What do you do when forms must be updated?

- How do you distribute it?

- How do employees know that they are using up-to-date versions of forms?

- Does data on completed forms have to be transcribed to a database? If so, how do you make sure that no errors are introduced by the transcription?

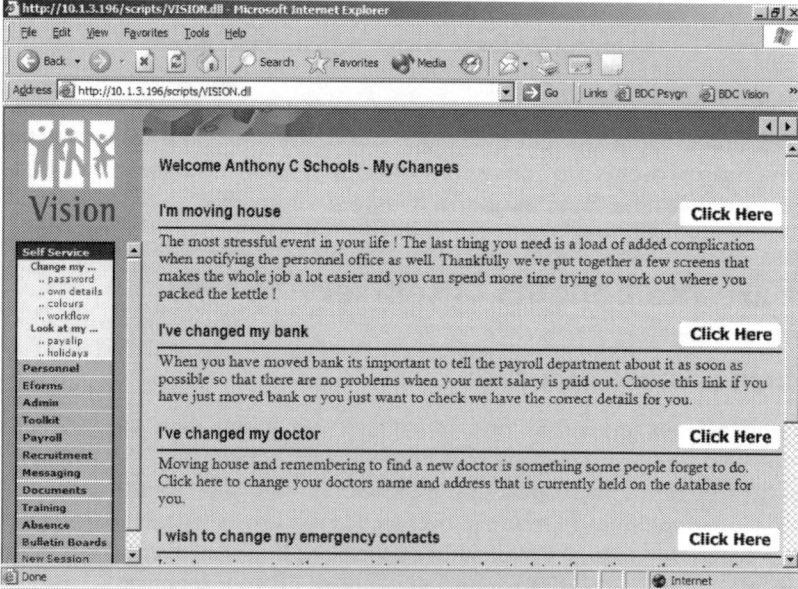

© Selima Software, www.selima.co.uk

Figure 4.3
Which form do I need today?
Employees have instant access to whatever request form they need. Forms do not need to be printed, stored and distributed.

The list of questions such as these is endless. The overall result of this is that a considerable amount of effort is devoted solely to keeping the administrative system working – definitely not an activity that contributes to the profitability of the organisation. With an e-HR system all forms can be on-line. Employees enter the information and submit it to the central storage system, where it is automatically available in a database. In fact, the most significant savings come not from reducing the costs of moving paper around the organisation but from the streamlining of business processes.

HR systems become proactive

Database integration means that it is possible to put together information about employees from different sources and recognise when the organisation or an employee needs to take some special action. For example, think about the need for organisations to retrain their qualified first-aid staff. This is usually a manual operation, where perhaps the first-aider makes a note in their diary to remind themselves that in 12 months' time they must attend another training courses to requalify. All sorts of things can happen here: they may forget to transfer the reminder to the next year's diary or they may leave the organisation. When they do remember that they need to arrange the training, they will have a number of administrative tasks to perform. Now how could an e-HR system deal with this? Take a look at Figure 4.4.

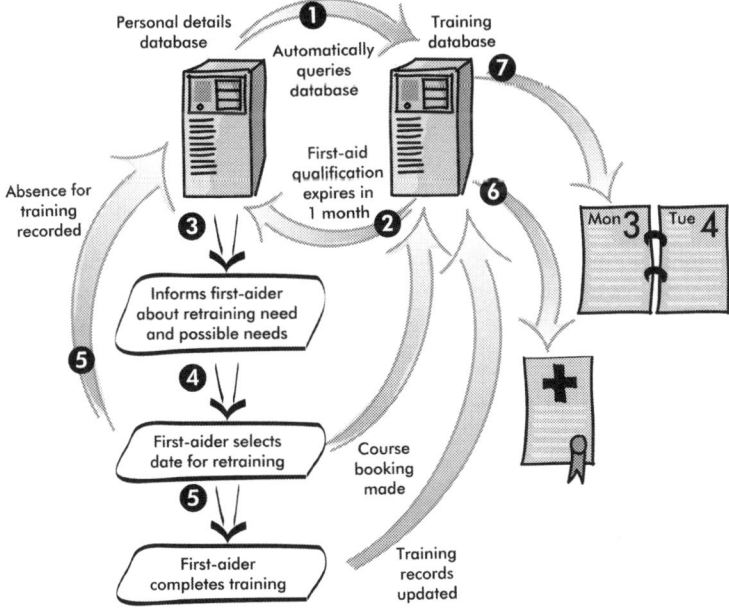

Figure 4.4
Proactively arranging training

The process starts with the e-HR system sending a routine daily query to the Learning Management System (LMS) holding the training database. The query asks for information about any regular training requirements that will be due for renewal within the next month. Sooner or later the LMS will respond and say that one particular employee needs to renew their first-aid qualification within the next month. It automatically checks the database for first-aid courses to see when they are available within that time and sends this information back to the e-HR system.

The system then generates an e-mail to the employee informing them about the need to arrange the retraining and telling them about possible dates. The employee decides which date is most convenient, selects this from the list provided and sends the confirmation. This simultaneously does several things. It:

- tells the LMS to book a first-aid course for this person for the chosen date

- inserts the course time and location details in the employee's on-line calendar

- updates the employee's absence record to say that they will be absent on that day for a training event.

This means that the line manager will always be able to find out which members of staff are going to be absent for training on any particular day.

The process is completed when the person completes their first-aid retraining. They or their trainer will inform the LMS that the training has been completed and the training database will be updated accordingly. The system could even automatically generate a certificate that would be sent to the requalified first-aider and insert a reminder in an on-line calendar that will send a reminder to the employee in 12 months' time.

You can see that this principle could be employed to watch for any event that happens on a regular basis. For example, the system could remind staff about such things as:

- the imminent end of a probationary period of employment, simultaneously doing such things as updating the Payroll Department's database so that their monthly salary is amended and generating a full-time standard contract of employment which would be automatically e-mailed

- the need to arrange a performance appraisal interview with their line manager, informing the line manager at the same time.

E-HR systems can also behave proactively by displaying a limited amount of forward thinking about the implications of an employee's action. For example, look at Figure 4.5.

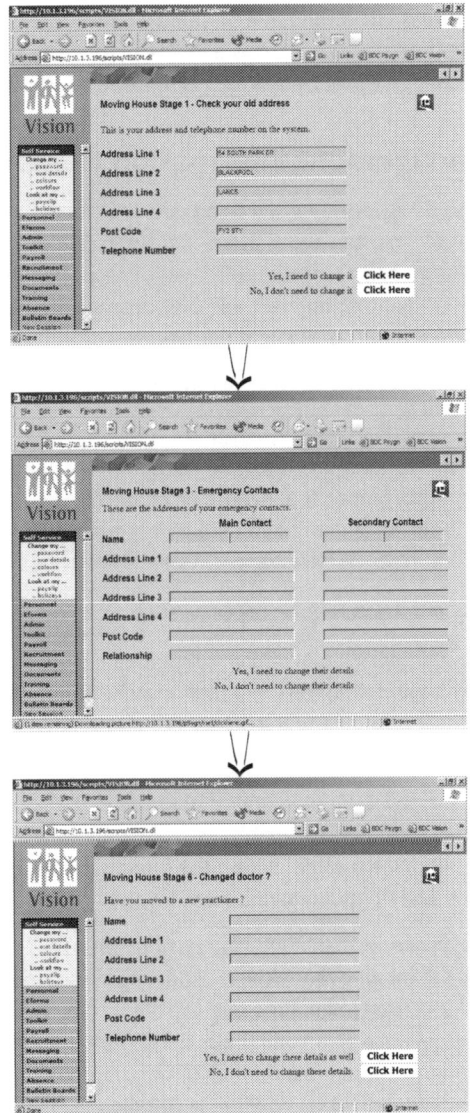

© Selima Software, www.selima.co.uk

Figure 4.5
Thinking ahead about change of address implications
After the user enters their new address details they move through a series of screens that prompt them to enter new information about related information – for example, emergency contact details and doctor's details.

When we change our address we often have to change other things as well, such as contact details for our next of kin and perhaps a new doctor. The system can look ahead and prompt the user to change these details as well if necessary.

The quality of management information is improved

Employees with managerial responsibility who log into the portal will be presented with various reporting options. These can allow them to interrogate the organisation's databases to a degree commensurate with their level of responsibility so that, for example, a team leader could look at data relating to their own team whereas a departmental manager could access data about the whole department.

Depending on the exact functionality of the system implemented, this reporting can take various forms:

- The manager may be able to request ad hoc reports based on whatever parameters are important at that time. For example, they may be about to attend a management meeting and want to take a report showing how their department's performance has changed over the previous few months.

- The system may generate regular reports, such as a weekly report about sales or sickness absence.

- The system may be event-driven. In other words, the system will automatically generate a report if particular parameters go past certain levels, for example, if absenteeism or overtime levels go more than, say, 10 per cent above normal levels.

While this information may have been available within a traditional client-server system, the advantage that an e-HR system offers is that the information is readily available to any employee with a browser and the necessary access levels.

Think about a real-life example. A manufacturing business installed an e-HR system and one of the line managers set up an event-driven reporting system to provide a warning if sickness levels exceeded a certain level. One day the alarm was raised through the portal, and very quickly the manager was able to find out that employees in one particular part of the shopfloor were starting to report in sick with back pain. When the manager went to take a look at the area they found that a new piece of machinery had been installed and, by talking to the people working on it, discovered that using it meant bending down more than was comfortable. Hence the back pain. It was then a simple matter to reinstall the equipment at a higher level so that people no longer had to bend. Very quickly sickness absences dropped back to normal and productivity went back up to normal. In the absence of a system that was able to spot a trend and alert the line manager involved, this situation would have continued for some time, leading to short-term losses in productivity and long-term damage to employees' health.

Workflow status can be monitored

'Sorry, haven't seen it', goes the cry when asked what has happened to a paper-based authorisation request. And the vagaries of internal distribution systems mean that it is often a legitimate excuse. But if nobody has the form, where is it? Such problems become a thing of the past with an e-HR system. Anyone with responsibility for a form can pull up a summary of where all such forms are in the system, which will indicate who needs to provide the next stage of authorisation. Figure 4.6 shows an example of what that might look like.

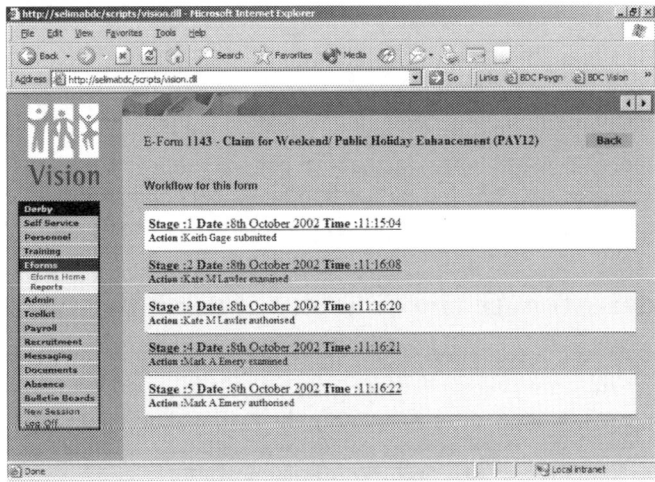

© Selima Software, www.selima.co.uk

Figure 4.6
Example of a workflow status screen
From this screen a manager can check to see where an authorisation request is in the system. It shows the path it is following and who has received, examined and authorised the request.

Easier compliance with the Data Protection Act

One of the requirements of the Data Protection Act is that anyone whose details are stored on a computer should be able to demand to see this information at any time. Organisations typically collect large amounts of information about members of staff, usually distributed across a number of different systems. This means that the administrative effort needed to identify and assemble it all can be significant, should an employee ask to see all the information that is held on them.

With an e-HR system the administrative effort disappears. An employee can simply click on one button and all relevant information will be drawn from the separate databases and delivered.

Families can be integrated into the life of the business

'What did you do in the office today, mummy?' can be brought to life. If staff can access their portal via a domestic Internet connection they can involve their families in HR-related issues. A good example of this is in planning flex packages. Rather than the worker thinking through what balance of holidays, childcare and pension provision they will opt for in the office and then bringing it home to discuss, families can sit together around their home PC and discuss it, play with the possibilities and, when happy, press the 'Submit' button together. After all, families that flex together, stay together

However, it should also be noted that making the portal available to the public gaze does mean that its image becomes important.

What challenges can self-service HR present?

Challenges presented by e-HR were discussed in general terms in Chapter 1. However, as self-service HR systems are intended for use by all members of staff, particular care must be taken to make sure that they do not present any particular problems.

Do not underestimate the difficulty of using the system

It is easy for people who are familiar with using browsers to underestimate how difficult they are to use. If implementing e-HR represents the first exposure people will have had to using a browser you will need to think seriously about what training will be needed. Suppliers may well say that their systems are intuitive and need no training, but they would say that, wouldn't they? Implementations of many systems have gone awry because the training requirements were underestimated, and e-HR systems will be no exception. The big challenge with this is that if an implementation fails because it puts off the potential users, relaunching is much more difficult.

This actually happened with a supermarket chain that implemented an e-HR system. Many of their employees were part-time and consequently difficult to train. Many of them did not use a computer in their work, nor had they used them anywhere else, but it was assumed that they would find the browser interface easy to use, and so no training was provided. Unfortunately users did find the interface difficult to use and they quickly became frustrated with the system.

Avoid raising a barrier to people with disabilities

Moving away from paper-based or telephone HR systems to those dependent on the ability to use a browser can present difficulties to people with some types of disability. This depends to a large extent on the nature of the disability and the way the system is designed.

This issue is covered in more detail in Chapter 1 where you will find information on how browser-based systems should be designed to minimise such difficulties.

Keeping personal information secure

It is absolutely vital to make sure that personal information is kept secure. Access to personal details should be restricted to the individual and only other people who have a legitimate right to know. This will clearly raise issues regarding the different types of information that are held and the levels of management who have access rights, and these issues must be resolved prior to implementations by full and open discussion with employees' interest groups, such as trades unions.

 For more information about implementing security, see Chapter 8.

Making sure people have access to the system

You will need to make sure that everybody in the organisation has easy access to a computer and hence the e-HR system. For people whose everyday work does not involve a computer, that may mean installing kiosks and making sure that working practices allow people to use the system as and when they need to. Such groups may require considerably more training and performance support than others.

Compensation and benefits administration

Rewards to employees come in a number of different forms:

- Pay, the most obvious. This may be a regular weekly or monthly amount or be based on the number of hours worked. To the base pay may be added variable amounts resulting from performance-related pay agreements, bonuses, commission or allowances.

- Routine expenses, incurred by employees during the course of their work such as car mileage, train fares and subsistence while away from the office.

- Pension plans. Many organisations operate pension schemes for their employees or contribute to an individual's own personal pension planning.

- Health-care schemes. Organisations and individual employees may jointly contribute to private health-care provision.

- Holidays. These are example of a non-financial benefit, the days off on holiday being provided as part of the overall package, with employees being paid for the days they take off.

- Sick pay. Employees who are forced to take time off work due to illness will continue to be paid for a certain time.

Individual employees are rightly interested in what their total benefits package is and what its status is at any particular time. For example, people will want to know how many days, holiday remain in the holiday year and whether their health-care package provides for a particular treatment. In a traditional setting an individual wanting to make enquiries about these benefits would probably need to refer to one of many different telephone numbers or ask to be sent a paper-based form.

E-HR systems provide a single portal through which any of these benefits can be investigated.

- Pay. The employee can look up how their pay is calculated, look back at previous month's payments and request payslips.

- Routine expenses. The employee can claim for expenses on-line without needing to complete a paper-based form or make calculations about miles covered and mileage rates.

- Pension plans. The employee can see how plans are performing and make changes to payments, if they wish to do so.

- Health-care schemes. The employee can check up the details of their scheme and add, amend or remove elements from the package instantly.

- Holidays. The employee can check to see how many days they have used and how many days remain. They can also arrange on-line to take days off.

- Sick pay. The employee can look to see what their position is if they are taking an extended period of sick leave.

Let us now take a look at payroll administration and claiming expenses in more detail.

Payroll administration

Payroll systems perform a number of different functions:

- They do the mechanical work of calculating such things as tax, National Insurance and pension payments, generating payslips to be sent to employees.

- They can generate correspondence to be sent to employees on a variety of pay-related matters.

- They allow managers to perform a variety of calculations, such as 'what if?' scenarios or payroll cost projections.

Payroll systems vary considerably in their sophistication. When selecting a system you need to make sure that it is capable of dealing with particular factors within your organisation – for example:

- multiple employment by the same member of staff

- varying rates of pay

- holiday and shift differentials.

There are a number of useful ways in which e-HR systems can enhance existing payroll systems.

Closer integration with time and attendance systems

In the case of an hourly-paid workforce, employees can clock in and out using a convenient computer and the data can be easily accessed by the payroll system.

 There is more information about how browser-based time and attendance systems work in Chapter 5.

Easier administration of payroll procedures

Payroll Departments spend a considerable amount of time each month printing off and distributing payslips for employees. Even if the process is completely automated a considerable amount of effort is required and the expense of distribution cannot be avoided.

Browser-based payroll administration avoids this. Employees need not actually be sent paper versions of their payslips; instead they are sent as e-mails, or the employee is able to access the payroll administration system and view their payslips on-line. They can therefore print them off if they so wish and never have to worry about losing them.

Faster response time to changing employee circumstances

If we tell a small child that they have done something well and that we will as a consequence give them a reward we need to give them that reward immediately. If we wait a week, the link between the achievement and the reward is lost and if we were hoping that the offer of a reward would drive the child on, we would be disappointed.

Employees are adults, but much the same psychology applies. If an organisation offers any form of performance-related pay, the reward for good performance needs to be delivered as near to the performance as possible. And organisations today are certainly moving away from traditional notions of rigid pay structures, where increments are based on slow-moving and predictable factors such as length of service. Salaries nowadays can take into account a variety of different factors:

- performance-related pay, where salary depends on perceived levels of performance

- target-driven incentives, where bonuses may be paid if someone achieves agreed targets

- knowledge-based pay, where salary is influenced by the levels of knowledge or skill demonstrated by an employee

- competence-related pay, where salary is influenced by the employee's performance against the organisation's competency criteria.

Whatever type of incentive structure operates within an organisation, the traditional way of dealing with it is essentially the same. The performance triggering the salary increase or bonus must first be acknowledged. How easy this is to do depends on what the trigger is and how it is recorded. Often it may have to be found manually. Once found, the appropriate person must inform the Payroll Department of what has happened and what salary implications this has. The Payroll Department can then amend the employee's salary instructions accordingly.

Of course, this all takes time. Information will probably be recorded in different databases held by different departments. The shuffling of authorisations from one part of the business to another will take time. However, the integration of databases through an e-HR system can eliminate many of these delays.

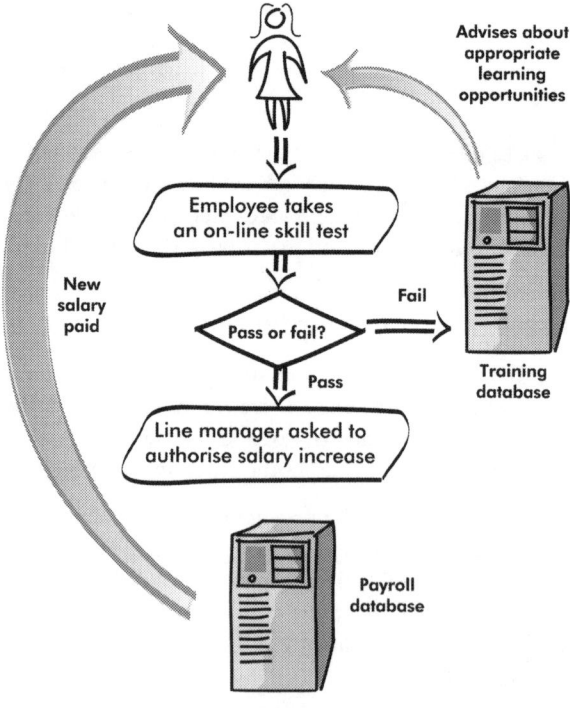

Figure 4.7
Updating a skill-based salary

Take the case of someone whose salary can be boosted by being able to demonstrate certain levels of knowledge about their work. They can take an on-line assessment test whose results will be forwarded to the appropriate person for review. If the person has been successful, the manager can authorise the salary increase on-line so that, possibly within minutes of having completed the test, the employee's salary details have been amended. At the end of that month they could receive a salary that reflects their newly recognised knowledge levels. This is providing as an immediate a linkage as possible between the desired performance and reward.

Of course, the person may not achieve the necessary score, in which case the system can assess the areas of weakness demonstrated and by reference to a Learning Management System, identify learning opportunities that the employee would find useful.

Savings in administration costs

Cutting out the need to produce and distribute paper versions of pay information can lead to considerable cost savings. One large borough council printed out and distributed payslips each month to each of its 6000 employees but implementation of an e-HR based system enabled them to save £150 000 each year. They were also able to reduce the size of their payroll administrative staff from 14 to 8, with the other employees being redeployed to other, more strategic functions within the HR Department.

Salary reviews in action at Cisco

Many companies regard annual salary and bonus review rounds as something of a nightmare, and the process often takes many days and nights. Cisco is an example of a company that has used e-HR to address this problem. On-line technologies allow it to complete its salary and bonus reviews in about a week.

The e-HR Department agrees the size of the pot available and the allocation rules with senior management, and then on a given day all the first-tier managers release their allocation on-line to their team. The rules are built into the software. Exceptions are escalated upwards to the next level. After making the first-tier allocations, the next tier reconciles the allocations between their teams and so on through the organisation. Adjustments are communicated as appropriate back down to the previous tier. By the time it reaches the top, the allocation is complete and has been carried out to common standards throughout the organisation.

Processing routine expenses

Processing expenses claims is traditionally a somewhat laborious process. The employee completes a paper form, digs out all the necessary expenses and sends it off to the Payroll Department. If they do it by the month's cut-off date they should be remunerated that month, but they may have to wait longer. This can be frustrating, and if an employee has incurred significant expenses, financially embarrassing!

An e-HR system can automate this process. Instead of providing the employee with the information so that they can drive the expense claim procedure, the procedure drives the information. The employee:

- selects 'Make an expenses claim' from the HR homepage

- selects 'Mileage claim' from a list of possibilities

- works through an on-line form that gathers information about important information such as engine size, miles covered and purpose of journey.

The system then automatically calculates how much the claim will be for and forwards the details electronically to the Payroll Department. At any stage the employee can ask to see more detailed information from the on-line expenses claim manual, but in many cases they will not choose to do so. However, if they do, the system will take them to the precise point in the manual so that they do not have to spend time searching. And they may be happier people for not looking up information! After all, how much time in organisations do people waste by looking for information that they only need very occasionally? A good example is mileage rates based on engine size. An e-HR system can automatically calculate expenses just by knowing the engine size of the employee's car (for which it may already have details provided by the employee). There is no need for the employee to use look-up tables of some sort to find out what rate is applicable to their particular engine size.

Look at the real-life example of how Cisco Systems, e-HR system, Metro, automates the expense claim process.[1] After completing a business trip, employees complete an on-line form with details of their business expenses. If they have used a corporate credit card they can access details of these expenses and transfer them to the on-line claim form. They then submit their claim, and can receive their reimbursement, in their pay cheque or directly into their bank account within 72 hours rather than the five or six weeks it took previously.

 You can find more information about other aspects of reward management, such as total benefits and on-line flex packages in Chapter 7.

Accessing e-HR systems through a portal

As administration of personal information touches everyone in the organisation it makes sense to make the self-service HR homepage the gateway, or portal, to other on-line HR services. However, its function as the portal to other services means that it is important that it is well designed.

Watson Wyatt[2] suggest a number of guidelines to ensure a portal is successful.

Make sure the site is attractive and usable

This is the fundamental thing to get right: if a system of any sort is not easy to use people will quickly get fed up with it and avoid using it. Self-service HR only works if people do actually serve themselves! All parts of the site, and not just the portal, must be designed from a user's point of view. To make sure this happens, look actively for feedback from users and make it easy for people to provide feedback through the site. Use the feedback to make improvements.

Allow a single log-on

Badly-designed computer systems require the user to log on several different times, perhaps to the particular computer they are using, to the network and then to individual applications. The end result of this is that users resort to strategies such as writing passwords down on pieces of paper near to their computer or using easily-cracked passwords such as their name or the day of the week.

Well-designed systems enable the user to log on just the once and then have full access to all functionality and systems.

Use rapid prototyping methods

Build prototypes with limited functionality quickly and let users try them out. Use their feedback to make improvements as the system grows. This approach is much more preferable to developing a fully-functioning system in secret and then implementing it only to find that there are unexpected reasons why users do not like it.

Allow customisation and personalisation

Those of you who shop on-line may have noticed how the more sophisticated shopping sites seem to know something about you when you arrive. They remember previous purchases and suggest items that you might now be interested in. This works on the theory that the more relevant to a user a site, is the more likely it is that they will use it.

Self-service HR systems should do this. The system picks up log-in details, checks to see who the person is and what their responsibilities are within the organisation and then presents them with a customised screen. Personalisation can do such things as:

- provide functionality relevant to the user's grade or role
- provide links to services that the user has accessed recently.

Such systems are often described as role-based, in that the functionality that the portal to the system provides is configured according to the individual logging on. Employees with no management responsibilities may have access to nothing more than self-administration of their personal details, whereas line managers will be able to access various reporting functions. This means that the system can be as powerful as it can be without compromising security. Figure 4.8 is an example of a portal. The box down the left side of the screen contains a list of functions, but only those appropriate to the grade of the person logged on would be available.

Taking this a stage further, the system could also present non-business function information of interest to that particular user, in the same way that sites such as amazon.com® remember what books and music you have purchased from them previously and suggest new items that you may be interested in. Some organisations are offering direct links from the employee portal page to those of external businesses offering useful services, such as on-line supermarket shopping or financial services planning. People who use such services regularly could find these links having a more visible presence on their particular page than other people might. People who are interested in weather forecasts could find a link to a weather forecast site while people who have never shown any interest in this would not have such a link.

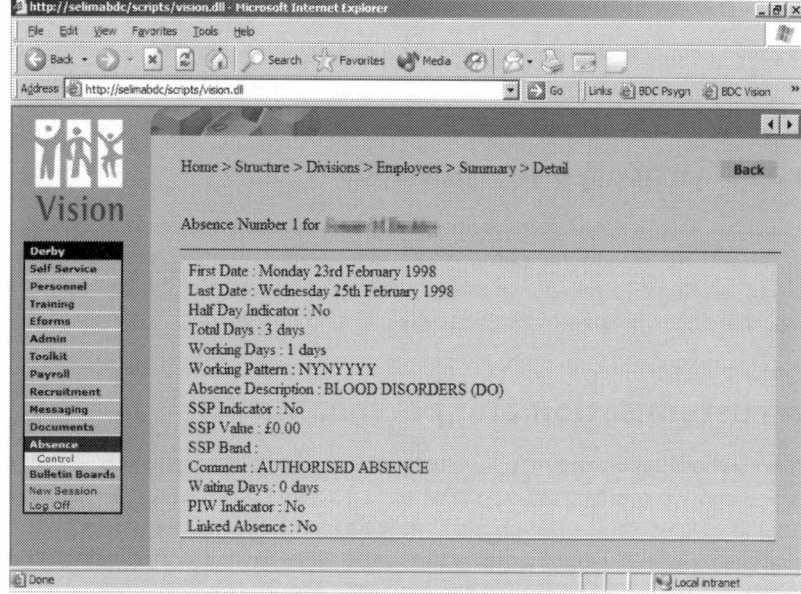

© Selima Software, www.selima.co.uk

Figure 4.8
Example of a line manager's page
Here a line manager is looking at an employee's absence record. Such information would be restricted to managers with the appropriate responsibilities.

Implement step-by-step

Roll out services gradually so that users have the chance to get used to the new system. Knowing that new services are continually coming on-line makes it more likely that people will call back from time to time to see what is new.

Make sure content is kept fresh

Everything on a web site should have a clearly identified owner who has responsibility for making sure that it is kept up to date. Find ways to keep users updated with new functionality. One way is to let users register an interest in particular functions so that, if they are updated, users are automatically sent an e-mail informing them of the changes.

Review processes before automating

You will not achieve the hoped-for benefits of e-HR if you merely automate an inefficient process: only automate processes when you are sure that they are efficient. For example, one large city council planning the implementation of an e-HR system discovered that it had 88 different paper forms for various aspects of HR administration. By carrying out a careful analysis of its processes and associated workflows it was able to reduce this to 25 on-line forms.

So before starting the automation process, set up cross-functional teams who can pick processes apart and put them back together so that they work properly. Make sure that process users are involved in this process, especially in geographically dispersed organisations. Procedures are often developed centrally with limited regard to local constraints. Involving representatives from all parts of the business will help make sure that the redesigned process meets the needs of the entire organisation.

Give the site an identity

Giving the HR site its own name and identity makes it easier to get it established as the place to go for HR-related information. For example, Cisco Systems' HR site is called Metro and BP call theirs myHR.

Remove alternatives

When you are confident that your site works effectively and efficiently you could take away the alternatives! Remove paper-based forms and let people know that the only way to do things is through the HR site.

Summarising ...

- Self-service HR systems allow employees to manage their own personal information.

- Employees access self-service systems through a portal, which can act as a gateway to all other e-HR services.

- Portals can be personalised to the person logging in, so that they offer the appropriate functionality.

- Self-service HR offers a number of benefits, including:

  - improved accuracy of data

  - reduced HR administrative costs

  - less paper shuffling

  - more proactive HR

  - improved management information

  - better control of HR processes

  - improved compliance with information legislation.

- Self-service HR presents various challenges, including:

  - staff finding it difficult

  - potential barriers to people with disabilities

  - security

  - access.

- On-line compensation and benefits administration offers a number of advantages including:

  - better integration with time and attendance systems

  - easier administration of payroll procedures

  - faster responses

  - reduced administrative expenses.

- Care must be taken to make sure that systems are usable.

Notes

1. 'Cisco Employee Connection: Exploring the Frontiers of Intranet Technology', www.cisco.com/warp/public/756/gnb_gen/intra_wp.htm

2. Watson Wyatt, 'Best Practice of e-HR Portals', republished at www.workforce.com/section/10/article/23/27/30.html

chapter 5

Managing people
more effectively

Chapter 4 focused on how we can use e-HR to reduce administrative tasks within the HR function. There is, of course, considerable overlap between managing people and administration, but the focus in this chapter is more on what can make the job of managing teams of people easier and more effective. This chapter looks at three areas where e-HR can help people to manage their teams more effectively:

1. recruitment

2. time and attendance

3. performance management.

Recruitment is one area where e-HR has the potential to change radically the ways in which the whole process of finding new staff (both internally and externally) works. Traditional methods can be extremely time-consuming, requiring a lot of administrative effort to make sure that everything happens at the right time. The process of filling a vacant position can therefore take a long time, which is expensive for a business. E-recruitment systems can simplify things by:

- making advertising vacancies easier, more accessible and more effective

- making it easier for people to find vacancies

- linking up with external organisations offering candidate validation services

- providing an easy-to-use tracking process for the application process

- automating many of the administrative processes needed

- making it possible to link in with other relevant sources of information, such as learning opportunities and competency requirements

Another area where the integration offered by e-HR systems can provide benefits is in recording time and attendance. Perhaps the key feature here is that time and attendance can be monitored in real time. As people come and go from work, the attendance database is constantly updated so that anyone logging in through an on-line system can find instant information about a wide range of information such as:

- who is in the building

- how many hours people have spent on particular projects

- trends developing in absence patterns.

Finally, the chapter looks at the role e-HR can play in performance management. The performance management process is sometimes seen as a largely bureaucratic exercise, a perspective that can detract from its value. Automation of the administrative aspects of the process, plus easier access to performance-related information such as learning and promotion opportunities, can help to strip away this perception.

e-Recruitment

One of the mantras for modern businesses is that they must be able to adapt quickly to the ever-changing marketplace. It follows therefore, that as 'people are our greatest asset', the way in which a business uses its employees must also be able to adapt quickly. It is consequently not surprising that many forward-looking businesses are finding ways of using intranet-based systems to speed up their recruitment processes.

What are some of the ways in which e-recruitment works? Let us look at some of the possibilities.

Advertising vacancies

You can advertise current vacancies in a 'Jobs' section of your intranet and, depending on the nature of the vacancy and your recruitment policy for the job, you may also make this available publicly on your Internet web site.

Traditional ways of advertising vacancies mean that the sponsor must decide what information to provide to potential applicants and then spend time gathering and packaging this. Intranet advertisements can provide links to relevant parts of the intranet that can give people interested in applying further information. Potential applicants can then use their own interest and initiative to help them decide what further information they need in order to decide whether they want to apply for the job. If you were to install a webcam in the office where the vacancy is, prospective applicants could even watch what goes on in the office and get a feel for the working atmosphere!

This all means that job sponsors can save a considerable amount of time and job applicants collect exactly what information they need.

Providing search engines

Search engines are now standard technology that can easily be installed within an intranet. This makes it much easier for employees to find a particular type of job. For example, someone may be looking for a job within the Marketing Department based in the Edinburgh office. They can ask a search engine to see if such a vacancy currently exists. If it does, they can find further information but, if not, they can register their interest in such a position with the system. Then, as soon as Edinburgh starts to look for a marketing person, an e-mail is automatically sent to that employee giving them full information about the vacancy. This could mean that the vacancy has attracted a number of applicants within minutes or hours of it being made public.

You can also, of course, register these vacancies with one or more of the many Internet and job search engines.

Links to previous employers and educational establishments

Checking the accuracy of a job applicant's claims regarding previous work experience and educational achievements is a time-consuming and somewhat tedious activity that, nevertheless, must be done. E-mail connections to and from intranet and Internet sites make it possible to streamline this process considerably.

Applicant tracking systems

Applicant tracking systems allow you to monitor and manage the progress of the application process. Systems typically include features such as:

- CV scanning software with Optical Character Recognition (OCR) facilities
- generation of standard letters, for printing and posting or for delivery by e-mail
- recording details about where individual applications are
- time scheduling for participants in the selection process.

You can see that many of these features are enhanced by the ability to link in with standard network applications such as e-mail and personal on-line calendars.

On-line testing

On-line systems are increasingly being used to test employees and potential employees. For potential employees this can take the form of an informal screening, where people expressing some interest in a particular position can take a test that will give them some idea about whether they have the necessary skills, knowledge and aptitude needed. Such tests can also be formal in nature, where the person's performance is used to make some decisions about whether or not to take their application further.

Psychometric testing is an obvious candidate for on-line delivery. Most of the major players in psychometric testing offer on-line testing services, sometimes done automatically and sometimes with a human moderator.

Using on-line delivery of psychometric testing for pre-employment screening has a number of advantages:

- It avoids the need to bring people to a central location, reducing recruitment costs.
- Larger numbers of people can be screened in the same amount of time.

The Canadian government has been using on-line pre-employment screening for a number of years and has reported cost reductions of over 50 per cent in the recruitment process as a result.

Of course, there are also some drawbacks:

- The possibility of the test being taken by someone other than the official candidate must be recognised (if done externally).

- On-line testing discriminates against people with limited computer skills, although this may be a relevant criterion for jobs involving technology.

- Care must be taken not to discriminate against people with disabilities.

Skills testing may also be used internally as part of regular performance appraisal procedures.

 Performance management is discussed in more detail later in this chapter.

What are the benefits of e-recruitment?

Speeding up the recruitment process

It is important to remember that people are adapting to the dynamism of the modern workplace. Few people expect to stay in the same job for a long period of time nowadays, particularly the more ambitious and talented members of the workforce. Businesses who want to keep hold of these people must therefore make sure that the internal job marketplace is more interesting and dynamic than the external marketplace.

The technology can enhance both internal and external recruitment procedures. Let us first consider how posts are filled internally in traditional organisations.

A manager identifies an opening within their department, say because of expansion within the department. As soon as they have drawn up a job description and perhaps a profile of the type of the person needed to fill the role, they will advertise the vacancy. Elapsed time, say, one week.

How will they advertise the vacancy? Noticeboards, internal newsletters and magazines are typical media for internal job advertisements, but we immediately find two problems with this. Firstly, posting these advertisements takes time. Newsletters and magazines may only appear monthly or quarterly and will have strict deadlines for going to press. Even pinning advertisements to noticeboards will take some time, especially in organisations operating over several sites. Taking these delays into account will mean that the time allowed for applicants to respond will have to be fairly generous. The clock keeps ticking. The second problem with the method is that it relies on people 'pulling' on the information: the advertisements sit there and wait for people to read them and there is limited control over who does actually read them. After all, the ideal candidates may be so focused on their present jobs that they do not read noticeboards and staff magazines and have not really considered the possibility of looking for new positions. Elapsed time, say, six weeks.

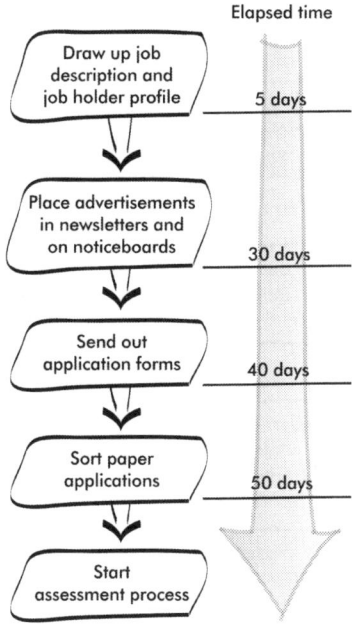

Figure 5.1
Timescales for internal recruitment using traditional methods

Interested people respond to the advertisements. They may do this by sending in a CV, which saves time but does mean that the selection process has to consider unstructured information from applicants. They may alternatively be asked to complete application forms which does make it easier to compare different applicants but again adds to the time taken for the recruitment process. By the time applicants have sent in their application forms, between one and two months could have gone by.

Let us now think about how an e-HR system could help to speed up this process. Firstly, advertising. Details about the vacancy could be given on a jobs page on the intranet. This still relies on people finding the advertisement, but the chances of this can be increased greatly by providing links to the advertisement from other pages in the intranet that people likely to be interested in the position would be using routinely. Supplement this by e-mail advertising: send out e-mails containing information about the vacancy to people working in departments where potential applicants are likely to be. But do this with care! People nowadays are increasingly being overwhelmed by unsolicited e-mail. This second tactic introduces the concept of 'push' technology: instead of relying on people pulling job information towards them you are pushing it at them. Strategies such as this have the potential to dramatically reduce the amount of time needed for advertising a job vacancy.

Instead of having to wait weeks to see the advertisement appear in the company magazine, information about the vacancy will be circulating within the organisation minutes after an agreement about what should be advertised. Elapsed time, perhaps six days.

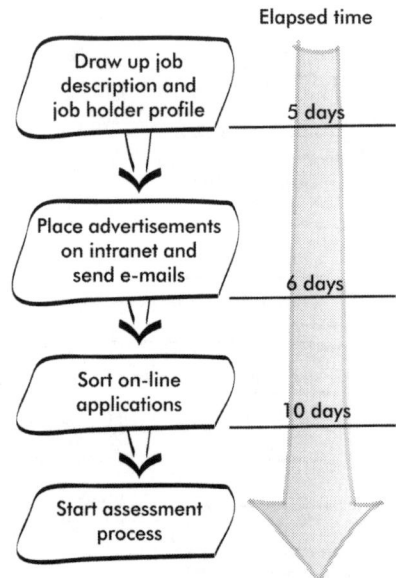

Figure 5.2
Timescales for internal recruitment using e-HR methods

The e-HR system can also help with responses. Intranet advertisements and e-mails can contain hyperlinks that take the potential applicants to an on-line form that they complete and submit immediately. Within hours of posting the job advertisements you could have applications pouring through your electronic letterbox.

So how does this compare with the traditional method? Instead of a total elapsed time of perhaps two months between identifying the vacancy and starting to sift the responses we are looking at perhaps one or two weeks. Time to fill is reduced by weeks and what is the value of that? The right person in post quickly means that they are quickly doing what is needed for the business and the opportunity costs of the vacant post are minimised. This must surely look attractive to an organisation wanting to adapt itself quickly to a changing marketplace.

The benefits for saving time do not end there. As applications are submitted using an on-line form, information on applicants will be held within a database. Therefore, as long as the form has been appropriately designed, it will be possible to sort applicants by any relevant factor – for example, years of experience in the organisation or relevant academic qualifications.

Depending on the sophistication of the e-HR system it may be possible to go even further. If occupational competencies are stored on-line, someone looking for someone to fill a vacancy could interrogate the system to draw up a list of everyone with appropriate competencies. They could then be sent e-mails with information about the vacancy. Such an approach would automatically mean that people with inappropriate qualifications and experience, who have no chance of getting the job do not waste their time filling in application forms. Such a system has really turned the job hunting process on its head: instead of people hunting jobs, the jobs hunt people. But beware! There are serious ethical issues that need to be considered and addressed with approaches such as these. These ethical issues are discussed later in this chapter.

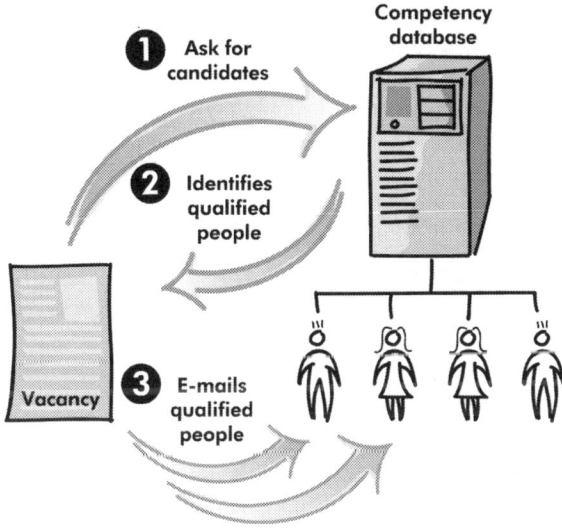

Figure 5.3
Jobs hunting people

It is also possible to set up systems where people looking for particular types of work can register their interest so that, if such vacancies come up, the system will automatically notify them. People registering an interest in particular work could also be directed to on-line assessment tests that would identify whether they have the necessary skills, knowledge or aptitude characteristics.

BP's intranet offers myProfile, where employees can enter information about their qualifications and experience. This information then feeds into myJobMarket, which deals with over 10 000 internal job vacancies each year. Vacancies are matched to skills in the organisation and e-mails are sent automatically to employees with the necessary requirements.

Cutting out intermediaries

Many organisations rely on temporary employees to cover for such things as peaks in workload or sickness absence. They therefore use agencies that maintain a database of freelance or casual workers. The advantage to the organisation is that the task of managing this database is left to someone else, but the disadvantages are that:

- the actual process of identifying a temporary worker can be fairly slow

- the intermediaries charge for their service, meaning that the contracting organisation has to pay a premium while the part-time worker probably accepts a lower hourly rate for the convenience of the agency finding the work.

E-HR can simplify this process. Let us consider the example of schools, which have a constant need for supply teachers. They often only know that they will need a supply teacher in the hour before school starts so it is important that they can identify a suitable teacher quickly.

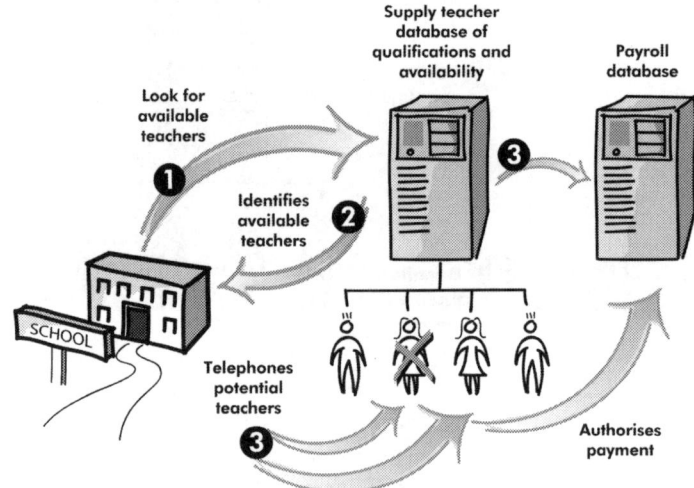

Figure 5.4
Identifying supply teachers

The local authority maintains a database which stores records about all the qualified supply teachers in its area. Each weekend the supply teachers who are actively looking for work log into the database through an Internet connection and indicate on which days of the following week they are available.

Now, Monday morning comes and a school realises that it needs a supply teacher for mathematics classes. It logs into the supply teacher site on the local authority's intranet and searches for a mathematics teacher who is available that day. Within five minutes they have identified a number of possible teachers and can contact them by telephone to see if they can make it into the school. One of them says yes – problem solved. The e-recruitment system has saved the local authority some money and has provided the school with a solution to its teacher shortage within minutes. The system records the unavailability of that teacher for the next enquirers.

But the advantages do not stop there. When the supply teacher has finished their day's work, the school again logs into the database and records this fact. This event automatically triggers a message that goes to the authority's payroll system saying that this supply teacher needs to be paid for this day's work. Yet more administrative savings.

Organisations can also use processes such as this to help with redeployment. Most businesses would much rather be able to redeploy staff than have to make them redundant. Staff needing to be redeployed can be identified on the capability database as being of high priority for internal recruitment. An e-recruitment system can quickly identify such people and place them in new positions.

Ethicality of computer-based selection

While in theory a recruitment process based on the yes-no neutrality of a computer system seems to eliminate human prejudice from selection, we have to remember that the selection criteria used by the system are, of course, created by people. Garbage in, garbage out. It is in practice just as easy for a prejudiced administrator to discriminate against people of a certain colour or religion with a technology-based system than with the traditional method of sifting piles of CVs. In fact, one could argue that it is easier as the selection process is hidden within the black box of the computer system.

There are particular dangers when such systems are used, or are thought to be used, to identify employees for redundancy purposes. This is such a sensitive issue that it is vital that decisions are made in an open, humane way.

Consequently there are some major ethical issues surrounding the use of e-HR systems such as those described here and any implementation of such a system should be done with a great deal of care and sensitivity.

Where such systems can be of value and the ethical issue is possibly less of a problem is where a project team must be assembled at short notice. The project manager knows that people with certain skills and knowledge are required and the capability matching system can be used to quickly identify suitable people within the organisation.

What do you have to do to make e-recruitment a success?

As is discussed in some detail in Chapter 9, the biggest obstacles to successful systems implementation are the organisational rather than the technical ones. It is not actually very difficult to post job advertisements on an intranet page, nor is it difficult to send e-mails informing people of the vacancy. What is difficult is in getting people to change how they manage their role within the recruitment process so that they take maximum advantage of the benefits e-recruitment can offer.

Develop standards for job descriptions and job holder profiles

The first organisational obstacle in the recruitment process can occur if everyone does their own thing as far as writing job descriptions is concerned. Standard templates for job descriptions and job holder profiles make it much easier to link competencies to job roles.

Make job recruitment decisions quickly

Technology makes it possible to advertise a job and receive applications within hours. But, of course, applicants realise this and expect decisions to be made correspondingly quickly. Long lead times in traditional recruitment processes often make people involved in the selection process adopt a somewhat relaxed attitude. After all, if it has taken eight weeks to get to the stage of sorting through a pile of applications, what does it matter if it takes a few extra days to draw up a shortlist?

Such an attitude will not work at all if you are using an e-recruitment process. Decision-makers in the recruitment process need to move quickly and to have strong personal discipline to take full advantage of the benefits gained by e-recruitment.

Develop systems for finding suitable candidates

Integrated recruitment and appraisal systems, linked by search engines, will make it much easier for managers to find the right candidates for the jobs.

Design easy-to-use job sites

Every intranet should have a site where current vacancies are advertised. Cullen[1] proposes some guidelines for such sites:

1. They should be easily accessible from the homepage.

2. They should contain an up-to-date list of openings. Expired vacancies must be removed immediately.

3. Job descriptions should follow the same format so that they can be easily understood.

4. Advertisements should contain links allowing applicants to easily send e-mails to relevant people.

5. The application process should be clear and concise.

Recording time and attendance

Time and attendance systems focus on recording the hours worked by employees and tracking absences, which may be for a variety of reasons:

- recording hours worked for payroll purposes

- recording billable hours worked on specific projects

- recording information needed for project management purposes

- recording who is in and out of a building, perhaps for health and safety purposes

- recording information about absenteeism, and generating reports based on parameters such as Monday-Friday absenteeism or Bradford Factors for employees.

Much of the functionality of on-line systems is similar to that found in existing client-server applications. However, the integration of databases and the universality of the browser interface offers a great deal of extra flexibility and functionality.

It becomes possible for people working at any location around the world to clock in for work. For example, someone staying in a hotel in a foreign city could clock in via the Internet using a public telephone connection. Information on where they are would then be immediately available to everyone else in the organisation.

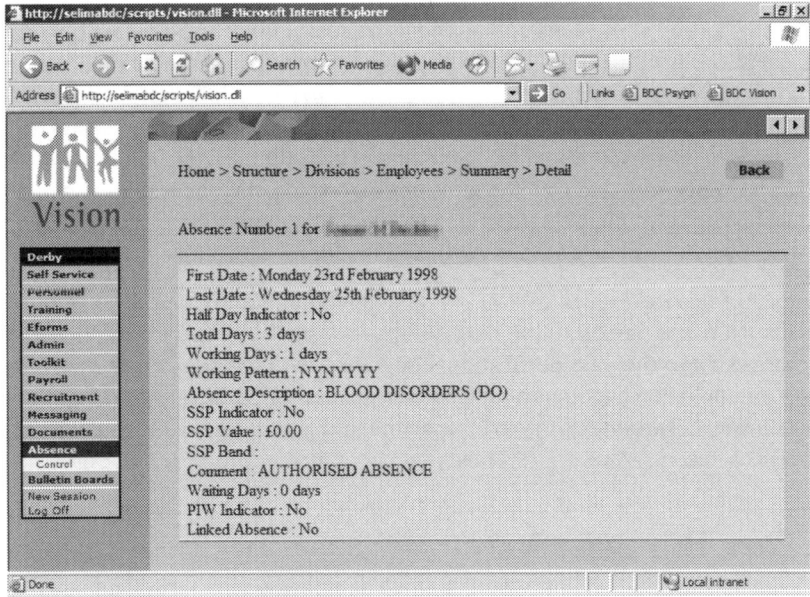

© Selima Software, www.selima.co.uk

Figure 5.5
Recording absence information
This shows a screen available to a manager that shows absence information for an employee.

As well as feeding the payroll and finance systems, the information could also be available to receptionists at the front desk or on the main telephone switchboard, mimicking the familiar dry-wipe board that is a feature of many offices. The advantage of the electronic system is that it is constantly up to date and available everywhere. For example, someone arriving at the reception desk for a two o'clock meeting could immediately be told that the person they have come to see is still at lunch, rather than the somewhat unsatisfactory 'I'm sorry, they are not answering their telephone. Would you like to wait?' A manager working in Tokyo could find out who is in the office in Tadcaster.

How do time and attendance systems work?

On-line time and attendance systems can work in a number of different ways. They generally allow people to clock in and out of using whatever technologies are appropriate to the business. Shopfloor workers can continue to clock in using a punch or swipe card system, while office workers can clock in and out through their desktops. Whatever the means employed, the data is fed to the central database.

It is important to make sure that any system you choose supports the method of time entry that is most appropriate for your organisation. Time clocks would probably not be acceptable in an office environment and computer entry may not be practical in a workshop setting.

Information recorded about time and attendance usually needs to go through an approval process, traditionally by a supervisor or line manager signing timesheets that are then passed on within the business. The information may then go in different directions for different purposes, to the Payroll Department for the calculation of salaries and to Production Management for monitoring hours worked and overtime implications, for example. The paper trail that this implies is often a source of error and delay, with timesheets ending up at the bottom of an overworked supervisor's in-tray or disappearing in the internal post.

E-HR systems can automate all of this. Workflow processes automatically route the information from one person to the next and, as soon as the necessary authorisation is given, it moves on to the next destination. Integration with e-mail systems means that timesheet authorisation becomes a much easier process to operate and monitor. If a timesheet is late arriving in the Payroll Department, it is an easy matter to check its workflow record and see where it is held up.

What are the benefits?

Improved accessibility of information

While client-server applications may be able to generate the same types of information that an on-line system can provide, it is only available to people with the client licence. That means that managers needing the information may well have to contact someone in the HR or Payroll Departments to ask for information. An on-line system can make the information immediately available to that manager, saving administrative time for these departments. This is a big advantage.

If a manager has the feeling that one of their employees seems to be taking Mondays off more frequently than would be expected, it is very easy for them to ask the system to provide them with the information. If the information confirms their suspicions, they are in a much stronger position to tackle this absenteeism with the employee concerned. With a client-server system they might have to complete a request for the information, which would waste time and might put the manager off.

For client-related information there may be advantages to granting access to the client to view information. For example, you may be invoicing a client for amounts that depend on the number of hours worked. If you were to provide them with on-line access to view who is working on their account and how many hours they are spending on it, this could provide a great deal of transparency in the relationship which would have positive benefits for generating trust.

Information available more quickly

As data is being fed into the system in real time, information can be obtained in real time. Think about the example described earlier of the manufacturing business losing employees to lower back pain. In a traditional system the employees would have probably completed a paper sickness absence form which would have passed through the internal postal system to an administrator in the HR Department. Depending on their workload and the importance they attached to the form, it may have sat on a desk for several days before it was entered into the system. Even assuming that the system identified the trend in sickness absence immediately, production could have been affected for at least a week longer than if the e-HR system were in use. How much would that have cost the business?

The availability of information in real time has other benefits. For example:

- The number of billable hours worked on specific projects is immediately available to project managers or people responsible for producing invoices. This has obvious benefits for shortening the cash flow cycle within the business.

- Employees and line managers wanting to know how many normal and overtime hours they or their staff have worked during the current month can find this out immediately.

- For many organisations salary costs are the single largest item over which there is some degree of control. Easy and immediate access to current information about salary costs for all makes managing the profitability of a business much easier.

Elimination of transcription errors

Whenever information has to be manually transferred from one system to another there is the danger of transcription errors. For example, if people are recording hours worked in a project management system and someone is reading off those hours and using them to calculate figures to go on invoices, sooner or later a mistake will be made. Errors lead to costs. Employees may be overpaid, and while some may keep quiet about it, leading to an obvious cost, the majority will report it, in which case time must be spent recalculating the pay and issuing a new payslip.

With an on-line system, the data from the time and attendance system is recorded in one database to which the invoicing system has access, so that the potential for clerical error is eliminated.

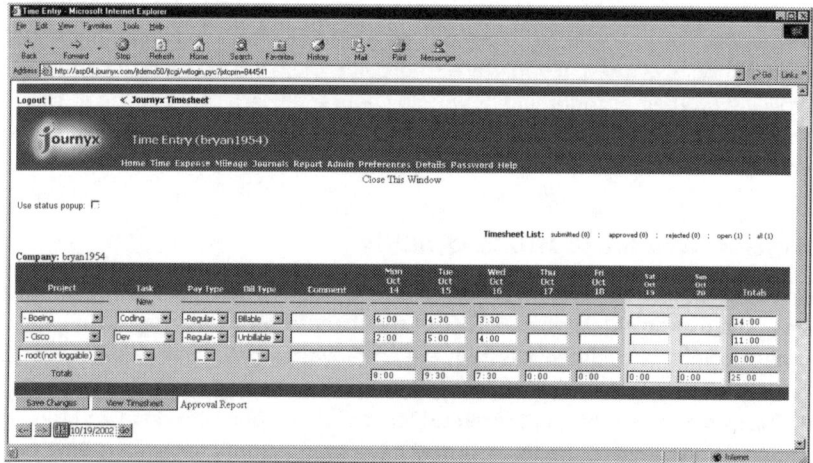

© journyx, www.journyx.com

Figure 5.6
Time recording system
This screen shows the timesheet facility within journyx. The user can enter their time spent against cost centres, and that information is immediately available for billing and project management purposes.

Automatic reminders

How much time does the Payroll Department spend ringing around other departments at the beginning of a week or month asking for the previous period's timesheets? On-line systems can automatically generate e-mails reminding managers of the approaching cut-off date for procedures such as verifying the electronic timesheets.

Managing performance

Here we will take a look at how on-line technologies can help the performance management process.

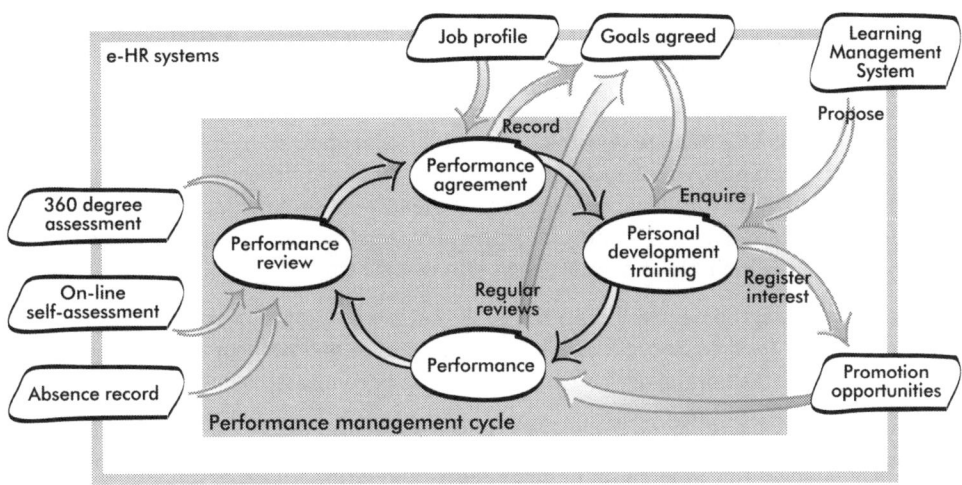

Figure 5.7
The performance management cycle

Figure 5.7 shows the performance management cycle, as proposed by Armstrong[2]. It identifies four stages in the process:

1.	**The performance agreement**	A formal statement of the requirements of the job in the form of objectives or competencies required.
2.	**Personal development planning**	The job holder develops a plan that will enable them to meet the requirements of their current responsibilities and prepare them for career developments.
3.	**Performance**	The job holder carries out their responsibilities.
4.	**Performance review**	The job holder meets with an appropriate person, possibly their line manager, to formally review performance over the previous period and to plan for the future.

Let us look at this process in more detail and see how e-HR systems could support it.

The performance agreement

The performance agreement is driven by the definition of the role, which will be contained in a document such as a job description or job profile.

Job descriptions became a compulsory part of every working person's life in the 1970s. Neatly typed lists of responsibilities, they soon found their way to the back of the Personnel Department's filing cabinets and employees' drawers. Often made somewhat worthless by the inclusion of catch-all phrases such as 'Any other requirements necessary for the functioning of the department' and rendered obsolete by the march of technology, they have become somewhat discredited.

However, the centralised nature of intranet technology makes it possible to provide job descriptions or profiles that are dynamic, constantly being updated to reflect changes in working practices. Employees should be able to click through to their own job description from their portal. Each individual requirement of the job can be linked with training opportunities recorded in a Learning Management System to make it easy for people to see what training is available to support each area of their job.

The performance agreement will drive the goals that the employee needs to aim for, and these can be recorded on-line, accessible by the employee and perhaps their line manager throughout the course of the performance period for ongoing assessment purposes.

People should be able to check the profiles for other jobs, perhaps ones that they think they may be interested in applying for. The profiles could provide hyperlinks that would take the people to on-line skill or knowledge assessments that would show the person whether or not they are ready for this set of responsibilities. The links provided to the LMS would show them what training they need to complete in order to prepare themselves for those jobs.

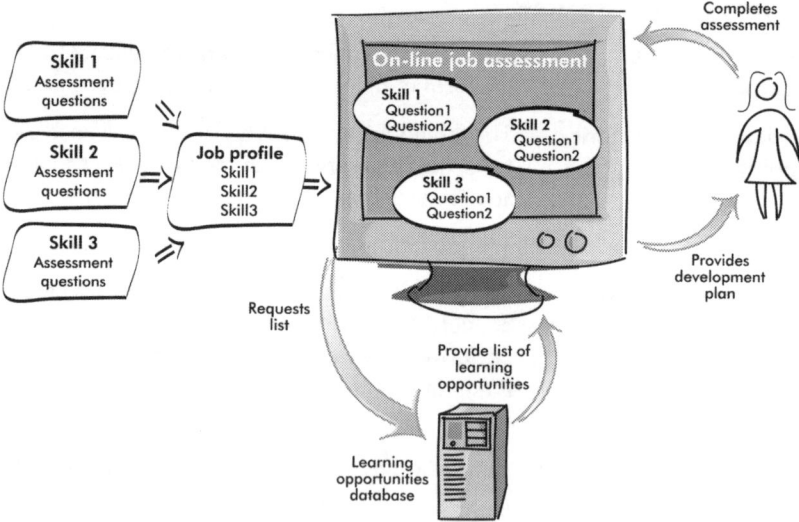

Figure 5.8
Constructing an on-line job assessment

Such a system could also be used as part of a recruitment process, where the results of the test were made available to the person responsible for selection. They would then have a good idea as to what the training needs were for each applicant.

Personal development planning

Personal development plans typically contain such things as opportunities for broadening experience and training requirements. An on-line performance management system should allow the person to investigate what learning opportunities are available and for them to make the necessary arrangements to attend courses or enrol for distance learning programmes.

The plan may reflect the individual's interest in promotion or transfer to another part of the business. They should therefore be able to register this interest in an e-recruitment system that will automatically notify them of suitable opportunities as they arise.

Performance

While the person is working they can review their performance against their on-line plan. This may imply some additional training, for example, which they can duly find and arrange on-line.

The performance review

Performance reviews are typically annual events, with an employee and their line manager arranging a date to meet and discuss what has happened in the previous year and agreeing on the goals or targets for the year to come. On-line systems can provide an effective support for this process.

At an appropriate time before an appraisal is due, the system can automatically e-mail reminders to the people involved, asking them to liaise and arrange a meeting. It may even be possible for the system to interrogate on-line calendars and identify times when all parties are free and suggest potential dates.

E-HR systems should not replace the person-to-person contact of an appraisal system as it is still obviously important for an employee to talk in person to their line manager. However, the system could provide a template for the interview to follow and fields where the manager and the employee can type in their record of the interview. The template could be constructed there and then, by accessing the job profile database and identifying what skills are needed for the employee's job. This would then provide a central and easily accessible record (by the employee and the manager) of what was agreed.

In organisations where this has been implemented, one enhancement has been to devise means whereby the recording process can be completed off-line. People often like to reflect on what has been discussed during an interview and make a record later, perhaps while at home or at their laptop while travelling on a train. The parties involved can then share what they have written before an agreed version is finally uploaded to the HR database.

In preparation for the performance review the employee could take an on-line self-assessment test or they could arrange an on-line 360 degree assessment. The line manager could also pull in information from other systems, such as the individual's absence record if this were an issue.

360 degree feedback

360 degree feedback is used by some companies as a method for assessing performance. The basic principle is as shown in Figure 5.9.

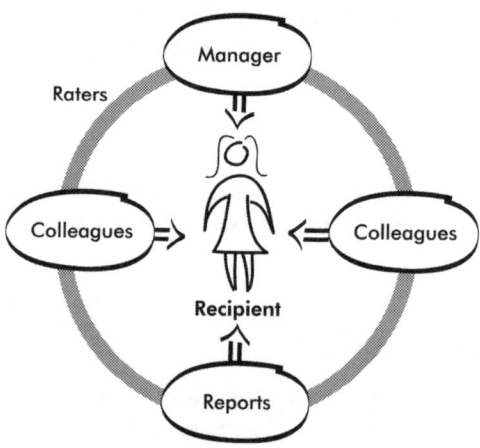

Figure 5.9
360 degree feedback

The individual employee (usually described as the **recipient**) seeks feedback on relevant aspects of their performance from their line manager, colleagues on the same or similar levels and from people who report to them (the **raters**). Sometimes levels above or below are omitted from the process and sometimes feedback is also sought from people outside the organisation – for example, customers or suppliers (in which case the process is sometimes described as 540 degree feedback).

One major US retail chain has implemented an on-line system for providing feedback on its store managers. Having recognised that there was a link between the working atmosphere in branches and the level of sales it decided to introduce a 360 degree feedback system that would provide its store managers with feedback on how sales staff perceived the management of the branch. On a particular date each month staff access kiosks and complete a simple questionnaire asking them for their opinions about how things are in the store. This information is collated and passed on to the manager, who can then take any necessary action. It has apparently proved to be successful in raising the performance of what were seen to be poorly managed stores.

360 degree feedback is usually collected in a structured way using questionnaires, and software solutions have been in use for a number of years. Increasingly these solutions are available on-line, which offers a number of advantages:

- Requests for feedback can be distributed using e-mail, with the recipient clicking on a link to access the 360 degree feedback application.

- Reminders to people who have not submitted feedback can be generated automatically, reducing the amount of administration needed.

- When everyone (or at least a quorum) has provided feedback a report is generated and delivered either on-line or in an Adobe Acrobat file.

However, there are some significant difficulties and disadvantages:

- People can be somewhat blunt in comments made on-line, and with the communication lacking auditory and visual clues, resulting feedback can be distressing.

- There is still a need for human intervention to make sure the process works smoothly, such as making sure that people do provide feedback when requested.

- It is better for a real person to moderate the feedback to make sure that nothing potentially damaging passes through the process.

- The speed at which the process happens can be a disadvantage. There definitely seem to be benefits to a slower process that allows people to reflect before offering opinions about someone else.

Best practice in on-line 360 degree feedback

360 degree feedback has become popular because of its effectiveness in the appraisal process. The effectiveness comes from its power, but this power can also make it a potentially dangerous and damaging tool to use. For this reason it must be implemented with care.

It is beyond the scope of this book to discuss best practice guidelines for 360 degree feedback in detail, but it is important to think about how best to implement on-line approaches. The UK government has made available a set of best practice guidelines[3], developed by a number of organisations involved in the field of appraisal, such as the British Psychological Society and the Chartered Institute of Personnel and Development. The suggestions below have been developed from these.

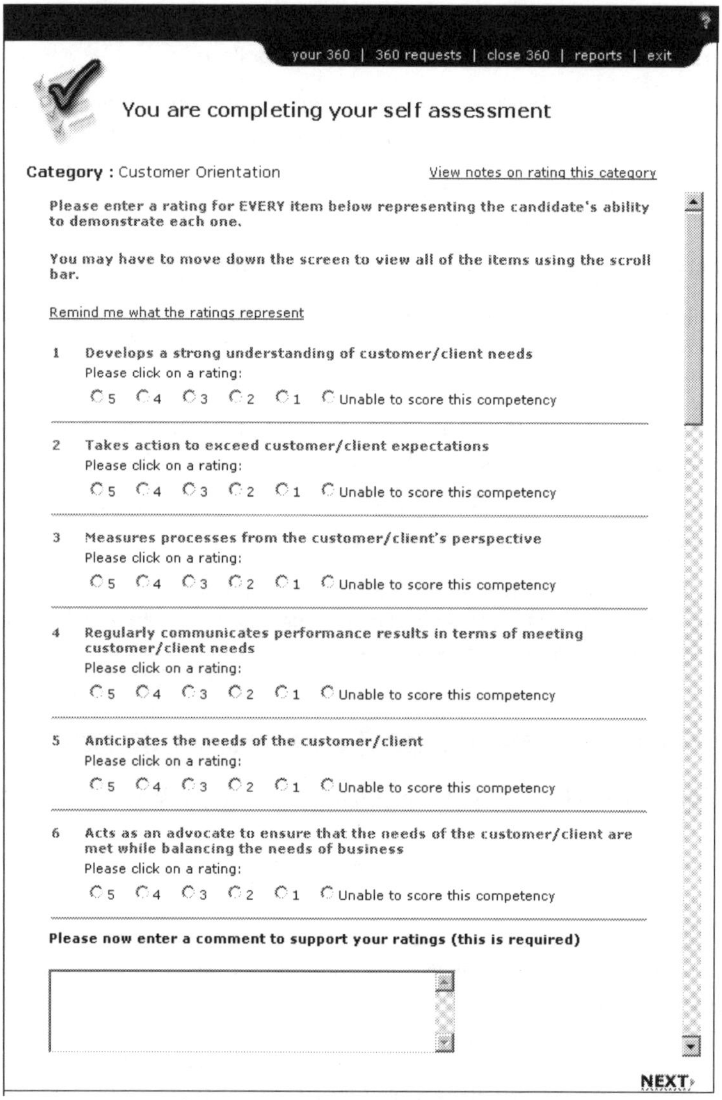

your 360 | 360 requests | close 360 | reports | exit

You are completing your self assessment

Category : Customer Orientation   View notes on rating this category

Please enter a rating for EVERY item below representing the candidate's ability to demonstrate each one.

You may have to move down the screen to view all of the items using the scroll bar.

Remind me what the ratings represent

1   Develops a strong understanding of customer/client needs
Please click on a rating:
○ 5   ○ 4   ○ 3   ○ 2   ○ 1   ○ Unable to score this competency

2   Takes action to exceed customer/client expectations
Please click on a rating:
○ 5   ○ 4   ○ 3   ○ 2   ○ 1   ○ Unable to score this competency

3   Measures processes from the customer/client's perspective
Please click on a rating:
○ 5   ○ 4   ○ 3   ○ 2   ○ 1   ○ Unable to score this competency

4   Regularly communicates performance results in terms of meeting customer/client needs
Please click on a rating:
○ 5   ○ 4   ○ 3   ○ 2   ○ 1   ○ Unable to score this competency

5   Anticipates the needs of the customer/client
Please click on a rating:
○ 5   ○ 4   ○ 3   ○ 2   ○ 1   ○ Unable to score this competency

6   Acts as an advocate to ensure that the needs of the customer/client are met while balancing the needs of business
Please click on a rating:
○ 5   ○ 4   ○ 3   ○ 2   ○ 1   ○ Unable to score this competency

Please now enter a comment to support your ratings (this is required)

NEXT

© Inch-perfect Ltd, www.inch-perfect.com

Figure 5.10
A 360 degree feedback assessment form
This is an example of an on-line 360 degree assessment questionnaire.
The rater is asked to assess the recipient on a five-point scale against a number of criteria.
The ratings can easily be stored and processed by the application.

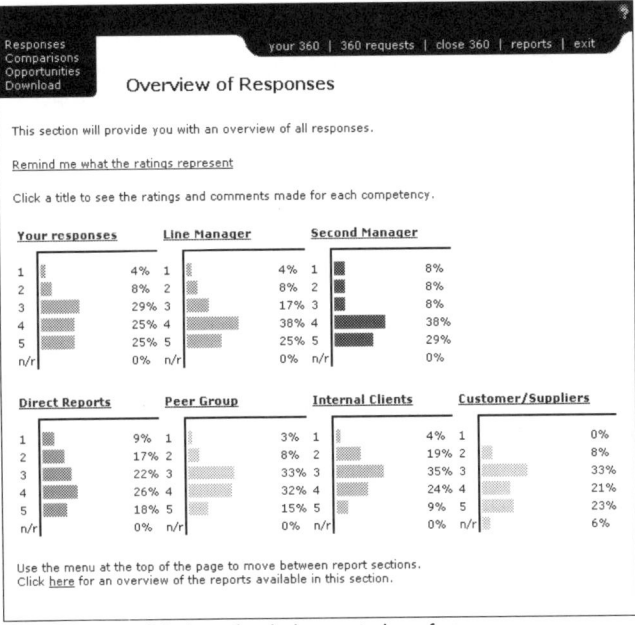

Figure 5.11
Feedback on the 360 degree process
This shows how feedback could be presented by the application, broken down by the different rater groups submitting feedback.

Make sure you are clear about the purpose of 360 degree feedback processes

On-line 360 degree feedback solutions are often sold with an emphasis on how much easier they make the process. This may tempt some organisations to rush into an implementation without thinking clearly about why they are doing it. It should only be implemented as a process in organisations that already have a strong performance appraisal culture.

Make sure you have clearly defined objectives for the process which link to organisational strategies and goals.

Decide how the raters will be identified

It is important to decide at the outset who will identify who the individual's raters are going to be. On-line systems usually allow the recipient to do this, and this may be acceptable as long as there are clear guidelines for who the raters must be and how many must be involved.

Decide how feedback will be presented

On-line systems compile feedback into a report that can be sent straight to the recipient or it can be delivered by a trained facilitator. Whether or not a facilitator delivers the report, it is most important that someone is available to discuss the feedback with the recipient.

It is generally considered to be important that feedback is kept anonymous so that the recipient cannot identify who has given what feedback.

On-line systems are often based around multiple-choice rating questions, which are easy to answer and for a computer system to aggregate, and then present a summary. However, such systems can hide differences in perspective that may be valuable.

If free-form answers are also requested, these should be provided in the feedback but human intervention will be necessary to make sure that this feedback is not potentially distressing.

Keep systems secure

It is important to make sure that the entire process for feedback is kept secure, and that only nominated people have access to the information.

Monitor and review the programme

Key people involved in managing the feedback programme should monitor and review it to make sure it is meeting its purpose. This will involve such things as:

- piloting before fully implementing
- making sure that the questionnaire works
- making sure that the feedback process is effective.

Summarising ...

- E-recruitment covers a number of related processes, such as advertising vacancies, applicant tracking and on-line testing.
- E-recruitment offers a number of benefits, including speeding up recruitment and cutting out intermediaries.
- The ethical issues surrounding e-recruitment must be treated with great care.
- E-recruitment works most effectively if you can:
  - develop standard job profiles
  - make sure that people involved in the recruitment process work efficiently
  - find ways of targeting suitable employees

- — develop easy-to-use job sites.
- E-HR offers a number of benefits for time and attendance systems:
  - — Information is more accessible.
  - — Information is available in real time.
  - — Data processing errors are reduced.
  - — Time management processes can be automated.
- On-line systems can provide useful support to the performance management process.
- 360 degree feedback can be delivered and managed effectively using on-line systems.

Notes

1. Cullen, B., (2001), 'E-recruiting is Driving HR Systems Integration', *Strategic Finance*, **Vol. 83**, No. 1.

2. Armstrong, M, (2001), *A Handbook of Human Resource Management Practice*, London: Kogan Page.

3. '360 Degree Feedback: Best Practice Guidelines', http://www.dti.gov.uk/mbp/360feedback/

chapter 6

Improving collaboration and learning

Previous chapters have looked at how e-HR systems can improve the flow of information within an organisation for quite specific purposes. In this chapter we will look at improving the flow of information for softer, less clearly defined purposes – for example, for general business communications, collaborative processes and training.

Many words have been written over the years on the subject of organisational learning, and it is not the intention of this book to try to further the debate. However, in order to set the contents of this chapter into a context, we need to provide a simple explanation of what organisational learning is so that we can show how e-HR can contribute to it.

In essence, an organisation is learning when it acquires information, uses it and changes as a result. It is the third part of this process that proves to be the difficult issue for most organisations – the leap from what Argyris referred to as single-loop to double-loop learning. Fortunately for the authors, this stage is beyond the scope of this book, and what we shall concentrate on is looking at how intranet technologies can help organisations to acquire and use information.

This chapter therefore covers a number of different topics, all of which are linked by the fact that they are means by which information can be circulated within an organisation. This includes:

- making information available on the intranet
- what knowledge management means in the context of e-HR systems
- managing documents
- carrying out organisational surveys
- improving collaboration
- managing and delivering formal learning opportunities.

Making information available

Given that the World Wide Web (which is actually just one specific function within the global network we call the Internet) was developed as a way of sharing information amongst computer professionals, it is hardly surprising that its intranet spawn spent its formative years delivering organisational information. Businesses quickly realised that such things as telephone directories, policy guides and procedural information could very easily be transferred to the intranet. This makes a lot of sense, as it makes the information instantly available to everyone, eliminates printing and storage costs and means that information is always up to date (as long as changes are implemented on the server!). Word processing software quickly acquired the ability to 'Save as HTML' so that documents originally designed to be printed out suddenly became available as web pages.

This remains the situation while organisations' intranets stay in the first- and second-generation stages. This terminology was explained in Chapter 2 but, as a reminder, these are intranets that rely heavily on simple HTML to produce static pages – in other words, pages whose content is fixed and where users cannot enter information into or extract information from databases. E-HR systems take intranets into the fourth generation, where information is routinely added to and extracted from databases. This opens up a number of new possibilities.

Information becomes active

Documents, such as procedural manuals stored on an intranet, often remain passive. If someone wants to find out how to, say, make an expenses claim for a car journey, they will possibly have to:

- access the on-line manual covering expenses claims

- search for the page covering mileage allowances

- make a note of the allowances and the procedure to follow

- complete an expenses claim form

- send the completed form to the Payroll Department.

An e-HR system can automate all of this. Instead of providing the employee with the information so that they can drive the procedure, the procedure drives the information. The employee carries out the particular procedure on-line and the system draws relevant information from the person's records and asks the person to provide other information as necessary. For example, the system could automatically calculate mileage expenses just by knowing the engine size of the employee's car, which may already be recorded in the personal information database.

Of course, the manual can also provide links that will provide the user with an on-line form so if someone does choose to read the manual they can easily jump straight to carrying out the procedure that they are investigating. However, there is an argument that there is no need to provide static, generic information if embedded personal information can be used to construct dynamic personalised information as required.

Information can be targeted to people who want it

E-HR systems allow people to sign up to receive information about subjects they are interested in, which could be from within the organisation or external, via the Internet. These could be work-related, such as new clients or market research feedback or personal, such as the latest news from Sheffield Wednesday Football Club (or perhaps not).

There are various mechanisms for making this happen. One common way is by providing a bulletin board. When a user loads the bulletin board page the system calls information from a database that displays on the screen as a list of topics, within which there are contributions from different people. The user can then read the contributions and add to them or start a new topic. They can also asked to be informed as and when new contributions are added. If they do this, every time they open their e-HR portal page they will see a message indicating that a new contribution has been made. Alternatively they could be sent an e-mail of the contribution itself.

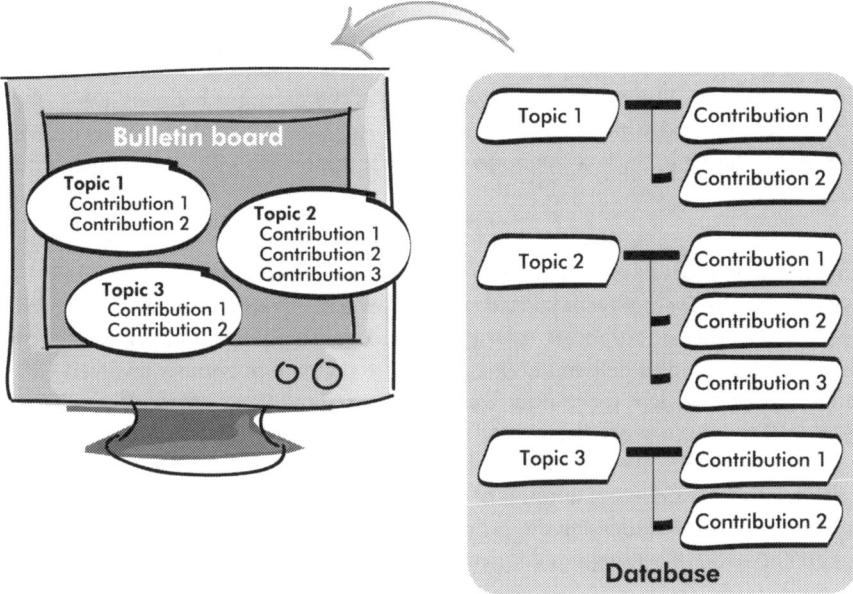

Figure 6.1
How a bulletin board uses a database

Answers to important questions can be made more accessible

As with probably most aspects of life, there are a certain number of questions that people tend to ask over and over again. Certainly, if you are using a call centre to provide an HR service you will have developed a clear picture of what commonly concerns your employees. It therefore makes sense to provide a link from your employee portal to a part of the site where they can look up the answers to frequently asked questions (FAQs).

This can be provided as a static page, but it is also possible to make the page specific to the person logging on. For example, questions about holiday entitlement may require different answers depending on the grade and length of service of the enquirer. An integrated e-HR system can look up the records of the person making the enquiry and deliver a personalised response. This greatly reduces the possibility that the enquirer will read the answer and think, 'Yes, that is all very well, but it doesn't apply to my situation' and then call the HR Department anyway.

Enhancing information using streamed video

As long as your network has the necessary bandwidth (and that is a significant 'if') it is easy using industry-standard streaming technologies to allow employees throughout the organisation to watch video clips. Streaming technology is software within the browser (installed as a plug-in) that allows the browser to interpret data received from the server in a continuous stream. The streaming plug-in decodes the data as it receives it and displays it on screen. Without the streaming plug-in the browser would wait until it had received all the data before using it. Such technologies are most important with such data sources as sound and video.

Cisco Systems, an organisation with the benefit of high-speed data networks, uses streaming technologies to deliver training and communications videos across their network.[1] With 7000 employees spread across over a hundred world-wide locations, they needed a way to deliver corporate information and training quickly and easily. It proved its value when being used to deliver a training initiative that had previously involved 18 presenters delivering eight three-hour training events. Traditional methods would have required staff to have travelled to central locations, incurring substantial costs for travelling and accommodation, as well as opportunity costs for time spent away from desks. It would have also taken a considerable amount of time to have delivered the sessions to all necessary staff. After videotaping the presentations they were able to stream them across the entire network, delivering the information simultaneously to all relevant employees.

New technologies are now appearing that make it possible to introduce interactivity into such sessions. While the presenter is broadcasting live, viewers can ask questions and interact with the presenter and other viewers by web cameras or instant text applications.

 On-line collaborative tools are discussed in more detail later in this chapter.

Information and knowledge

Intranet technology makes the delivery of organisational information to the workplace much easier. Of course, that has a value in itself, but it does not necessarily make it any easier for the organisation to find out what individual parts of the business know and for that knowledge to be spread upwards and horizontally.

However, it is becoming increasingly apparent that modern organisations live and die according to how well they utilise what they know about what they do and the marketplace. As part of this acknowledgement, we have seen Peter Drucker's term 'knowledge worker' come into the business lexicon. Businesses are increasingly expected to manage their knowledge effectively, but in many organisations this is proving to be very difficult.

Firstly, for various reasons knowledge tends not to be spread about. There may be cultural traditions arising from the old belief that 'knowledge = power'. Especially in competitive environments, people keep useful information to themselves to maintain a competitive advantage over colleagues. There are often technical barriers. Knowledge can be stored on paper, perhaps in handwritten format, and so cannot easily be exchanged. Even where information is held in computerised format, this may be within a client-server system, limiting the availability of the information to those employees with access to a client. However, the advent of intranets made people realise that here was a technology that could make it possible for information about how the organisation worked to be readily available to everyone, whenever they needed it.

In contrast to the inadequacy of information, there is also sometimes the problem of a surplus of information. People returning from holidays brace themselves for the avalanche of e-mails that pour into their desktop computer, most of which may have little or no relevance to them but which they have been sent 'just in case'. The overload of information enabled by e-mail means that the important nuggets can easily be overlooked.

'Knowledge management' has therefore appeared as a discipline, albeit one that many people find hard to understand. This difficulty may have something to do with the function implied by the word 'management', which suggests an administrative, rather than a creative, function. This is perhaps why linking 'intranet' with 'knowledge management' leads people to think about systems that can catalogue every existing item of paper held within a business, usually described as document management systems.

However, knowledge is much more than what exists on pieces of paper. We prize knowledge for its usefulness, for its allowing us to create new ideas and new opportunities. Bawden[2] considers this from the perspective of scientific researchers who are constantly trying to create something new, but although the field of work may be specialised, the principles are applicable to all of us. Bawden's research led him to believe that studying previously published information has a limited effect on helping people develop new concepts. He says that claims from the information community that access to relevant literature is crucial to scientific development is more of an act of faith than an opinion based on reality. Going further, he suggests that close study of one particular area can actually be damaging in that it inhibits one's creativity, quoting Lord Byron 'To be perfectly original one should think much and read little...'. We should not take this warning too far: there is clearly much that can be gained by looking at what has been discovered and documented in the past and, for this reason, document management systems certainly do have a place in any knowledge management initiative.

But, in Bawden's opinion, in order to synthesise useful knowledge from previous documentation we must find a spark, and that spark can come from a number of different sources. Chance plays its hand. Many important leaps forward have come because someone was in the right place at the right time. Fleming's discovery of penicillin is sometimes attributed to a culture dish being placed close to an open window, whence drifted in a penicillin spore. Apocryphal or not, this does highlight the randomness of whether or not that particular window was open. Analogy and the examination of exceptions and inconsistencies are also important, as is contact with people from different disciplines. These factors all help to look at a problem from different perspectives.

So where does this leave us with e-HR and knowledge management? It shows that, while the accessibility of previously recorded information is important, a more significant factor in how effectively knowledge can be developed and disseminated is technology that allows contact with a range of different people, and not necessarily planned contact. Think about how often you have suddenly thought about a new answer to a seemingly intractable problem when having a chance conversation with someone in the corridor. Technology needs to be able to replicate this, and magically, e-HR can! On-line collaborative software applications can supplement meetings in the corridor, and of course, enable meetings to take place that would otherwise be impossible because many miles separate the participants. With such tools it becomes possible to collaborate with people from different professional backgrounds and different cultures without leaving your desk. This is not to devalue the importance of face-to-face contact. We should probably all try to get out more and talk to other people about issues facing us, but on-line collaborative tools allow us to do this more and with a wider range of people.

 You will find more information about how on-line collaborative tools work later in this chapter.

Delivering an effective knowledge management strategy

The most important strategy to follow when trying to make sure that an intranet-based knowledge management tool realises its full potential is to remember that knowledge is essentially a human asset. It therefore becomes very important to involve people in the knowledge management process, and not to rely solely on technology.

Support working practices that encourage inter-departmental collaboration. On-line collaborative tools can provide a valuable way of enabling chance and planned interactions between people from different departments, but there may be a need for training initiatives to make people aware of the value of on-line collaboration within the context of knowledge management.

However sophisticated the technology that you employ, knowledge management can only succeed if the human issues are addressed and sharing information becomes part of the organisation's culture. Geraint John[3] has identified a number of initiatives being employed by different organisations in order to encourage such a culture:

- Within one professional community of about 100 people in BT, a bottle of champagne was given each month to the person offering the most innovative idea and also to the person making most use of other people's ideas.

- Specialist staff have been nominated as 'knowledge facilitators' at ICL.

- Ernst & Young developed specific knowledge sharing competencies to be included as part of regular appraisal processes.

- Ernst & Young also instituted a three-monthly raffle where the names of people who had contributed knowledge were entered, ten winners each receiving prizes of £1000.

VisionCor, a knowledge management consultancy, offer a number of guidelines about how to include the human element.[4]

Identify the most useful 20 percent

It is probably fairly safe to assume that just a small percentage of the knowledge captured within a knowledge management system will be of most significance. Remember the 80:20 rule: applying it here, 80 per cent of the time just 20 per cent of the information will be of value. You should therefore set up ways of identifying the most important 20 per cent of the information.

The only way to do this is to involve experts within the organisation. Set up a small group of experts and high performers who can regularly review new knowledge and:

- correct inaccuracies

- delete out of date or irrelevant knowledge.

Make sure that your chosen software system is able to filter out information according to a user's needs – for example, not displaying information older than a particular date. It should also be possible for a system to identify which knowledge artefacts have been accessed most frequently (and so are possibly the most useful) and to display them at the top of a list of search results.

Work with experts to capture their knowledge meaningfully

Much the best way to capture knowledge from experts is for a skilled interviewer to ask the expert about what they do and why. Not only will this flatter the expert (usually a good strategy) but it may be the first time that they have been acknowledged as such. It will also mean that the resulting information can be structured clearly and presented in a format consistent with other items in the knowledge database. This is the process followed by an experienced instructional designer when capturing information to be presented within a training programme. Sometimes referred to as a **knowledge audit**, the instructional designer will ask questions such as:

- How will you know that you have been successful?

- What are the actions you will take to make sure that you are successful?

- When starting to do this task, what patterns or clues do you look for that you know will ensure success?

- What shortcuts do you have?

- When you start, what issues do you consider?

- What do you do to monitor your own performance?

- What do you do if you see that a situation is different to normal?

- Is there any special equipment that you find useful?

This approach has a number of benefits. The expert becomes aware that they are an expert (if they do not know this already) and they come to spend some time analysing what they do and why they do it. This will help them think about ways in which they can improve their own performance and will also mean that they learn something about the approach needed to capture and transfer knowledge to others in a consistent and meaningful way.

Provide a context for all knowledge

A knowledge audit, if carried out thoroughly, will provide you with everything you need in order to give other users a rich explanation of a process or procedure that includes:

- the basic way of approaching the process or procedure

- examples of where to apply the knowledge (and examples of where not to apply it)

- case studies or anecdotes showing where the knowledge has been applied and how it worked

- demonstrations of how to do it, perhaps using audio or video

- performance aids (such as checklists or flowcharts) or tools (simple software utilities, for example)

- practice scenarios or simulations where a user can try applying the knowledge

- contact details for experts who are able to discuss the subject in more detail than is possible through a page on the intranet.

Managing internal documents

Paperwork within an organisation can be made more accessible through the use of document management systems, which make an electronic record of paper documents. High speed-scanners can read perhaps 100 pages per minute, and the software then converts the output to an appropriate format and stores it. The documents must then be indexed. To do this, the software scans the stored pages and performs Optical Character

Recognition (OCR) so that it has a record of the text on each page. It then makes a record of every word on the page and includes this in an index.

People looking for documents addressing a particular subject can then use a search engine that looks through the index and compiles a list of all pages having the required keywords. It will then deliver either just the text or an image of the page to the user's browser.

Document management systems should have various refinements. For example, they should also have filtering mechanisms so that searches can exclude some types of material. They should be able to attach security classifications to every page, so that only people with the appropriate access can view them.

A major new development in this area is what is sometimes known as **data- or text-mining**, a process through which software attempts to extract the meaning of a document rather than just the list of words that it contains. To understand this better, think about carrying out a simple text search on the Internet for a word such as 'domino'. A simple search would return pages containing information on such diverse subjects as the Lotus groupware product, the game, historical analyses of why the United States became involved in Vietnam and women in James Bond films. Now, if we were to apply text-mining principles to the search we could specify which application of the word 'domino' we were interested in and the search software would read the documents and decide what type of domino the pages were talking about. The search results would therefore be much more focused.

Limitations of document management systems

Although document management systems can make it much easier to find, share and disseminate document-based information, certain things must be taken into consideration.

Different types of knowledge need different solutions

Some types of knowledge are more amenable to storage and reuse than others. For example, organisations following standard processes, such as assembly-line manufacturing, will find it easier to record information than organisations that are constantly doing new things. This does not mean that knowledge sharing is less relevant to the innovative organisation; rather; that how it is done will need to be different.

Documents only tell part of a story

Capturing the content of documents and e-mails can only tell part of the story. Such documents become rather like the pots and tools that archaeologists retrieve from prehistoric sites. We know that this is a pot and that is a spoon but how they were used is pure speculation, albeit informed by previous experience. But, however experienced the archaeologist, they can never know for sure exactly how an particular artefact was used.

It is the same with captured text. The context of why this particular procedure rather than another was carried out may not be clear from documents that were prepared without the particular aim of being documents from which another person could learn.

Finding relevant knowledge becomes harder as the amount stored increases

The ease with which computers can soak up data means that the size of an organisation's knowledge bank can increase very rapidly. As it grows, it becomes ever harder for individuals to find exactly the information they need. Expert use of the search engine becomes more important – a skill which many people will find themselves unable or unwilling to acquire. If you have ever spent time searching the Internet will know that unless you use the search capabilities of a search engine carefully you are likely to find yourself having to sift through hundreds of thousands of hits. Very quickly you tire of this and go on to do something else! As described above, text-mining technology can help to improve the quality of information searches.

Information goes out of date

The world changes very quickly these days and information that is hot today could be old hat tomorrow. Document management systems can therefore find themselves guarding an increasingly large amount of out-of-date information, which further complicates users' searches.

Knowledge systems need constant maintenance

A major cultural barrier to knowledge management systems is that people will not submit information as the knowledge management enthusiasts amongst us would want. People may:

- not submit any knowledge that they hold, seeing it as a precious asset for them to keep to themselves

- submit information to the knowledge database that should actually be kept secret

- submit information that is of little value to anyone.

Much of this is to be expected. The knowledge that is of most value to an organisation is held by its experts and high performers, who should be being rewarded for their skills by the organisation. Few people in such positions will voluntarily give up the secrets that they see as being key to their exalted positions and salaries. Also, less obviously, experts often have such an intuitive feel for what they do that they cannot present, in any meaningful form, the mental processes that they follow in order to achieve their success. If they do provide knowledge, it often comes completely detached from the context in which it is used and so loses much of its significance.

Of course, the opposite may be true. Some experts maybe so committed to the idea of sharing their knowledge (for whatever reason) that they come to be the only people contributing to the database. This can then have the effect of putting off other people from submitting knowledge or even searching for it.

Knowledge out of context can become meaningless

Merely providing information about how to do something without providing information on the situation in which it is done can make information meaningless or, worse, dangerous. What works very well in one situation may not work at all or have unfortunate consequences in another.

Gathering information from the workforce

Regular users of the Internet will know that web sites seem to have an insatiable demand for information about us. Registering to search within a site or to receive information almost always requires that we complete an on-line form that sets us up as a marketing opportunity. But the technology that allows Internet sites to collect information about its viewers can also be used to collect information from within an organisation.

On-line survey tools are becoming an important way for organisations to get feedback from its employees. They are used in such things as 360 degree feedback processes, but they can also be used to gain feedback on anything from the quality of the food in the cafeteria to industrial relations issues. But, as with all questionnaires, they must be carefully designed. As a useful guide, on-line surveys must be:

- short enough so that people actually complete them (people should be able to complete the survey in less than 20 minutes)

- meaningful, so that people are motivated to complete them

- statistically relevant, which means that they must explore the subject in sufficient detail without becoming too long and that a satisfactory percentage of people complete them.

On-line surveying offers considerable advantages over traditional approaches – principally those speed and cost.

It is quicker: survey forms can be distributed virtually instantaneously. A bulk e-mail with an embedded hyperlink informs people of the survey, they click on the link and complete the survey on-line. In theory results can start to come in within minutes of the e-mail being sent. The tedious step of transferring answers from paper to PC is also eliminated: feedback flows directly into a database. Postal surveys always have to allow people enough time to complete the form and return it, but this delay also allows people to forget all about it. With on-line technology there are no postal delays and the (hopeful) ease of completion makes it less likely for people to forget about the form. Motivation to complete it is another matter, and one that relates more to the perceived importance of the subject than the medium. As the technology matures, statistics about relative completion rates for postal and on-line surveys should appear, making the situation clearer.

It is cheaper: there are no reproduction costs for questionnaires and no postal costs. With traditional surveying methods each recipient costs a certain amount, so numbers may be limited by budget. E-mail essentially costs the same for one recipient as a thousand (as spam e-mailers know only too well!).

Keeping up to date with the outside world

As the Internet has become the principal way by which information is spread around the world, many businesses have sprung up offering specialist news and information services.

These services can offer many different facilities:

- Streamed news services, where external news stories are fed from the supplier to your intranet servers and it then displays automatically within browsers. An example of this is the share price information fed to financial organisations by companies such as Reuters and Bloomberg's.

- Newsletters, where information on particular subjects is compiled in an e-mail that is sent to you on a regular basis. These usually provide links to relevant web sites that can provide more extensive information than is possible in an e-mail. For example, an HR professional could be interested in:

  - news about the HR community in the UK, through subscribing to the HR Zone (www.hrzone.co.uk)

  - a free regular newsletter from the journal *Workforce* (www.workforce.com) that provides regular information about human resources in the United States. This provides links to an on-line version of the journal, which of course allows you to subscribe to the paper version!

- Bulletin boards – special e-mail-based systems that allow messages to be linked together by subject. Someone posts a message or question to the bulletin board and other people with comments or questions can attach responses to it.

There are various models for paying for such information. You may pay a flat fee or on a sliding scale according to how much the information is used. Until you have established how much the information is being used, it is usually more cost-effective to pay for it on a per usage basis.

Improving collaboration between people

The word 'organisation' has a number of different meanings. We talk about the organisation of something as being a quality that indicates how harmonious that thing is. We talk about an organisation when referring to a body that has a particular purpose. Putting the two together we come up with the idea that an organisation requires its constituent parts to be working in harmony: in other words, collaborating.

Collaboration within organisations takes many forms: people talk across their desks or in corridors, they have meetings, sometimes in their own building but sometimes in other continents, they attend briefings, they go on training courses together. Although these forms of collaboration are all different, they are all characterised by people getting together. Now, over the years technology has come up with many new ideas that help us communicate, such as the telephone, television and e-mail, but none of these is ideal as a collaborative tool. Each has its strengths but also its limitations, and we often find ourselves using a combination of different technologies in order to collaborate with colleagues. Having to do this may be awkward and even impossible to achieve synchronously: the media get in the way of the message.

So what is the difference between communication and collaboration? Let us take a look at what these terms mean, and by identifying the crucial difference we should be able to see why on-line collaboration is likely to become what the jargon refers to as a 'killer application'.

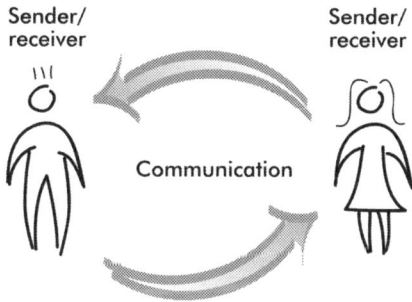

Figure 6.2
Communication

Communication is an instant and transient process. We speak to someone, they reply and we move on. What was said and heard a few minutes ago is quickly forgotten. It is also a very fragile process: we are easily distracted when trying to talk to someone in a noisy room, and long-distance telephone conversations can be ruined by time delays or echoes on the line. Also, the essence of most conversations is the **exchanging** of information rather than sharing it. As Michael Schrage puts it, 'The serial and ephemeral nature of conversation, then, subtly works against collaboration[5]'.

So what is the crucial difference between communication and collaboration? As Figure 6.3 shows, collaboration requires a shared space. This need not be sophisticated: it could be as simple as the proverbial back of the cigarette packet. Think about conversations you have had with friends and colleagues where someone suddenly picked up a piece of paper and started drawing a picture or making a note. Almost certainly everyone involved suddenly became more engaged and probably remembered more about the interaction: the communication had become a collaboration. One of the best examples of a shared space is the traditional blackboard (or nowadays the dry-wipe whiteboard). There is probably not a single research establishment anywhere in the world that does not have something such as a blackboard where people can collaborate, adding, amending and rubbing out ideas. Famously, Crick and Watson developed their initial ideas about the DNA double helix on a blackboard: '... the blackboard... will commonly be found covered with logical trees. On the top line will be the hot new result just up from the laboratory or just in by letter or rumour. On the next line will be two or three alternative explanations..., suggested experiments or controls.'[6]

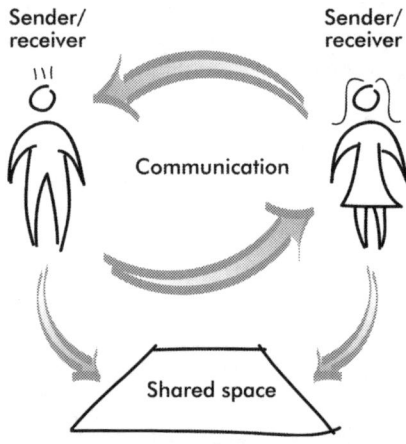

Figure 6.3
Collaboration

Intranet technology now offers a way of providing people, separated by time and distance, with a shared space. And this new technology-enabled shared space offers a number of significant advantages:

- Unlike a blackboard, which once it is wiped has lost its value, the electronic shared space can remember everything that it has contained. Communication may be ephemeral, but on-line collaboration lives on forever in a hard disk.

- Participants have all the computational power of a computer at their hands. The shared space can be occupied by a spreadsheet performing complex calculations or by a graphics package where the subtleties of an image can be adjusted by several people working together.

If we now think back to the connection between the two definitions of 'organisation', we can start to appreciate that enabling true on-line collaboration between everyone in a business, regardless of where they are, possibly represents the Elysian Fields of e-HR, and that the current excitement about self-service HR will come to be seen as just a staging post on the journey.

On-line collaborative tools – for example, Microsoft's NetMeeting® – have been available for a number of years. However, it would seem that although many people have tried such solutions out once or twice, few have welcomed it in as a regular part of their working lives. Why? Chris Reed[7] suggests that this is because of the fact that collaboration with other people can take many different forms, each of which requires many different subtleties. Face-to-face contact allows us to display all these subtleties and adapt to the changing requirements of the situation. We can classify collaborative events in a number of different ways.

1.	How the event is set up	Who arranges the event, you or someone else? Does it happen regularly or is this a one-off? Is it planned ahead of time or does it happen spontaneously?
2.	How people relate in the event	Is it a peer group discussion or is there a leader?
3.	The content	Does it require listening, speaking, writing or just doing? Is the content textual or graphical?
4.	Interactions required	Do people need to just talk with other participants or to actively work together?
5.	The outcomes	Does the event need to produce some sort of physical output?

When you think about collaborations in these terms you can begin to see why computers have struggled to reproduce the incredible flexibility that face-to-face interactions are capable of. Early collaborative tools recognised this difficulty and sidestepped it by focusing on enabling specific types of collaboration. For example, application sharing, videoconferencing and instant messenger applications all do one thing more or less well, but if you want to interact with other people in different ways you need a different application! More software to be installed and learnt – more hassle. No wonder they have remained niche applications.

Where they have become significant is in applications where they offer significant benefits and where the numbers of users can be high. For example, electronic classrooms (discussed later in this chapter) are a form of collaborative tool designed to mimic classroom-type situations. Because they can directly replace classroom training events they have become relatively well established as tools.

This offers us a clue as to how on-line collaborative tools can move forward to gain wider acceptance: by enabling the flexibility to mimic real-life collaborative events as closely as possible. They should enable spontaneity if that is needed, they should allow people to talk and see each other and they should allow a large number of people to be involved and relate to each other hierarchically or equally during the same session.

Reed identifies a number of attributes that the new generation of on-line collaborative tools possesses:

1.	Full flexibility of content	The application should be able to deliver any type of content necessary, whether it is text, graphics, audio, video or simulation.
2.	Synchronous or asynchronous	People should be able to collaborate simultaneously or at different times, so the application must be able to save and retrieve full records of the collaboration. Real-life collaborations are often unplanned – for example, the chance meeting in the corridor.
3.	Co-ordination of interactions	The application must provide electronic methods to allow people to co-ordinate their interactions, as we do in face-to-face meetings by such means as raising our hands, using body language to show that we want to speak and emotional reactions. These methods should mimic interpersonal methods so that they are easy to learn.
4.	Flexible arrangement of events	Users should be able to easily manage events, so that they can do such things as set up one-off or repeated events, check availability and send out invitations.
		The application should also be able to allow participants to propose and agree agendas collaboratively.
		It should be possible to have completely spontaneous events. For example, when someone is using Microsoft's Instant Messenger, anyone who appears in the user's address book can join in with the on-line conversation. In a business context, the newcomer happening by chance on a discussion about a particular problem could offer a valuable insight that the participants need.
5.	Compatibility with accepted business practices	Collaborative events must be able to follow standard business practices and work within accepted security policies to achieve what is required.
6.	Capability to deal with informal communications	Face-to-face interactions are characterised by a mixture of outcome-focused formal interactions as well as unstructured and less formal interactions that serve to develop rapport between the participants. The application should therefore allow people to communicate in informal and unstructured ways.
7.	Generation of outputs	The application must be able to allow a decision-making process to occur and for the results of that to be captured. For example, people must be able to vote for a particular outcome and the results of that vote must be recorded.

8. Recording and reuse of the event

People often scratch their heads after a meeting, trying to remember exactly what someone else said. One advantage of a collaborative software tool is that everything can be recorded and replayed as necessary.

9. Integration with other systems

The application should be able to integrate as necessary with standard organisational applications, such as standard office applications, enterprise software, e-mail and document management systems. For example, a person could join the on-line meeting by clicking on a link in the e-mail invitation and actions agreed during the course of the meeting could be automatically e-mailed to the appropriate people as a reminder.

How do you use an on-line collaborative tool?

You run an event using an on-line collaborative application in the same way as you would a face-to-face event. You first arrange a time for the event using the integrated e-mail function. This can scan calendars and identify times when all the necessary people are free (although this would have to be done manually for external people).

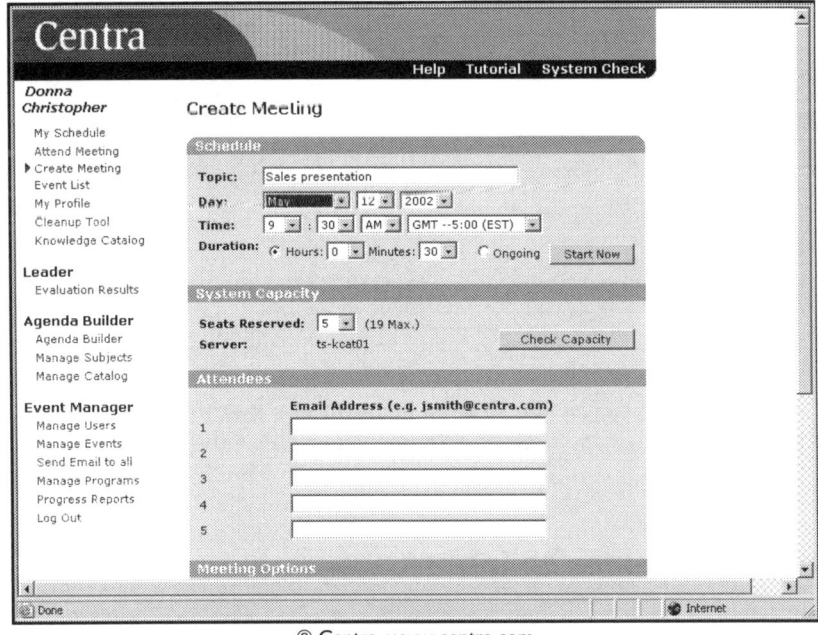

© Centra, www.centra.com

Figure 6.4
Setting up an on-line meeting

This shows Centra being used to arrange an on-line meeting. The person arranging it sets up the time and date and adds the e-mail addresses of the participants. They will join the meeting by clicking on a hyperlink in the e-mail notification they receive.

People join the event by clicking on a hyperlink in the invitation. They then have access to whatever tools the particular application they are using allows. For example, Figure 6.5 shows an on-line meeting in which participants are working together on a spreadsheet.

The system tries to replicate the practicalities and possibilities of a real meeting. For example, there is an agenda that will be worked through and participants can express emotional reactions to the proceedings by clicking on the appropriate button. They can also leave the meeting through the door!

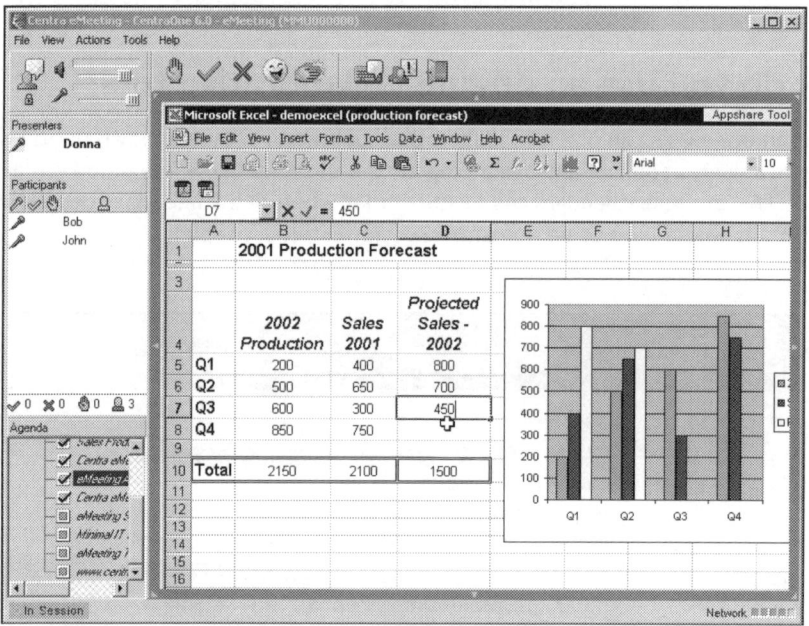

Figure 6.5
Application sharing in an on-line meeting
Participants can jointly run applications and collaborate just as if they were sitting at the same desk and computer.

Benefits of on-line collaboration

Improved opportunities for informal learning

We have already described the importance of such factors as chance and inter-disciplinary exchanges for stimulating new ideas, so it seems reasonable to extend this and propose that they are important factors in learning. But, of course, they are by definition unplanned and informal, as opposed to the formal training that we usually associate with individual learning. The importance of such informal learning is often underestimated, although many of us instinctively feel that we have learned more from day-to-day experience than by attending training courses. Some studies confirm this: according to research carried out by CapitalWorks LLC 'Approximately 75 percent of the skills employees use on the job were learned informally ... through discussions with coworkers, asynchronous self-study (such as e-mail-based coursework), mentoring by managers and supervisors and similar methods. Only 25 percent were gained from formal training methods such as workshops, seminars and synchronous classes.'[8]

Increased flexibility of business activities

The ability to take part in collaborative events without moving from the desktop is a major attraction of on-line collaborative tools. People can attend meetings and take part in classroom training or listen to presentations without having to spend time travelling.

This is not to say that there will no longer be any need for face-to-face activities. Physically meeting people and pressing the flesh is a fundamental part of human activity and it is impossible to conceive that physical meetings and training events will disappear: they offer too much value to do so. However, travelling can be reduced to more comfortable levels, improving the quality of people's working lives and reducing the amount of transport-generated pollution. Increased numbers of collaborative events may happen because it suddenly becomes easier to arrange them, improving the levels of communication.

Replaying meetings

Unlike face-to-face meetings, everything that happens in an on-line meeting can be recorded and replayed. True, you can video a meeting but this will not capture detailed work done on laptop computers, for example, whereas an on-line application will. This makes it possible to revisit the event and check just what that person did say or remind yourself what you agreed to do before the next event!

Broadening contacts

The costs of travelling (both time and money) mean that opportunities to travel and meet people in other offices or even countries are limited. Some people may not travel at all, and so never have the chance to meet colleagues in other parts of the world. As discussed above, meeting different people plays a large part in stimulating new ideas and helping to solve old problems, so any technology that makes it possible to do this without costing a lot of money is to be welcomed. So use on-line collaborative tools to encourage more contact between dispersed parts of your organisation.

Challenges of on-line collaboration

Making the cultural shift

It will be relatively easy to lead people to an on-on-line collaborative application, but it will be much harder to make them drink. Electronic meetings will represent a huge cultural step forward for many people and there will need to be a carefully designed change management programme in place to encourage people to take the step.

 The subject of managing the cultural changes needed when implementing new systems are discussed in more detail in Chapter 9.

Underestimating the training requirements

Computer-literate people often underestimate how difficult it is for others to learn how to use new computer applications. This seems to be particularly the case when applications are delivered through a browser as 'Surely browsers are very easy to use?' The reality is that people often need more support than 'techies' realise, either through formal and informal training or through built-in electronic support systems.

People's first reaction to a new system is often to play around with it, and if they work out how to use it quickly, everything is fine. However, if they initially find it difficult they may be put off using it completely. Also, learning must be done in a non-threatening atmosphere, and a collaborative event may be perceived as anything but non-threatening. Everyone else seems to know which buttons to click, everyone else seems to be contributing, and the people who are still climbing their way up the learning curve may well just disappear into the electronic background, never to be seen on-line again. It may therefore be necessary to design and run fun, non-pressure events that people can take part in so that they can gain confidence.

Bandwidth, bandwidth, bandwidth

Network administrators often seem to be fighting a continual battle against everyone else in the business who wants to send data down their pipes. Kilobytes shuttling through the network to create web pages are bad enough, but the megabytes needed to provide a streamed video feed can rapidly bring a network to its knees. You will therefore need to think very seriously about your network's capacity. What volume of network traffic do you expect from on-line collaboration? What about in six months' time? What if it becomes popular more quickly than you expected but people find that the network constraints make it completely unusable so that it loses its attraction and credibility?

Implementing on-line collaborative tools requires a long, hard look at network capacity.

How to implement on-line collaborative tools

The widely differing needs of each type of collaborative events mean that you must be very careful about selecting a collaborative tool. To do this you must be systematic in the way in which you approach your buying decision.

Establish your business objective

Decide how the implementation of a collaborative tool is going to support your organisation's strategy. Based on what that strategy is you can formulate an objective. You should then be able to obtain the buy-in from senior management that you will need.

Find out what collaborations currently take place

As discussed above, collaborations can take many forms. However, we can generally classify collaborations as either meetings, presentations or classroom events. Each of these modes of collaboration presents a different set of challenges to the application software. You should find out what forms of collaborative events different areas within the business currently run. Each area will probably have its own slightly different needs:

- Some will be purely internal while others will need to be able to run collaborative events using the Internet, for example, with customers or people working from home.

- Some will be using the tool to manage the development projects while others will be using it to help in the selling cycle.

- Some will be arranging formal meetings while others will want informal, perhaps asynchronous, contacts.

Find out if people are currently using any on-line collaboration tools and, if so find out about their successes and failures.

Develop your specification

Based on the needs expressed by different business areas, you should collaborate with IT staff to develop a specification for the tool that you need. Potential suppliers can help you in this by demonstrating what their products can do both now and in the near future. Be especially careful if you must cater for people working outside your organisation: they may use different browsers and have limited bandwidth.

Your specification should also require that the collaboration tools integrate with your existing standard applications and, where appropriate, conform to international standards – for example, AICC and SCORM standards for e-learning products.

 SCORM, AICC and other e-learning standards are discussed in more detail later in this chapter.

Decide how to move forward

Furnished with information about the business objectives for on-line collaboration, what types of collaboration are required and your technical specification you can now make some decisions about your implementation strategy. There are a number of issues that you need to consider:

1. **Will one package meet all your needs?**

   You may find that the range of collaborative approaches that your organisation needs cannot be met by a single application. Deploying several different packages may be the best strategy if you can satisfy the ROI requirements. This may not be difficult given the potentially high return and the relatively low cost of applications.

   You may find that this solution is thrust on you if a number of functions are already using different collaborative tools and do not want to change them.

2. **Will you install the system internally or use an ASP?**

   ASPs (Application Service Providers) are a business model that is growing rapidly to meet the demands of the on-line application market. With the application mounted on the ASP's hardware, you link to their servers via an external connection. This considerably simplifies issues surrounding installation and implementation but does introduce security concerns.

   The ASP route may be particularly attractive if you do not envisage using such a tool very often.

    You can find more information about ASPs in Chapter 8.

3. **How stable is the supplier?**

   As in all other fast-growing marketplaces, the on-line collaborative tools high street is littered with the debris of collapsed businesses and merged companies. You will therefore need to take great care to reassure yourself that any supplier you choose is likely to remain trading throughout the life of the application.

4. **How will your network cope?**

   The capabilities of your network will have a profound effect on how well the application works.

   Bandwidth is a major issue. Collaboration using rich data methods such as audio and video place huge demands on a network: organisations already using collaborative tools extensively have reported that half of their network traffic is due to collaborative events. If your network is groaning under the strain of present-day traffic, implementing collaborative solutions will have serious hardware implications.

If the collaboration is going to be moving beyond the confines of your intranet you will need to make sure that the collaboration will be able to move through any firewalls in place.

5. Is the application scalable?

You will be implementing a collaborative tool in the hope that it will prove popular and successful. So, if this is the case, can the application be easily expanded to deal with larger numbers of users than you initially expect?

6. What will the training requirements be?

Training required to support the implementation will depend very much on the profile of the typical users. As this is a somewhat specialist application, it is perhaps safe to assume that users will be technically competent, and that they will be able to learn how to use the package quickly. But then this may be a dangerous assumption! Senior management may be less technically competent than junior staff, and be less inclined to spend time learning how to use such applications. They may also be deterred by the thought of being exposed in a collaborative event as technologically challenged!

It is likely that the biggest challenge will be in learning the etiquette of on-line collaboration rather than in mastering the software. And really for an issue such as this there is no substitute for experience.

Tread carefully, and allow a contingency in your budgets of time and money for training.

Managing and delivering learning

In Chapter 1 we referred to the concept that the essential function of any HR Department is to enable the development of high-performance work systems. There are a number of ways in which HR can do this.

HR plays a central role in the co-ordination of training. Note that, although there is a vogue towards the use of the word 'learning' rather than training, we shall use both words in this book. 'Training' suggests what is done to people, and 'learning' suggests what people do, and, as much of the emphasis within this chapter is in what HR can do to its people, the word 'training' produces, hopefully, more elegant sentences. Where we are discussing what learners themselves do, we have tried to use the word 'learning'.

The role of HR in training is to identify training needs, develop and run training programmes and maintain individual training records. Some HR Departments even evaluate training to see how effective it has been!

Training is intimately linked with the other two areas. Knowledge management (as discussed above) is a developing field concerned with the capture and dissemination of knowledge held within the organisation. Training is one means by which that dissemination can occur.

Training should also be closely connected to performance management processes. The monitoring of how well individuals and departments are performing should feed into demands for new training or for existing training to be improved in some way.

 Performance management is covered in more detail in Chapter 5.

The increasing importance of e-learning

The delivery of learning materials through an intranet or the Internet (commonly referred to as e-learning) is becoming an increasingly important means of providing training. In 2001 the International Data Center predicted that classroom training in US organisations would decline from 77% in 1999 to just 35% in 2004, with e-learning enabling the change in emphasis[9]. They also predicted that by 2003 US businesses would be spending $11.4 billion on Internet-delivered training by. Within the UK, there are predictions that 85 per cent of organisations intend to have implemented an e-learning strategy by 2003.

However, it is important to remember that e-learning is merely another stage in the development of what was previously called computer-based training (CBT), so let us take a quick look at how the evolution of e-learning has occurred.

Mainframes

As mainframe computers started to appear in organisations, people started to think about ways in which they could be used to provide training. The training materials that could be delivered were seriously limited by the unavailability of graphics, but these were networked computers and it was relatively easy for Training Managers to store information about training usage.

Desktop PCs

The next stage in the development of CBT came with the increasing ubiquity of the desktop PC. Computers now became available to a larger number of people, and as computer applications became more and more important within organisations, it increasingly made sense to provide training through these computers. Also, as the graphics capabilities of computers developed, the visual quality of training materials improved.

CBT materials were generally distributed using floppy disks whose contents could be installed on hard disks. Where computers were networked it could be possible to store information about learners centrally, but this often proved difficult to do in practice. Updating disks was also difficult: once disks had been duplicated, the only way to change content was by subsequent releases of updated disks, which led to the immense logistical problems of making sure that users had the correct versions.

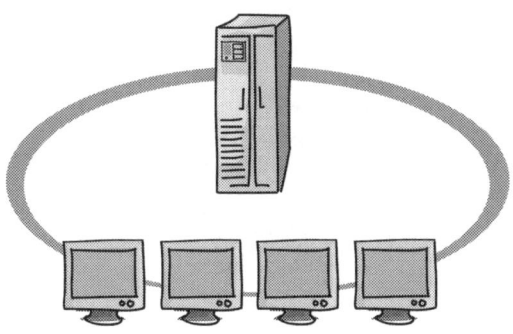

Figure 6.6
Mainframe CBT

Figure 6.7
CBT

Multimedia

In certain respects, multimedia made little difference to CBT. Learning materials were still distributed on a disk but now the disk could store 650 MB instead of 1.44, which made it possible to include video and audio in training programmes. However, as sound cards and CD-ROM drives became standard equipment on PCs, multimedia revolutionised CBT as audio and video made it possible to introduce different types of learning material.

Problems still remained over storing learners' records, although improvements in network technology simplified things, but updating incorrect or out-of-date material on the disk remained.

Figure 6.8
Multimedia

E-learning

E-learning represents both a completion of, and a step backwards in, an evolutionary cycle at the same time. Completion because it is a networked approach as in the days of the mainframe: learning materials and learners' records are stored centrally and are distributed over the network rather than using a disk. A step backwards because most existing networks are unable to provide the bandwidth necessary to show audio and video. Early e-learning programmes therefore bear more resemblance to the CBT of the early 1990s rather than the multimedia of the late 1990s.

Figure 6.9
E-learning

The storage of all materials on a central server removed at a stroke the problems of keeping disks updated. Interest rate changes affecting decisions in a learning programme? No problem, just update the central file.

However, although e-learning in the early years of the 2000s may lack the visual and auditory sexiness of multimedia, this is only a temporary problem. As organisations upgrade their network hardware, more and more will find that they are able to deliver video and audio throughout their organisation without finding that their network comes to a complete halt.

Also, e-learning makes it possible to integrate learning experiences with other aspects of the business's operations. Learning materials can link directly to operational manuals and other resources, whether they be stored locally on the intranet or externally on the Internet. Learners can communicate with subject experts by e-mail or video conferencing.

How can e-learning be delivered?

The most exciting aspect of e-learning is the flexibility that it offers. The ability of web-based technology to utilise different types of data and the delivery of these through a common interface has opened up a wide range of possibilities for delivering learning opportunities. Let us look at what these are.

Self-paced individual learning

Self-paced individual learning refers to the sort of 'open' or 'distance' learning that many of us are familiar with. The learner works on their own, studying a mixture of text and graphical materials delivered to their browser from the server. It is technically quite easy to also deliver video and audio materials, but this is often impossible due to bandwidth restrictions on the network. As businesses upgrade networks and data compression technologies improve, it will become normal for such materials to include all types of media. (At which point learning materials will contain so much rich data that the networks may once again slow to a crawl, but that will be another story!)

The early days of e-learning have seen an explosion in the amount of such material, often simple conversions from existing materials originally developed for CD-ROM. The promise of cheaper unit costs for training has also seen a big demand for conversion of paper-based distance learning and workshop materials into e-learning, which often proves to be less than successful. This is often because, for all its strengths, e-learning is not the ideal media for delivering all types of training. It is very good for delivering knowledge-based learning and assessment but cannot be expected to help people learn practical skills, for which the best type of training is some form of real-life or simulated practice. It is also an expensive medium for which to design materials. While it is relatively cheap to produce simple static web pages that mimic paper-based materials (and for certain subjects and target groups this may be adequate), materials that require more sophistication can be very expensive to design and develop.

One major advantage intranet-based distance learning materials is that they can be connected to other parts of an intranet or the Internet. So a learner working through a self-paced course on marketing could be given links to the organisation's own marketing materials, to internal documents relating to marketing policies or to Internet sites showing interesting examples of marketing or other reference material. Links could also be provided to webcams, so that the learner could watch events happening in another part of the business or on the other side of the world. Such flexibility can greatly improve the effectiveness of learning materials, although it often seems that the design of self-paced materials is driven more by the need to display technological sophistication than to provide a rich and effective learning experience.

Self-paced individual e-learning materials offer the same advantages as other forms of distance learning – for example, independence from the availability of a trainer or subject matter expert and the ability for learners to work at their own pace, fitting studying in with other commitments. It has long been recognised that this often produces better quality learning than traditional classroom-based approaches.

If you decide to use a self-paced individual learning approach you will need to decide whether your needs can be met by an off-the-shelf package or whether you will need to develop your own bespoke materials. Off-the-shelf materials have the advantages of being available and relatively inexpensive. You should also be able to review them and decide whether or not they meet your needs. For many generic subjects they may well prove to be perfectly adequate, but if you decide that they are not, or if your subject matter is specific to your organisation, you will need to develop your own materials.

Again, you are presented with a decision: should you try to develop your own materials or ask an external supplier? If you decide on the former route, be aware that developing effective e-learning materials requires a wide range of specialist skills. There are a number of software packages available that claim to make it easy for people to develop e-learning materials quickly, but while this may be true for the programming side of the development, it does not apply to the instructional design aspects. Designing training for e-learning is very different to designing training for workshops, so unless you have access to these specialist skills, tread very carefully.

 If you decide to commission an external supplier to develop materials for you, you will find the guidelines on selecting a supplier in Chapter 9 of interest.

Tutor mediation

Linking browser delivery to other intranet technologies such as e-mail or video streaming makes it possible for learners to have contact with a tutor or subject expert. Tutor mediated e-learning is much more common in the educational sector than in business. The approach mirrors traditional lecturer-student relationships much more closely than the trainer-trainee relationship in business, and higher education has had a much longer track record of networked communications. The demands placed on higher education to educate more and more students with static resourcing levels has also meant that they have had to think about alternative delivery methods much more seriously than has business. Many companies may find providing effective on-line tutors difficult in their early years with e-learning, but there are an increasing number of external suppliers who are offering tutor mediated e-learning for generic subjects. Most of these cover technical subjects, such as advanced computer skills, but there are some suppliers who can offer training in generic business skills. There are also an increasing number of training courses available for teaching on-line tutoring skills.

There are two different ways in which tutor mediation can be provided, **synchronous** or **asynchronous**.

The easiest to consider is asynchronous (or not at the same time) communication, as this makes less demands on technology. Look at some examples:

- A learner working through self-paced learning materials completes an assignment and e-mails this to the tutor. The tutor reviews the assignment and sends comments back.

- Learners on a self-paced course may be working in groups. Assignments require them to collaborate and submit a joint response. They can exchange information with each other using a bulletin board or by e-mail.

- A tutor may send learners assignments that contain necessary reference information and links to relevant intranet and Internet sites. The tutor can be a source of information via e-mail or the telephone.

- The tutor can video record a presentation and store this on the server. Learners stream this to their browser when they need to.

You can see how this asynchronous tutor-mediated learning is simply a way of speeding up and enhancing traditional 'correspondence' courses by using technology. Nevertheless it is a relatively easy and cheap way of providing tutor support.

Synchronous (at the same time) e-learning generally relies on altogether more sophisticated technology. The essential difference is that tutors and learners come together electronically, and again there are a number of ways in which this can happen, such as video conferencing, virtual classrooms and instant messaging.

Video conferencing – Learners and the tutor can use video conferencing. The tutor could deliver a lecture to the participants using the video camera or run a PowerPoint® presentation that would display simultaneously on the learners' screens. The group could hold a discussion or carry out a syndicate activity as if they were physically together in the same management training centre.

Virtual classrooms – The group could use a **virtual classroom** application. These are a particular application of on-line collaborative tools, discussed in more detail earlier in this chapter.

Figure 6.10 shows an example of such an application, Centra Symposium, in action.

Virtual classrooms are an enhanced form of video conferencing which includes the possibilities described above as well as offering techniques that would be employed in a real classroom:

- Video and audio streaming so that participants can see and hear each other. The tutor can talk to individuals publicly or privately and participants may be able to communicate with each other. Although it is not yet possible for participants to pass chewing gum to each other over the Internet, it will be when such systems incorporate Star Trek transporter technology!

- Electronic whiteboards so that the tutor can draw diagrams and scribble notes that appear on the learners' screens.

- The ability to split classes may be split into virtual syndicates, which the trainer can then virtually visit.

But one major advantage that the virtual classroom has over its real-life counterpart is that sessions can be saved to disk and reviewed later.

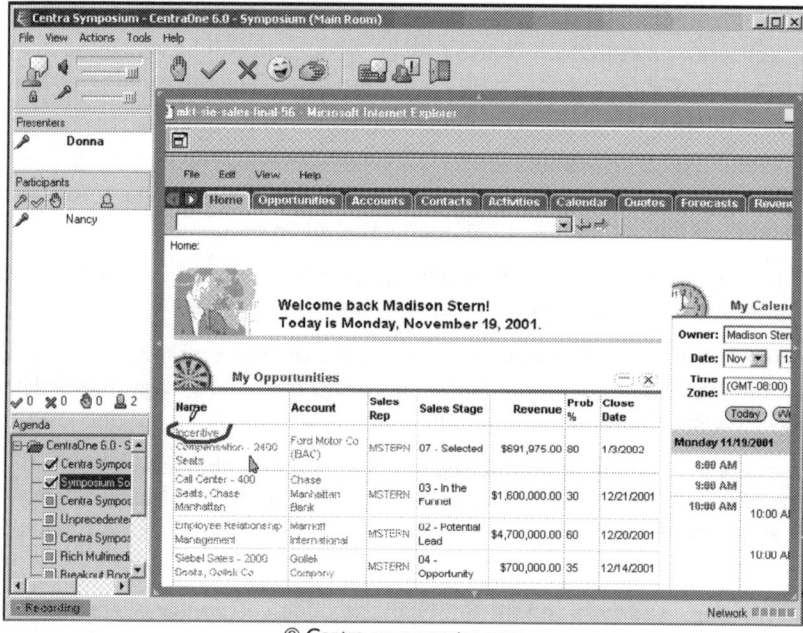

© Centra, www.centra.com

Figure 6.10
Virtual classroom application
This figure shows a virtual classroom application, Centra Symposium, being used to illustrate an aspect of a spreadsheet. The trainer is using a tool to highlight one cell within the spreadsheet, which is a live application.

Virtual classroom applications are complex and expensive and, unless an organisation is confident that it can use such systems extensively, it may be more attractive to rent time on a system from an Application Service Provider (ASP). Tutors also need to be extremely confident and competent in using the system, otherwise sessions can waste a lot of time.

 You can find more information about ASPs in Chapter 8.

Instant messaging – Learners and the tutor can use an instant messaging application to have a discussion, much as Internet chatroom users do. This can be a somewhat frustrating experience, however, as it is limited by participants' typing speeds and by the difficulties of typing what may be complex questions or answers under the perceived pressure of other participants waiting. Thinking about what you are typing while watching other conversations going on also taxes one's concentration.

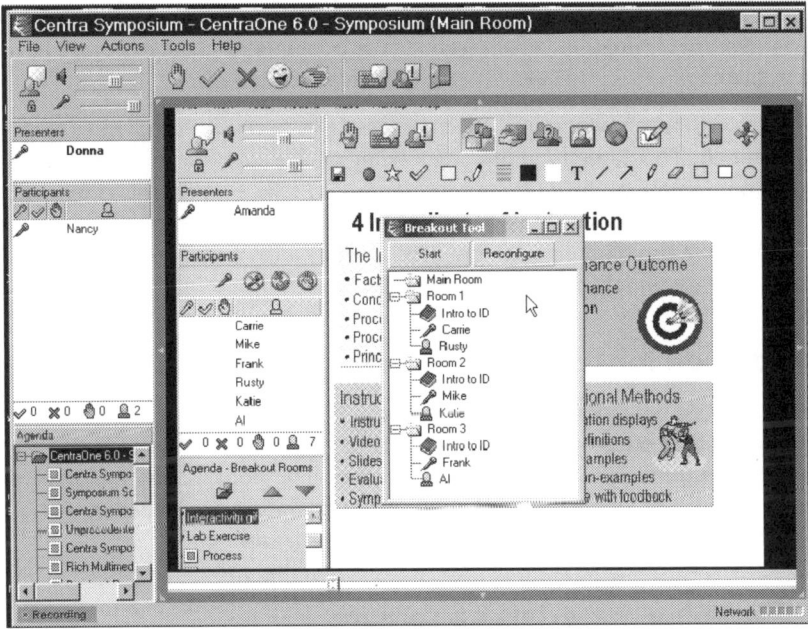

© Centra, www.centra.com

Figure 6.11

Virtual classroom application

This Centra Symposium screen capture shows a trainer dividing a group of participants up into syndicates. Each syndicate group will have its own shared space for collaborative working.

Blended learning

This is not an e-learning approach as such, but is a term often used to describe the use of a range of media to suit the training need. Despite what e-learning vendors might say, it is not an effective medium for delivering training in all subjects. Training in skills requires the learner to practise; after all, how would you feel about being operated on by a brain surgeon who had done all their studying over the Internet?

So training usually requires a blended approach to be successful. Training specialists should be able to identify what type of medium is most suitable for what aspect of a training course, the secret being to relate as closely as possible the learning medium to the ultimate performance expected from the learner.

What are the benefits of e-learning?

Reduced training costs

By eliminating or reducing the need to provide trainers and for learners to travel to central destinations in order to attend a course, e-learning approaches, can in some situations, offer significant cost savings. It can also reduce the opportunity costs of people having to leave their places of work and spend non-productive time travelling.

However, against these savings must be considered the relatively high cost of developing e-learning materials. This can vary widely, depending on the sophistication required and the consequent complexity of the development. It can also take a significant amount of time to develop an e-learning solution. E-learning only starts to become a cost-effective solution when the materials can be used over and over again by a large number of people, especially if they are widely dispersed geographically.

Reduced need for travelling

Travelling can often be unpopular with employees. People who travel regularly to carry out their normal jobs often appreciate being able to stay in their office or even access learning materials from their home over the Internet. The global political uncertainties following the events of September 2001 also served to make people more conscious of the benefits of e-learning in terms of reducing the need for travelling.

Ease of keeping materials up to date

All the assets (in other words, the individual files containing web pages, graphics, audio and video files) in e-learning courses are stored centrally, so it is easy to keep materials up to date. You never need to worry about the logistics of distributing new versions of CD-ROMs and devising ways of making sure that people use the latest versions of materials.

Integration of media

With an e-learning infrastructure in place it becomes possible to integrate the delivery of different types of distance learning material. Paper-based materials can be stored in Adobe Acrobat® format, for example, so that learners can download them and print them off as required. Links to do this can be provided in e-learning courses, providing an elegant integration of different ways of delivering learning. The increasing use of XML (see Chapter 2) also makes it possible to display materials on-line exactly as they appear in their native application.

Reuse of learning materials

As e-learning assets are stored centrally it makes sense to make them reusable over a number of courses wherever possible. For example, a learning sequence covering how to lift safely may be relevant to a specialist health and safety course, in an induction course or to someone who needs just-in-time training about how to lift a box. Rather than re-create it three times, the content is designed to be generic and is stored in a database. The three different training courses pull this 'learning object' out of the database and slot it into fields on pages that are themselves specific for the particular course.

Provision of just-in-time training

Learning materials that are delivered through the standard browser interface at the employee's desktop computer can be accessed instantaneously. The employee does not need to go to a special computer in another part of the building. You suddenly have to create a database to store some information and you have never used a database in your life? No problem. Access the relevant learning objects, study them and then just do it!

Support for using an unfamiliar application may also be provided through some form of Electronic Performance Support System (EPSS). An EPSS is a more sophisticated help systems that can steer a user through a specific problem, perhaps using multimedia or expert system approaches. Services such as these can be available through the intranet.

Comprehensive record-keeping

LMSs can store vast amounts of information about what learning is going on in an organisation: who has completed what training, how well they did in their assessment, what they got right, what they got wrong, how long they took. This data could then, say, be cross-referenced against departmental or organisational performance to generate information showing just how effective, or otherwise, particular training is proving to be.

Access to external materials

The Internet is a vast repository of information, some which is actually useful. You can supplement internal e-learning materials by providing links to relevant Internet materials. For example, a course on e-marketing could give learners links to examples of e-marketing out there in the world or to academic papers discussing specific aspects of the subject.

Integrating learning into everyday work

As people will often study e-learning materials from their normal desk, it becomes possible to design learning materials so that they integrate more closely with day-to-day responsibilities. This makes it easier for people to associate learning with their normal work, rather than as something they do in a training room. Adding in the possibilities of tutor-mediation and e-mail opens up the possibilities of learners developing an ongoing relationship with their tutor that continues even after their formal training has finished.

What are the challenges for e-learning?

The loneliness of the long-distance tutor

Although being an on-line tutor sounds like it is little different than being a teacher or trainer, it does call for a wide range of skills that may be difficult to find in one person. As well as being an expert in the subject matter of the course, the tutor also needs to be something of an IT trouble-shooter. However well tested software is, things will always go wrong – bulletin boards will hang, people will lose assignments, some users will be fearful of the technology. The tutor needs to be completely confident in using all the media and be able to sort learners' IT problems out for them at a distance.

They need to be self-disciplined to keep on top of the work involved. As with many types of IT solution, users expect speedy responses and on-line tutors need to make sure they review assignments quickly. They need to keep a close eye on how individual learners are progressing and how groups are getting on with collaborative assignments – and all this without possibly ever meeting any of the participants.

Potential problems of converting existing materials

In order to justify the investment that will have been made in order to deliver e-learning across an organisation, it can be very tempting to convert existing learning materials into an e-learning format. However, this needs to be done with care. Before embarking on a conversion process, there are a number of questions you need to consider[10]:

1. Are you prepared for the effort that delivering an e-learning course requires?

    Tutor-mediated e-learning courses place great demands on the tutor. They may no longer have to organise themselves to stand in front of a group of trainees, but they will have to respond to learners' e-mail questions, assess assignments, monitor bulletin board activity and solve technical problems, to list just a few of their responsibilities. They will almost certainly spend more time delivering a course using e-learning than in a workshop format.

2. Do you really understand how much effort is involved in the conversion?

    Just how difficult the conversion is depends on a number of factors:

    - Do you have electronic copies of the original materials? If they have dropped out of your recycling bin then you will have to re-create everything. Not such an issue for text, as this will probably have to be substantially rewritten anyway, but it could be time-consuming for graphics.

    - If you do have the assets you need, are they in a usable format? You may have to convert all graphics to intranet-friendly formats, for example.

- Do you have the right to convert material into electronic format? Depending on the age and source of the material, ownership of paper materials may not give you the freedom to make electronic versions.

- Will you need extra material? Classroom trainers always fill in gaps in workshop notes with their own material, and workshop plans are sometimes only skeletons outlining the programme, rather than being replete with detail. Allow time for more research and writing.

- Do you have the technical skills needed to produce e-learning materials of an acceptable quality? E-learning design calls for a range of skills quite different to those needed for workshop design.

3. **Are you prepared to change the delivery format?**

While technologies such as virtual classrooms and video feeds make it quite feasible to replicate the format and structure of a traditional classroom event as an e-learning course, this does not use the medium to its strengths. Classroom lectures are often effective because of the personality of the lecturer and the rapport that they establish with the group, and this does not come across on a recorded video feed. It also places heavy demands on the network, so needs to be kept to a minimum.

So where, in the past, a lecturer has delivered a formal lecture, you need to think about alternative ways of presenting this material, ways that use the medium to its best extent, such as tutorials with self-assessment questions, simulations or threaded group discussions using asynchronous bulletin boards. Use video for demonstrations or for explaining concepts visually.

Virtual classrooms allow learners to collaborate and learn together, even if they are separated by thousands of miles. However, such synchronous learning can be difficult to co-ordinate, especially where people are working in different time zones.

4. **Do people have the necessary access?**

E-learning requires that people have access to the intranet or Internet. Is this the case? If you are assuming that they will have access using their normal office computer, take into account the difficulties of studying in such an environment, where they will possibly be continuously distracted by colleagues, telephones ringing and their day-to-day responsibilities that are no more than an arm's reach away.

5. Will people keep going on an e-learning course?

All distance learning courses require discipline and persistence on the part of the learner. Most people find it much easier to stick with a course if they do it as a social activity, and while distance learning may be attractive to an organisation, individuals often see it as a second-best option. You therefore need to ask a fundamental question as to whether people in your organisation will accept e-learning as an alternative to the classroom-based events that they have known in the past.

If you do feel confident about this, then you also need to make sure that the e-learning that you provide is engaging. Will it continuously stimulate and provide feedback to the learners? Is it easy to use? How will you deal with learners who resist e-learning?

6. Is the subject matter appropriate to e-learning?

E-learning is best suited to delivering knowledge and skills that can be replicated using a computer. If the subject matter does not fit either of these categories then you would probably be best using the traditional methods: '... people can read about, discuss, see videos of, or listen to experts describing how to swim, but eventually they have to get wet.'[11]. But consider how existing courses could be converted into blended learning, with the knowledge elements being delivered using e-learning and the skill-based elements staying in a hands-on format.

Think about how much of the material does actually need to be incorporated in an e-learning format. Knowledge and skills about dealing with areas that the learner will not come across very often, such as special cases or alternative techniques, may best be dealt with by providing information on them as reference material or an EPSS solution, on the intranet, perhaps.

7. Are intranet-based assessment methods adequate?

It is very easy to develop certain types of test such as multiple choice or drag and drop questioning in e-learning materials, but it is much harder to use the medium to demonstrate skills or show fine degrees of judgement. You must think carefully about the performance criteria for the training and decide whether or not these can be demonstrated using e-learning methods. If not, you will need to persist with current methods of assessment.

High initial expense

E-learning is often sold on the basis of its low cost, but this is only true if many people use it. There are a number of significant up-front expenses that need to be made before you can enrol your first learner:

- Buy in or develop e-learning courseware.

- Install a Learning Management System for managing the delivery of courses. This subject is covered in more detail below.

- Train administration and delivery staff in the new skills they will need.

Developing e-learning materials is not cheap. It takes time to do it properly and, as we all know, time costs money. The design and development process requires specific skills, and these will have to be purchased. This is particularly true if you decide to incorporate audio and video, which are particularly expensive. And do not be tempted to save money by shooting video on your home camcorder: unless you are particularly skilled at such things as sound and lighting and have a willing cast of competent actors, the end result will look amateurish.

Capability of the infrastructure

E-learning can place heavy demands on network infrastructure, especially if it tries to send audio and video down the wires. If network administrators do not allow these, the materials must be well designed so that the lack of glossiness compared to CD-ROM multimedia materials does not become a problem.

Do all employees have easy access to a browser? If they do not, you may have to consider installing kiosks in convenient areas, where people who do not ordinarily use a computer can study.

Where should the learning take place?

A commonly quoted benefit of e-learning is that it allows people to learn at their desks, and that they no longer need to waste time travelling to and from classrooms. However, ask anyone who has tried to work through any form of distance learning at their desks how well it went and you will almost certainly get a somewhat negative answer.

Colleagues see the learner sitting there and assume that they are available for work-related conversations or personal chats. The telephone keeps ringing. The line manager may wonder why they are not doing their day job. People complain about the audio soundtrack being played over speakers. The learner associates their desk with work, rather than with learning. The list goes on. So in reality the only way to provide a proper learning environment is to provide a learning centre, which at its simplest may be nothing more than a room away from the main offices where learners can go to complete individual learning activities.

How is e-learning managed?

While e-learning materials can sit happily on a normal intranet server and be accessed just like any other intranet material, many of e-learning's advantages are lost unless it is managed by specialist software called a Learning Management System (LMS). This can do such things as:

- record what materials learners have studied and how well they have done

- show learners a catalogue of courses that are available, indicating if there are any prerequisites, whether the course leads to a qualification and how long the study time is likely to be

- allow learners to register for a course

- record information about a learner's progress through a course

- produce reports for managers showing who has done which course.

Learning Management Systems can usually also be set up so that they can record information about classroom-based courses and other non-e-learning programmes. Some LMSs may also be able to function as librarians, providing a list of books and journals available in a library, recording borrowers' names and issuing reminders for return automatically by e-mail. More sophisticated versions can also help with planning, by doing such things as:

- suggesting an individual employee's training needs based on their competency profile and training record

- proposing a training plan for an employee moving to a new job.

Working at a lower level are systems known as Learning Content Management Systems (LCMS), although many LMSs are also able to carry out such functions. These look after the individual files used to make up an e-learning course and will also monitor a learner's progress through an individual course. For example, if a learner needs to leave a course temporarily, the LCMS will record where they left the course so that they can pick it up again later from the same point. They also make it possible to share the same content across a number of different courses. This is because, in order to make the most of the central storage of learning materials, e-learning courses are often designed using **learning objects** – discrete pieces of information that are generic. Specific courses are therefore built up from material that is specific to the subject and generic learning objects.

Selecting an LMS

Selecting the right LMS for your organisation is not an easy task. They are complex pieces of software, can take a long time to install and can be extremely expensive. Depending on the system and its complexity an LMS can cost anywhere between £25,000 and £500,000.

Be confident about the supplier's viability

LMSs are something of an emerging technology, with all the complications that that introduces. The enthusiasm shown for e-learning in the 2000-2001 period convinced a large number of companies to develop and market LMSs, and of course, as time has gone by, some of these have disappeared or have been absorbed into larger organisations. It is therefore vitally important that, before choosing an LMS supplier, you find out as much as possible about their financial stability and make contingency plans. Will it be possible to transfer information and courseware to another LMS should you need to do this?

Make sure the LMS is compliant with standards

Choosing an LMS that complies with industry standards should make it more likely that you can change to another supplier, should this be necessary. It should also make it much easier when choosing e-learning materials that you want to run within the LMS. Again, the emerging nature of the technology means that the standards are still somewhat fluid, but there are some standards that the major players in the LMS market are working to. These include[12]:

- SCORM (Shareable Content Object Reference Model), a standard developed by the United States government drawing on specifications developed by AICC and IMS (below) – probably the most important of the standards and the one for which all new e-learning courseware should be designed.

- AICC (Aviation Industry CBT Committee), a United States-based organisation that has worked for many years to develop standards for CBT in the aviation industry

- IEEE (Institute of Electrical and Electronic Engineers), again a United States professional institution

- IMS (IMS Global Consortium Inc), an organisation working closely with the IEEE to help define standards

- CEN/ISSS LT (European Community Information Society Standardisation System for Learning Technology), a European group concerned with making sure that emerging standards meet the requirements of different languages within the European Community.

You can find more up-to-date information about e-learning standards at these sites:

- http://www.adlnet.org/

- www.ltsc.ieee.org

- www.manta.ieee.org/p1484

- www.imsproject.com

- http://www.cenorm.be/isss/cwa_download_area/cwa14040.pdf

Clearly, before making any decisions about buying an LMS, you should familiarise yourself with the current state of play in the LMS standards game by taking a look at the latest information from these organisations.

Remember that compliance to standards also applies to e-learning materials: if an e-learning course is described as AICC-compliant this means that it generates information which an AICC-compliant LMS should be able to manage without any difficulty. Of course, whether this is true in practice may be a different matter.

Make sure the LMS is compatible with existing infrastructure

It is absolutely vital to make sure that you involve your IT Department in the selection process to make sure that the LMS you choose is completely compatible with your existing IT infrastructure. If you are using an HR information system you should make sure that it is possible for the two systems to exchange information. For example, can an on-line appraisal system access the training database to identify appropriate courses for someone? Other compatibility-related questions you should ask include:

- What about existing training materials? Will you be able to run these under the LMS?

- Does the system allow people working externally to access learning materials via the Internet?

Plan for flexibility

You should have a clear strategy about what training you are going to be delivering over the next few years, and this, of course, should be derived from your business's strategy. Make sure that the LMS will be able to cope with what you plan to do and with any unplanned changes that you may have to make.

Make sure that you develop a Service Level Agreement with the supplier that meets your needs and ask them how this will be honoured in the event that they cease trading or are taken over by another company.

Be clear about what you are paying

Each LMS supplier has its own different way of charging for its system. Some may charge a flat fee while others may charge a rental, and this may be dependent on the number of users. Having a clear idea about how you are going to use the system will help you to make the correct decision.

Also remember that you may need to pay for upgrades over the life of the system and that the cost of these may be significant. Establish clearly what these are going to be so that you can budget accordingly. There will be other charges for training your administrative staff, consultancy advice and for system configuration.

Suppliers may be prepared to negotiate on pricing if they feel that your organisation offers the potential for long-term business. This may be an advantage if you are confident that e-learning will form a major part of your training strategy over the next few years (and also feel confident that the supplier will remain in business over that time).

Do you actually need an LMS?

Although LMSs are often seen as a vital component of an e-learning strategy, they are not without their critics. Clark Aldrich[13] identifies a number of serious problems inherent in the concept of the LMS.

The difficulty of choosing a supplier

LMSs vary widely in what they do and how they work, and Aldrich points out that it can be very difficult to get clear answers from suppliers as to just how their own product works and how it differs from other systems. The need to customise the LMS to fit in with each organisation's unique infrastructure means that every implementation is different so you cannot get a straight answer to the simple question, 'How much does it cost?'.

Also, the infancy and dynamism of the marketplace means that products are constantly developing, with new features appearing almost while you review the system's brochure. Aldrich suggests that '… most enterprises buying a system still feel like beta customers.'

What learning do LMSs actually manage?

The difference between the hype and the reality of e-learning means that many LMSs costing hundreds of thousands of pounds may not actually be managing much e-learning. Probably in time, as e-learning does become more widespread, their databases will fill up with records, but currently they are often sledgehammers being used to crack nuts.

They also formalise and quantify the notion that learning only happens in a course. Although many LMSs can record information about workshop attendance and completion of other non-e-learning activities, this relies on manual inputting of information, which is never totally reliable. They also completely ignore the informal learning that goes on in all organisations, the conversations, the sitting-by-Nellies, attending conferences and exhibitions and studying information on external Internet sites, for example. Most LMSs are very poor at recording the use of 'learning nuggets', the on-line delivery of bite-sized pieces of just-in-time training that are increasingly being seen as a major attraction of on-line delivery. They also find it difficult to cope with simulation training, such as business-oriented games, where the measurement of a learner's success does not fit comfortably into the requirements of a SCORM-compliant database.

The danger is that because an LMS can provide data on learning activities quickly and easily, people will assume that it accurately represents the sum of learning that is going on in the organisation, which patently it is not.

How meaningful is the information?

People in organisations do things – in other words, they demonstrate skills. Organisations in which people perform these skills poorly are likely to be poorly-performing businesses. But most of the data held in LMSs actually reports on knowledge and the theoretical implementation of those skills, which can be very different than how people perform in reality. You therefore cannot assume that LMS information showing a highly trained workforce actually means a high performing one.

Making e-learning work: a strategy for success

As with any other e-HR initiative, the implementation of e-learning is more likely to be successful if you follow a careful strategy. Watson Wyatt suggest[14] a strategy that incorporates a number of different steps.

Obtain high-level commitment

Make sure that the introduction of e-learning fits in with the organisation's vision. If this is the case, it will be much easier to obtain the necessary funding and managerial support needed.

Prepare a strong business case

You will need to be able to justify the expense needed to implement e-learning and develop high-quality materials by showing that it will produce a satisfactory return on the investment. To do this you will need to have a clear idea about the current costs of training and how e-learning can help to reduce these.

Plan the introduction carefully

Introduce e-learning solutions gradually, starting with those that are most important from an organisational point of view and that will produce significant financial savings. This will make sure that users become positive about e-learning and will show managers that your promises of financial savings are actually coming true.

Develop e-learning champions

Make sure you have people spread throughout the organisation who are committed to the success of e-learning and who will demonstrate their enthusiasm to others.

Allow people to adjust to the new medium

E-learning may present a cultural challenge to people within the organisation, especially if they have not previously been exposed to other forms of technology-based training. You should expect a certain amount of suspicion or cynicism at first, but as long as you choose your first e-learning subjects carefully and deliver well-designed materials, you should be able to overcome this.

Terri Anderson[15] identifies some other significant potential cultural barriers to the success of e-learning. The empowerment of employees implied by e-HR means that individuals would be encouraged to identify and organise their own training plans, using the information that e-HR systems give them. Indeed, this is cited as a major attraction of the medium. However, managers in many organisations may see this as a threat to their autonomy and influence if they have seen training needs identification as their responsibility or the granting of attendance at a training course as a gift to favoured employees.

She also comments on the need for the organisation introducing e-learning to realise that traditional measures of training success, such as the numbers of 'bums on seats' or hours of training delivered, will no longer work. The success of a training course will become measured by the ability of the learners to pass performance-related assessments and, increasingly as other parts of the organisation's systems provide the data, by measurable improvements in actually doing the job.

Give people the chance to provide feedback

The ability of e-learning materials to link in with e-mail systems makes it very easy for you to give learners the chance to provide feedback. Ask people for their comments on such things as inaccuracies in the material, whether or not they enjoyed using the materials and whether they have found them useful in their jobs. Give such feedback serious consideration and make sure that people can see that you have done so, by correcting mistakes and strengthening any weaknesses identified.

Choose suppliers carefully

With e-learning development you have a choice as to whether to do the design and development yourself or to look for an external supplier. If you choose the internal route make sure you have staff with the necessary specialised skills. Developing e-learning is completely different to developing any other form of training so do not assume that existing staff will be able to pick up an authoring package and develop effective learning materials.

If you decide to look for an external supplier be aware that, as with any other industry in its infancy, the e-learning market will need a little time to settle down as some suppliers prosper while others disappear. Make sure you choose your suppliers carefully and that your implementation plans are sufficiently flexible so that the disappearance of a supplier does not cause you serious problems.

You can find more information about how to choose suppliers in Chapter 9.

Evaluate the effectiveness of the e-learning

Most organisations fail to evaluate how effective any training has been. What evaluation takes place is usually at a fairly low level, what is often referred to as Levels 1 and 2 (derived from Kirkpatrick's model for training evaluation). Basically, Level 1 asks whether the learner has enjoyed the training activity and Level 2 tests to see whether they have learned anything from it. Level 3 evaluation tests to see whether people's performance at work has changed as a result of the training intervention.

One reason why Level 3 evaluation does not usually take place is that the learner has disappeared from the training room or is no longer working through self-paced learning materials and there are practical difficulties in contacting them. The quantifiable aspects of their job performance may also have been inadequately defined. However, it should be possible to configure an LMS to contact the learner or their line manager (or both) after an appropriate amount of time and ask whether or not there has been a measurable change in performance. Depending on the nature of the performance it may even be possible to give the learner a link to an on-line assessment test.

All training should be evaluated, not just e-learning. However, there is particular value in seeking to evaluate a new medium, such as e-learning, as a way of proving its worth, so that it is easier to obtain future investment.

Summarising ...

- On-line systems make it easier to deliver organisational information by:
    - allowing information to become active
    - pushing information to people who want it.
- Gathering information from the workforce becomes much easier.
- On-line systems make it easier to keep up to date with the outside world.
- On-line collaborative tools make it possible for groups of people to work together even though separated.
- On-line collaboration offers a number of advantages, including:
    - improved flexibility
    - the ability to replay meetings
    - making it possible to work with a greater number of people.
- Challenges to on-line collaboration include:
    - cultural challenges
    - training requirements
    - bandwidth.

- E-learning can be delivered in a number of ways and allows different media to be integrated in a blended learning solution.

- There are a number of benefits to e-learning but some significant challenges as well.

- Learning Management Systems are used to manage content and learners' records.

- It is important to have a carefully worked out strategy for the introduction of e-learning.

Notes

1. Cisco Employee Connection: Exploring the Frontiers of Intranet Technology', www.cisco.com/warp/public/756/gnb_gen/intra_wp.htm

2. Bawden, D, (1997), 'Information Systems and the Stimulation of Creativity', in Ruggles III, R.L. (ed.), *Knowledge Management Tools*, London: Butterworth-Heinemann, 1997.

3. John, G. (1998), 'Share Strength', *People Management*, 13 August.

4. ViosionCor (2001)'The Human Element: Knowledge Management's Secret Ingredient', www.learningcircuits.org/2001/dec2001/visioncor.html

5. Schrage, M, (1997), 'Collaborative Tools: A First Look', in Ruggles III, R.L. (ed.), *Knowledge Management Tools*, Butterworth-Heinemann. p. 169

6. Ibid.

7. Reed, C. (2002), 'Building an Enterprise Strategy for Digital Collaboration', www.centra.com/products/

8. Lloyd, R. (2000), 'Informal Learning Most Effective', *Knowledge Management Magazine*, www.destinationkm.com/articles/default.asp?ArticleID=576

9. Watson Wyatt 'e-HR: e-learning in the Knowledge Economy: Industry Outlook and Implications for Business', www.watsonwyatt.com/research/printable.asp?id=W-527a a&page=1

10. Sevilla, C. and Wells, T. (2000), 'Converting to Web-Based Training: Choices and Trade-offs', www.learningcircuits.org/may2000/may2000_elearn.html

11. Anderson, T., (2002), 'is E-learning Right for your Organisation?', www.learningcircuits.org/2002/jan2002/anderson.html

12. Technologies for Training (2000), *Technology based training and On-Line learning: an Overview of Authoring Systems and Learning Management Systems Available in the UK*, London: Lifelong Learning & Technologies Division, Department for Education and Employment.

13. Aldrich, C. (2001), 'Can LMSs Survive the Sophisticated Buyer?', www.learningcircuits.org/2001/nov2001/ttools.html

14. Watson Wyatt, 'e-HR'.

15. Anderson, 'Is e-leanring right for your organisation?'.

chapter 7

Enhancing employees' benefits

This final perspective on the uses of e-HR looks at a number of ways in which e-HR solutions are being used in what might be described as motivational ways, providing extra services and information to employees that can enhance their working lives in some way. These include:

- total compensation statements, allowing employees to explore in more detail the full extent of their rewards for working, over and above their take-home pay

- on-line flex, where employees can choose the mixture of extra benefits offered

- concierge and other external services.

Total compensation statements

There has been a trend in recent years for organisations to present the packages they offer to employees in terms of total compensation, rather than just salary. This is because many new employers offer packages with cash and few benefits, so organisations offering a mixture of cash and benefits need to find ways of showing how the package they offer compares. For example, how does a total compensation package of, say, £40,000 a year compare with a salary of £30,000 a year plus car?

Figure 7.1 illustrates what this might look like.

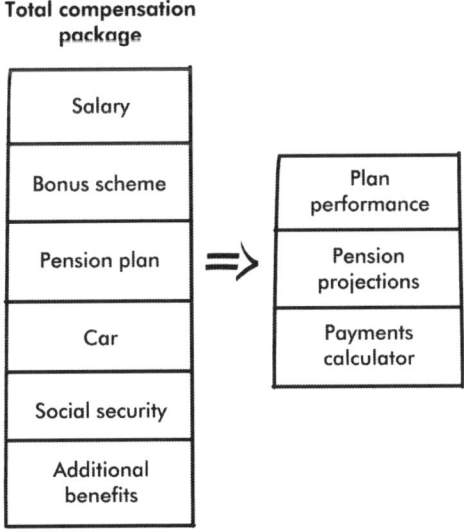

Figure 7.1
What a total compensation statement application might contain

When the user accesses their total compensation package application they will be presented with a list of all the items that are in their package, along with their notional financial value. This is often enhanced by relevant tools. So, for example, while the simple list will say what the employer contributes each year towards a pension, the employee can investigate this further. By clicking on the appropriate link they could find out more information about such things as:

- how their pension plans are performing

- what level of pension they could expect if they were to continue funding for a pension at this level

- how changing their contributions would affect their pension (by using an on-line calculator).

Similar functionality can be provided to allow people to do such things as look at the performance of their employee share scheme holding or how their current level of performance will be reflected in bonus payments.

Such applications can help to make employees feel more secure about their employment by appreciating more fully how well they are being looked after.

Different organisations will have different needs for such applications. For example in BP's e-HR system, myHR, employees can use the services of Expat Calculator. This provides instant information about compensation and allowances for overseas postings. This allows employees considering taking an overseas posting to make quick, informed decisions. Prior to the introduction of myHR it often took employees weeks to find the information they needed.

Lucent Technologies have operated a 'Benefit Answers' site on their intranet since 1996.[2] This provides extensive information on benefits available to employees. These include categories such as:

- health and well-being, offering information on health-care plans ranging from life insurance to eye care

- savings information, where employees can find out about such things as employee share ownership schemes

- work and home, covering benefits available to family members

- changing lifestyles, information about changes to their benefits that would arise as a result of lifestyle changes such as getting married, becoming a parent or taking leave of absence.

On-line flex

On-line flex applications have been popular in the United States for a number of years, mainly because of the need for private health-care policies, and they are just starting to become popular in Europe. Figure 7.2 illustrates the principle of how they work.

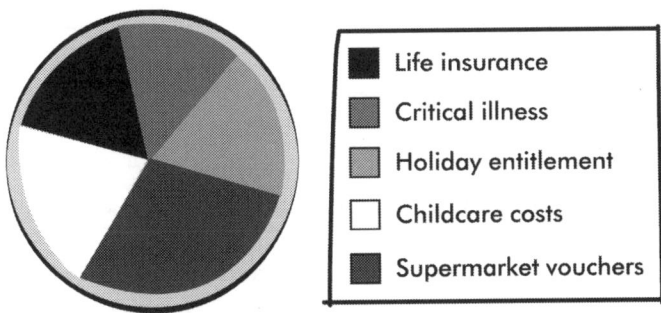

Figure 7.2
On-line flex

As part of the total compensation package, an employee is provided with a flexible benefit package that has a fixed value. Within that package they can pick and mix a range of benefits, which can include such things as life insurance, critical illness cover, insurance for a partner, childcare costs, supermarket vouchers, holiday entitlement and subscriptions to leisure facilities. Some items may be compulsory but there is some flexibility. For example, if an employer offers private health-care, the employee must accept it but may be able to upgrade it.

The attraction of packages such as these are that they allow employees to choose benefits that are relevant to them. For example, a single person with no children would probably not be interested in childcare provision but may be interested in more holiday. However, should they become a parent, they may want to trade off some of their holiday for childcare provision and enhanced life insurance.

While such flex systems have been available for many years, they have been complicated to administer because of the complex calculations involved, especially where the benefit has tax implications. Making changes to such packages could therefore take a considerable amount of time. However, with an on-line system the employee can literally sit at their desktop and play with the various permutations possible. Having identified some possibilities they could take them home, discuss them with their partner and return to the office, click on the 'Submit' button and their flex package is updated immediately.

The passing of the Electronic Signatures in Global and National Commerce Act into US law in 2000 also meant that it became possible to accept digital signatures as valid authorisation for transactions where ink and paper signatures had previously been obligatory. This meant that, as well as reading about benefits available and providing basic details to the benefits provider, it became possible to complete the entire application process on-line. This offers considerable savings to the benefits provider and increases the convenience to employees. Lucent estimates that it saved $1.2 million during its first year of operation through eliminating the need to distribute paper-based information on benefits to employees.

Lucent also recognised that publicising benefits available to employees could be a useful way of attracting high-quality staff. They therefore made information on these benefits available on their Internet site rather than just to existing staff on the intranet. As the director of HR compensation and benefits communication at Lucent says[1], 'To go forward profitably, productively and competitively, making this information widely available gives us an advantage overall.'

Concierge and other external services

As virtually all intranets provide connections to the Internet, it becomes possible to provide a range of external services provided by outside suppliers. Many of these fall under the heading of what are becoming known as concierge services, where a supplier can provide a wide range of services which are all characterised by being simple yet needing time. For example, you may need to take some clothes to a dry cleaner, buy some flowers, have your cat fed while on holiday or queue at the Passport Office.

Internet technologies have opened up new potential for such services, as they make it easier for the supplier to bundle up requests into more cost-effective single journeys or actions. For example, a large multinational organisation might have several people all needing to go to the Passport Office during the same week. The concierge supplier may be able to send one person out to go to the Passport Office, buy flowers, feed a cat and drop off dry cleaning at the same time, and all for different people.

The economies of scale offered by a group of people can allow employers to set up on-line shopping facilities on their intranet that offer competitive pricing. This might cover such services as:

- travel agents

- on-line shopping with a supermarket

- insurance companies and other financial services.

For example, Cisco Systems Metro e-HR intranet system gives employees access to hotel booking, airline reservation and car rental systems so that they can plan their own business trips according to their own preferences[3].

Such systems can offer various benefits.

Businesses derive an income from advertising. Businesses allowing external suppliers to have access to their employees will be able to charge for the privilege, meaning that the system provides a steady income from that source.

Employees may find more competitive prices.
Having access to a large, almost captive, market may mean that suppliers can offer more competitive prices. It can therefore be more attractive to employees to shop on-line through their employer's intranet than to do it externally.

Employers may be able to take advantage of the cash flows.
In some cases an organisation may be able to take advantage of the money flowing through on-line shopping.

For example, consider a bank offering on-line shopping opportunities to its employees through its intranet. As a condition of employment bank, employees must always have their salaries paid into an account within the bank. However, because of the competitiveness of high street banking, it may be advantageous to immediately transfer that salary to an account held at a competitor bank. The employer therefore loses the advantage of holding the money.

However, if the on-line shopping facilities require that payments be made from employees' accounts within the bank, it will be necessary for staff to keep their money within the employer's system.

Miscellaneous motivators

There are, of course, many other ways in which on-line technologies can be used to provide small services or functions that can motivate employees, and the scope is limited only by an employer's imagination. Consider these examples:

- Some employers have set up webcams in the company crèche so that parents can check up to see how their child is.

- In some organisations employees have a mood meter on their portal. This may take the form of a line of faces, ranging from sad to smiling, and the employee clicks on which they feel describes them. The system can provide a continuous, real-time summary of the mood in the department or the organisation as a whole.

- Quizzes can be set up to provide some light relief.

- Newsfeeds, perhaps displaying the company's share price, can be run across the portal.

- Chat-rooms and noticeboards can provide fora where people can have on-line conversations or advertise cars for sale.

Summarising ...

- Total compensation package applications allow people to check what benefits their employer is offering and to explore 'What if ...?' scenarios.

- On-line flex applications allow people to change the balance of benefits offered by their employer.

- External suppliers can provide such facilities as concierge services and on-line shopping.

- There are many possibilities for providing on-line motivational applications.

Notes

1. Wells, S.J. (2001) 'Communicating Benefits Information On-line' in *HR Magazine*, Society for Human Resource Management, February, **Vol. 46**, No 2.

2. Cisco Employee Connection: Exploring the Frontiers of Intranet Technology', www.cisco.com/warp/public/756/gnb_gen/intra_wp.htm

3. Ibid.

chapter 8

Planning your e-HR
implementation strategy

If you have worked through all the preceding chapters in this book, particularly Chapter 3, where we looked at how to decide what e-HR applications are right for you and how to prepare a blueprint, you should now have a fairly clear idea about how e-HR can help your business. You will have identified those parts of your value chain where e-HR can make the most effective contribution and will have developed a business case justifying the necessary investment. The next step is to decide how to put this into practice.

Of course, exactly how you will go about this will depend on the solutions you want to put into place, but there are some general points to consider. Let us look at some of the questions you may be asking yourself:

- Should I upgrade, add or start from scratch?

- How do I choose a supplier?

- Should I rent or buy?

- What should I do about security?

This chapter will look at answers to each of these questions in turn.

Should I upgrade, add or start from scratch?

Should I upgrade my existing HRIS?

Most organisations already use some form of HR Information System. According to the Watson Wyatt B2E/eHR survey for 2002,[1] 88 per cent of European businesses use an HRIS, so for many of these businesses a valid question may be to consider whether to simply ask their existing supplier to quote for the necessary upgrading. However, this needs to be considered against another finding of the survey which was that 42 per cent of the respondents said they were thinking of changing their HRIS supplier, often because of bad experiences with implementation. Also, upgrading with your existing supplier will mean being constrained by what they offer. If they offer what you want, great, but if not, think again. The change from client-server to intranet-based technologies may therefore be an opportunity for such companies to look for another supplier.

There is therefore no simple answer to this question. If you are happy with your existing HRIS and have a good relationship with the supplier then, provided that the cost of upgrading to an e-HR solution is within your budget, this may be the best solution. However, whatever your final decision is, make sure you start your decision-making process with a blank sheet of paper and work through the process outlined in Chapter 3 to develop a blueprint of what your business really needs. Do not work backwards from what your existing supplier can offer.

Should I go for an integrated application or a best-of-breed?

Those of you with an interest in hi-fi will be familiar with the debate over whether to buy an integrated 'midi' system or to go for the best separate amplifier, CD-player, speakers and cassette deck that your pocket will stretch to. There is a similar issue to face when buying an e-HR system.

Integrated packages, such as those offered within ERP systems will work together seamlessly but may not offer the functionality or flexibility you want, while best-of-breed solutions may be more flexible and future-proofed but can be harder to integrate.

Fortunately, compromises are appearing: some vendors offer packages that contain applications developed by different suppliers (often similar packages competing against each other) but which are designed within a common template and so will integrate more easily. You can then choose the particular applications that meet your particular needs.

Should I start from scratch with our intranet?

The third approach, and probably the most daunting, is to go back to basics and build or install systems that work directly on your intranet. You can approach this gradually by upgrading second-generation sites to offer more functionality and looking to install one of the new generation of intranet-based portal systems.

As client-server technology passes on into the history books this is probably the strategy that everyone will follow, but in these early days of e-HR the situation is not so clear. This will probably be the most expensive solution and may be politically difficult to justify and technologically difficult to implement.

How do I choose a supplier?

No doubt about it, choosing a supplier for any HR management system is a difficult and stressful activity and the old advertising slogan 'Nobody ever got fired for choosing...' does not really help very much. If you have an existing HR management system and you are happy with the supplier, you may well find that they offer an intranet-based system that provides you with the functionality you require. However, if you are looking to change your supplier or are starting from scratch with a management system you will find the following guidelines[2] of help.

Be clear about what you want

Although this may appear to be a statement of the obvious, purchasers often ask suppliers to provide something that is not what they actually want. This can happen for a variety of reasons. Purchasers may not completely understand what they want, so express their requirements too vaguely.

On the other hand, requirements may be written to minute levels of detail but not adequately describe the big picture. This is often the case where specifications are written by IT departments rather than the business.

Choose a supplier to suit your budget

Perhaps the most important factor in choosing a supplier is price. You can only choose from suppliers who can deliver a product that meets your budget. But there are several things you must bear in mind when considering the price a supplier is offering:

- It is a false economy to buy a product that is cheap if you think that it may not do what you need. If you cannot buy the functionality you want with the budget that you have available, think about what functionality you can dispense with for the moment and choose a supplier who can deliver this limited requirement adequately.

- Suppliers may offer you an unrealistically low price to win the business. Future upgrades may then turn out to be relatively expensive and you could end up spending more money in the long term than if you had initially chosen a more expensive option.

As well as asking for a price for the installation and initial support, ask the supplier to give you a total price for two years of operation, taking into account costs for installation, implementation, upgrades, training and support.

Test the application

One of the great advantages of web-based systems is that they do not require a special client. This makes it possible for suppliers to offer demonstration versions of their applications that can be set up and run with a minimum of installation problems. Many suppliers even allow you to do this using an Internet connection to their own web site. It is therefore very easy to try different suppliers' applications out and see which ones have the look and feel that you want without ever having to speak to a salesperson!

There are a number of sites on the Internet that provide lists and summaries of HR software suppliers, and a few hours spent surfing through these can provide you with a lot of valuable first-hand experience.

These sites will provide you with links to potential suppliers:

- www.softwaresource.co.uk/ (managed by the CIPD)

- www.hr-guide.com/

Alternatively, use your favourite search engines to track down particular types of application.

Buy from a supplier you like

Buying an e-HR system is not like buying breakfast cereal from the supermarket: you are probably going to be in a technological bed with this supplier for several years, so you should make sure that you feel comfortable with them.

Find out what you can about how the supplier's business actually runs. You may feel most comfortable with a supplier whose business is similar to your own. If you work for a large, international organisation it may be most appropriate to look for an internationally-based supplier which is used to dealing with companies such as yours. If your business is small, you may feel more comfortable with a small supplier who may be less formal and more customer-focused.

What sort of people work for the supplier? What are their backgrounds? People with a background in HR will understand the issues you face and so should be offering better designed products. You may feel less confident about this if they develop a wide range of IT products rather than focusing on HR systems.

Ask the supplier for a client list

Ask suppliers to give you lists of customers using systems similar to the one you are thinking of buying. You can then speak to these people and ask them for their opinion about the system and the supplier. The supplier may run user groups, which can give you an opportunity to meet other customers. See if you can visit these other customers and look at the supplier's systems in operation. But, if you do this, make sure you are clear about what you want to find out about the system and the supplier. Also remember that every business and implementation is different: what may work wonderfully for company A could be completely unsuitable for company B.

Look at the other businesses on the client list. Do they look like you? If they seem to focus on a completely different size of customer or market sector, you might feel that they would not understand your business. Systems designed to run the HR function in a multinational corporation might not be suitable for a business employing 20 people based on one site. They could provide inappropriate functionality or have hardware requirements that you cannot meet. If you are a public sector organisation it might be advantageous to consider suppliers that seem to have a specialisation in that area. This specialisation may be because their systems provide features that are particularly relevant to public sector customers. For example, local authorities often employ the same person in different capacities, so that they are effectively doing a number of different part-time jobs. The system needs to be flexible enough to recognise that the job holders are actually the same person so that national insurance and income tax can be calculated correctly.

Many suppliers doing market research aimed at improving their business talk exclusively to their existing customers. After all, they are the easiest ones to contact. However, such people have already made certain decisions about the supplier and are more likely to be positive. Market researchers need to think about people who are not their customers: why are they not? Likewise, when investigating potential suppliers, ask who used to be on the client list. When did they stop buying their products? Why did they do that? It may be difficult to elicit open and honest answers to these questions, but if you can find out the names of former customers you may be able to make discreet enquiries about what happened.

Go to user group meetings and ask other people attending what suppliers they have considered and dismissed or have used in the past and do not use now.

Be clear about what a supplier is providing

Is one supplier going to supply you with what you want or what it wants to sell you? You need to be very clear about what e-HR services you want to provide to your employees and how you want these to work. Ask potential suppliers to describe back to you what your specific needs are and what you are trying to achieve. Ask them to confirm that the product they are offering meets or exceeds the requirements you have identified through your value chain analysis process. Ask them to demonstrate the system doing what you want, ideally for another customer so that you can be reassured that it works in a real-life situation.

Be clear about the exact specification of the system the supplier is offering. As HR information systems move over from client-server technology to intranet technology some suppliers are offering what may be described as halfway houses where the client interface is designed to look like and work like a browser although you cannot use it to connect to your intranet. Such solutions may also require high-specification computers for the end users, rather than the basic specification needed for common or garden browsers. Just how open is the system? Will it really be able to integrate with existing and planned systems?

Ask the supplier to mock up its system to your specification so that you can get a better idea of what it will look like. It is always surprising how this can throw up previously unconsidered issues.

Think ahead. What will your company's needs be in a year's time? Three years? Five years? How scalable is the system? If you think that your workforce is going to double in that time, make sure that the system you buy can be scaled up accordingly.

Ask the supplier what enhancements it is planning to make to the system over the next 12 months. While those enhancements may be good news, they do highlight current gaps in what the system currently offers. And planned enhancements may not ever appear!

A supplier may be looking to sell you software and hardware, but you should appreciate that it is also selling you a philosophy about how to manage your HR function. It can also provide you with knowledge about how it see s other organisations managing HR and give you ideas about what current best practice is. Look at the supplier as a source of information and, perhaps, inspiration.

Find out what after-sales support will be available

Suppliers should be able to provide you with the after-sales support that you need. Suppliers often offer different levels of support, using terms such as Gold, Silver and Bronze, so think carefully about what level of support you need. Make sure that you have a written and signed service-level agreement with the supplier that meets your needs.

Will they be implementing the system themselves or will it be left to you and your IT Department? Find out what training they will provide to system users and administrators. How easy will it be to get problems fixed? What form will the support take? Will you have access to on-site engineers or will it be via e-mail or, worse, just shrink-wrapped user guides? If they offer telephone support, try calling the number a few times before making your decision. If you find that you always have to spend a long time listening to tinny classical music before your call is answered, you can be fairly confident that this will also happen just when your system has crashed taking the month's payroll data with it.

Most people like to see the same doctor each time they go to their local health centre. It is the same with nursing a sick IT system back to life. Ask the supplier about their staff turnover in their service and support function. If they have a high turnover you could find yourself talking to a different person each time you call in with a problem.

Decide who chooses the supplier

Choosing a supplier should be a team activity. It is all too easy for one person to overlook crucial factors or to be swayed by a particularly persuasive salesperson. A team to make a decision about an e-HR implementation should:

- have a diverse (and perhaps flexible) membership that represents all interested parties at different levels
- include someone from board level as a sponsor
- allocate enough time to the selection process for it to be meaningful
- be prepared for some complex decision-making.

Should I rent or buy?

This is a difficult question to answer, partly because it depends very much on a business's internal policies and partly because of the changing nature of the marketplace. Up until about 2001 most e-HR systems that were implemented were bespoke products, developed in-house or by specially commissioned software suppliers. However, as the sector matures, there is a trend towards off-the-shelf products, which is leading to a reduction in costs.

Because e-HR systems use industry-standard technologies such as browsers and intranet servers, many organisations will find that they have already made much of the necessary basic investment. However, many suppliers will charge per user, even though it may not be necessary to install separate client software.

Organisations that are already using HR information systems will probably find that it is possible to integrate their existing databases into an intranet-based system. It should not be necessary to start from scratch, as most HRIS suppliers are developing web-enabled versions of their systems.

Suppliers of e-HR systems sometimes claim that the common nature of web technology applications can also lead to reduced IT operating costs. The larger an organisation the more systems the IT Department will probably be maintaining but the commonality of web-based technologies means that the steady migration of systems to an intranet-based model will simplify their work. Also, the move away from client-server technologies to ones based on a standard browser delivery platform will mean that implementation and maintenance issues are greatly simplified. At least, that is the theory. Much of this is true, but in reality the increased complexity arising from demands for connectivity to laptops and new technologies such as mobile telephones and PDAs will counteract the increased simplicity in other areas.

E-HR systems do not have implications for the minimum specifications of computers needed in the workplace. Although the exact minimum specification will depend to some extent on the services being delivered and the browser functionality implied (for example, whether sound cards will be needed, and whether the browser will have to interpret Java or streamed data such as video), browsers adequate for an e-HR system should run comfortably on a computer with a standard specification.

Most businesses have always bought and operated their own systems. This offers a number of advantages, such as reducing dependencies on external parties and easier security management. However, if you do decide to buy, you will almost certainly be faced with the question of how best to integrate the e-HR system with other system purchases within the business.

This traditional view of departments owning and operating all of the systems necessary for their effective functioning is a thing of the past. Driven by concepts such as business process re-engineering and the introduction of new technologies, new models are appearing. For example, Shared Service Centres (SSCs) are now seen as ways of bringing together an organisation's administrative functions so that economies of scale reduce the overheads associated with routine data processing. Intranet technologies fit in very comfortably with the Shared Service Centre concept, with an SSC providing a physical home for the servers and the IT support needed.

For many businesses operating an e-HR system internally may indeed be the best solution. However, e-HR systems can be complex and expensive and HR departments may not be able to provide a sufficiently powerful justification for the necessary investment. For example, a 2001 survey by the Hunter Group,[3] an organisation in the United States, found that the average company spent about $1 million on employee self-service systems. In terms of cost per employee this ranged from $35 to $1600, depending on the size of the company and the sophistication of the system that it introduced.

In situations like this, outsourcing may be a solution possible. This could happen in various ways – partial outsourcing, through fully managed services or through an Application Service Provider.

Partial outsourcing

You can decide to outsource specific parts of your HR activity. Some businesses have been doing this for many years, relying on specialist third-party providers to manage such things as payroll administration or recruitment. Where this is done, it is almost certainly run using quite separate systems to standard internal systems.

Fully managed services

In Chapter 3 we discussed Porter's concept of the value chain, which distinguishes between an organisation's primary and support activities. Support activities, which include HR, are those that enable the primary activities to work more effectively but are not in themselves core to the business. As such, many organisations have considered ways of outsourcing the provision of these services.

All HR functions could be outsourced to a specialist supplier. This effectively means that the organisation closes its HR Department and contracts with another organisation to manage all its HR operations, using e-HR and call centres. This is obviously a drastic solution although, in many cases, it may be economically justifiable. As well as providing the staff needed to run the HR service, the supplier runs all the necessary systems. Fully managed services are not commonly employed: the Watson Wyatt 2002 survey reported only 4 per cent of companies in Europe outsourcing their entire HR function.[4]

Application Service Providers

Sub-contracting to an Application Service Provider (ASP) is a halfway solution and is generally less challenging to the culture of an organisation. An ASP is a third party that hosts software and customers' data on its servers. Customers link their intranet to the server using a secure telephone connection. This is invisible to the user: the interface is customised so that it looks exactly like centrally delivered parts of the intranet and the user is totally unaware that the server may actually be sitting many hundreds of miles away from their office (see Figure 8.1).

Surveys suggest that the number of organisations using an application service provider to manage their e-HR systems has increased from virtually nil in 1999 to 7.3 percent in 2000[5]. There are predictions that the ASP market in the United States will grow from its 1999 level of $296 million to $7.8 billion in 2004.

While many ASPs simply run standard industry software that they themselves have rented or purchased, increasingly the major players in the enterprise resource planning software industry are stepping forward as ASPs. Companies such as SAP, PeopleSoft and

J.D.Edwards now rent their software and space on servers or are making it easy for small ASPs to offer their software on a re

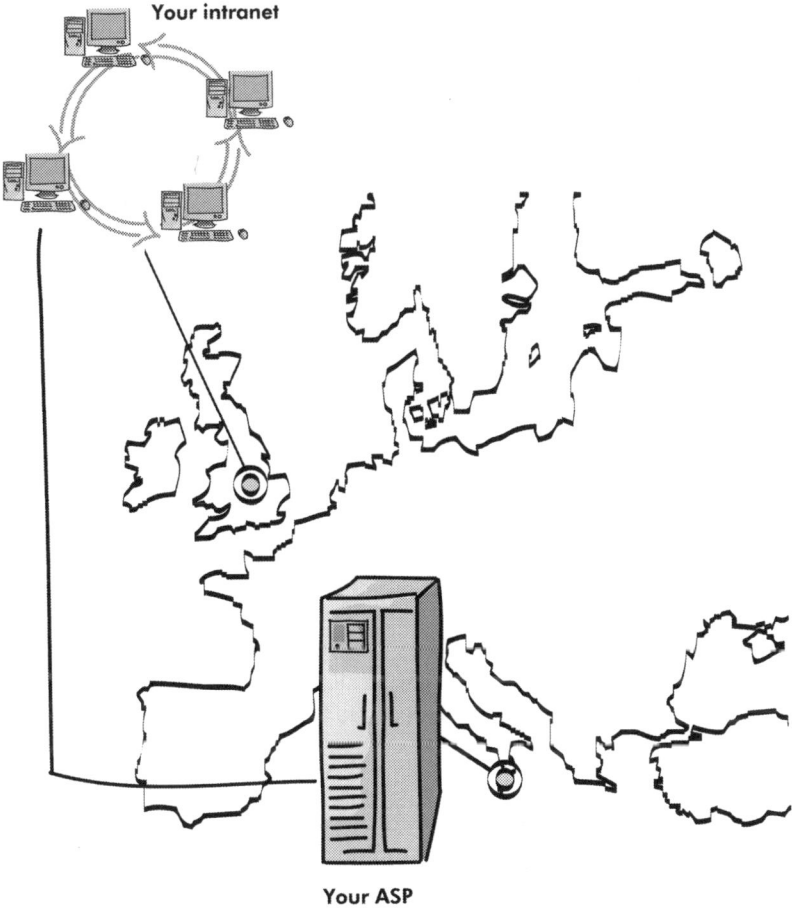

Your intranet

Your ASP

Figure 8.1
Application Service Providers
ASPs can be located anywhere in the world, but this is invisible to users.

There are several benefits to using an ASP rather than managing the system yourself.

Lower financial outlay

ASPs often sell their services on the basis of so much per employee per month, and the figures can seem very attractive, perhaps as low as £1 per employee per month. It could be much easier to justify this type of expense rather than a large capital outlay on hardware and software. The outlay is also predictable and you should not find yourself having to make an unexpectedly large investment to upgrade software that you have bought.

Renting may also make it possible to use software that would normally be out of your organisation's financial range.

Software kept up to date

You do not need to worry about your system going out of date as the ASP can make sure that you always have the latest versions of software in use. However well you research the marketplace before you buy, there is always the chance that you may buy from a supplier that goes out of business or that the technology you choose proves to be a dead end.

No need for dedicated in-house IT staff

All of the technical issues are managed by the ASP so you do not need to train or recruit new staff to manage the system.

Get up and running quickly

Rather than having to spend perhaps months installing and testing software on your own servers it should be a relatively quick and easy process to make sure that everyone in the organisation can connect to the system. You could have a fully functioning e-HR system working within days, which can be very attractive to a new or fast-growing business that needs to focus on its core activities. Surveys have shown that, on average, the implementation time for an e-HR system is reduced by 20 per cent when managed by an ASP[6].

However, there are also some drawbacks.

Dependency on a third party

You need to have as much confidence as possible in the ASP. If it proves to be technically unreliable, or worse, goes out of business suddenly, you could find yourself with a serious problem. If users perceive the system as being slow or unreliable, they may resist using it. It is therefore important to have a clearly defined service-level agreement and make payments based on the achievement of a satisfactory level of service.

Unexpected increases in price

As this is a new marketplace, many companies are scrambling to get established and may be offering unsustainable prices in order to build their own customer base. You could therefore find yourself signed up with a supplier who, some way down the line, increases their prices substantially, so you must think carefully about which ASP you choose and not necessarily opt for the lowest price.

Data security

Information about your workforce is valuable and you need to feel very confident that it is totally secure. You do not want competitors to find out about how you run your business, and employees would feel very unhappy if they found that their personal information had somehow leaked out. There are several aspects about security to consider.

Media-fuelled stories about Internet security and the (possible) lack thereof mean that the link between your intranet and the ASP's servers may seem like a security weak link. In practice it is virtually impossible to intercept data as it moves back and forth over a telephone line and then decrypt it. Security lapses are much more likely to occur through human error at either end: credit card fraud in Internet transactions is due largely to people losing credit cards or having them stolen rather than as a result of electronic eavesdroppers sniffing out credit card numbers and addresses.

This means that you must treat an ASP as if it were part of your own organisation. Whatever security precautions you have deemed to be necessary to protect your data internally must also be followed by the ASP. Paul Gilster suggests various questions you need to ask about a prospective ASP's security:[7]

- Where does the company keep its servers? Are they as physically secure as possible?

- Does the ASP have firewalls (hardware or software security systems) strong enough to keep out even the most determined hacker?

- What is the ASP's policy on disaster recovery? Do they keep sufficient backups of data and how quickly would your data be available should disaster strike?

- Does the ASP guarantee not to sell your data to third parties?

Only negotiate further with ASPs that can give you satisfactory answers to these questions, but remember that, in the ever-changing world of technology, what is secure today may not be secure tomorrow. Be prepared to constantly monitor data security policies and procedures at your chosen ASP to make sure that they keep ahead of the latest security threats.

What should I do about security?

Opening up HR records so that they can be updated by employees themselves inevitably poses a security risk. How do you make sure that the changes made to an employee's bank account details are legitimate?

Passwords

Passwords, which may be over and above the passwords needed to access the organisation's normal network, are the most common solutions at the time of writing. However, as any network administrator knows, they are far from being an ideal solution to security. Many people use obvious words (such as their own name or the day of the week) as passwords, and may compound this by writing the password on a sticky note left near the computer. Unless prompted to do so by the network, they do not change them often, if at all.

Also, simple password systems do not provide the necessary degree of authentication needed to guarantee from a legal point of view that the information received by a server is the same as the information that the user sent. For example, in a paper-based system, an employee informs the Payroll Department that their bank account details have changed by completing a paper form and then signing it with their approved signature. The Payroll Department can verify the signature and can see if any attempts have been made to tamper with the form. However, with an electronic system, this is not possible. When somebody logs in with another person's user name and password they become, as far as the network is concerned, that person. What e-HR systems need, therefore, is an electronic form of security that is as reliable as the old handwritten signature.

Digital signatures

The security offered by a handwritten signature could be met in e-HR systems by digital signatures. These have been used in e-commerce applications for several years, and they are now starting to be adapted for use in such applications as e-HR. So what exactly is a digital signature?

As far as a user is concerned, it is rather like a password in that it is a string of numbers or digits that must be memorised. However, unlike a password, it is generated by software that sits on the user's computer. This code that the user has is called, in digital signature-speak, the **private key**. This is related mathematically to a **public key** that is stored in the computer to which information is sent.

Let us look at the example of someone changing their bank account details. They log into the system and access the page where they can amend bank details. When they choose to submit this information, the digital signature software asks them to enter their private key. As soon as they have done this, the software reads the information they have entered and uses the private key to encrypt the data being sent into what is known as a **hash result**, essentially a digital representation of the information. This hash result is then sent along with the unencrypted information to the server. The digital signature software on the server decrypts the hash result using the public key and compares what it finds with the unencrypted information. If the decrypt and the original match, the server can be assured that the information:

- was signed by the correct person, and

- has not been tampered with.

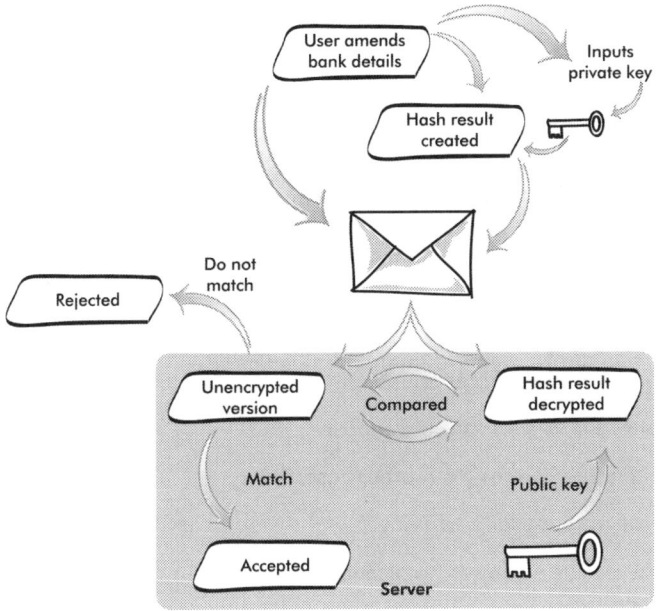

Figure 8.2
How a digital signature works

The enhanced security offered by digital signatures opens up extra possibilities for an e-HR system. For example, setting up new insurance policies or making changes to existing ones has always had to be done using paper because of the need for a real signature. Digital signatures eliminate the need for paper, saving a considerable amount of time in transmission through the post and administrative effort.

Firewalls: keeping the outside out

Virtually all intranets will provide some means for communicating with the wider world, either with other parts of the intranet located elsewhere in the world or through Internet connections available to employees. When this is the case, it is vitally important that security systems are in place to make sure that outsiders cannot snoop around in the internal network. Widely available software and information-sharing networks among hackers means that it is not at all difficult for people with the right level of knowledge to find their way into an organisation's network.

You therefore must make sure that you keep your intranet secure by installing firewalls. These can be software systems or hardware devices that constantly monitor all traffic going in and out of the system. They can recognise data attempting to enter the system from an unknown source and block it.

Summarising ...

- Your strategy will depend in part on what applications you want to implement, and this will depend on the business case you can make.

- Implementing an e-HR system can be by upgrading an existing HRIS, adding specialist applications or by building a system directly on your intranet.

- You must take great care when choosing a supplier, taking into account such things as:

  - budget

  - quality of the application

  - your relationship with the supplier

  - recommendations from other customers

  - what the supplier is offering.

- You may decide to buy an application or rent it from an Application Service Provider.

- Managing security is absolutely vital.

- Security procedures include such things as passwords, digital signatures and firewalls.

Notes

1. Watson Wyatt, (2002), *B2E/eHR Survey Results 2002*, Watson Wyatt, http://www.watsonwyatt.com/research/resrender.asp?id=2000861&page=1

2. Ball, K. (2000), 'Interface value (Human Resource Information Systems)', *People Management*, 6 January, **Vol. 6**, No 1.

3. Wells, S.J. (2001), 'Communicating Benefits Information On-line' in *HR Magazine*, Society for Human Resource Management, February, **Vol. 46**, No. 2.

4. Watson Wyatt 2002 survey.

5. Greengard, S. (2001), 'Handing off your HRMS', *Workforce*, January 2001, **Vol. 80**, No. 1.

6. Wells, 'Communicating Benefits'.

7. Gilster, P. (2000), ' Security issues take centre stage when it comes to ASPs ', *Workforce*, August 2000, **Vol. 79**, No. 8.

Implementing IT systems

Earlier chapters in this book have looked at specific applications of e-HR. However, an issue common to all types of computer system, whatever their function, is that of implementation: how do you make sure that the system is installed and operates as you hoped? This chapter addresses this question, and applies to whatever kind of e-HR solution you decide to adopt.

The implementation of new computer systems is a notoriously fraught activity. Newspapers regularly comment (often with some glee) on the latest disaster to befall some organisation that is trying to implement a new system and that is finding delivery to be months late, the budget to be going through the roof, and so on.

Studies of what happens during system implementation projects[1] make depressing reading:

- 90 per cent fail to achieve the goals stated at the beginning of the project

- 80 per cent are delivered late or over-budget

- 40 per cent are abandoned before completion.

What is more, these sorry statistics are not confined to particular sectors or sizes of organisation: public or private sector, large or small, any organisation is likely to run into systems implementation problems.

What makes implementation go wrong?

Organisations that have a specialised or unique function may find themselves having to develop software from scratch, and it is to be expected that projects such as these may face their fair share of technical problems. For example, programmers find that they cannot get the system to do what they want it to do or there are unanticipated conflicts with other systems. However, e-HR software is, to a large extent, generic across all sectors and so it is much more feasible to metaphorically 'pull a box off the shelf', install it and expect it to work satisfactorily. But does this happen? Of course, the answer to that question depends on what 'working satisfactorily' means.

There are two possible answers. Working satisfactorily from a technical point of view means that the system does what it is supposed to do. Working satisfactorily from an organisational point of view means 'Are people using it to do what we wanted them to do?'. This is where system projects often fail: users do not use the system.

Studies show that it is usually not technical issues that bring systems implementation projects to their knees but organisational ones. Doherty and King[2] report that in a survey 60 per cent of people involved in implementation projects agreed that organisational issues were more important than technical ones. Paradoxically, 50 per cent of their survey respondents thought that in less than 30 per cent of projects were these self-same organisational issues satisfactorily treated. Although Doherty and King's survey looked at the implementation of IT systems in general, the same will probably be true for e-HR systems.

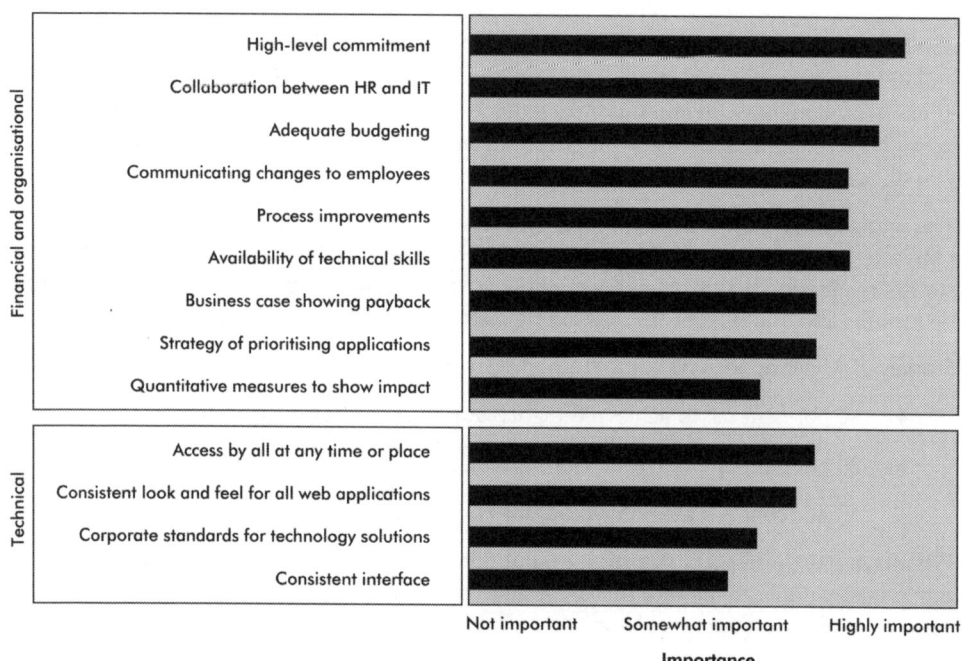

Figure 9.1
Success factors influencing self-service HR implementation

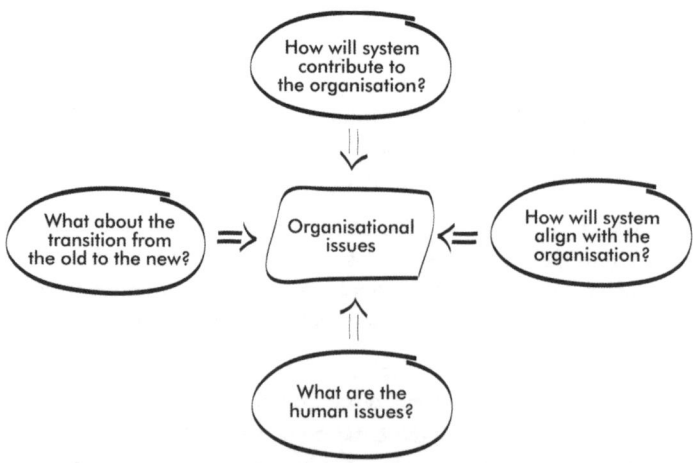

Figure 9.2
Organisational issues affecting systems implementation

The Cedar 2001 HR Survey[3] comments that '[organisations that] have successfully implemented self-service report that adequate budgets, strong executive commitment and collaboration between HR and ITT are essential to a good outcome. In fact, overall success depends on less on the features of a particular technology than it does on financial, organisational and internal communication factors.' Figure 9.1 summarises Cedar's findings.

This clearly shows the relative importance of financial and organisational and technical factors.

Doherty and King suggest that there are four main areas to consider: the system's contribution to the organisation, its alignment with the organisation, human issues and transition from old to new systems (see figure 9.2).

Let us take a look at each of these in turn.

How does the system contribute to the organisation?

This asks the basic question 'Why are you implementing this system?'. What is it going to do for the business in terms of direct and indirect benefits, how does it fit in with the organisation's strategy both now and in the future?

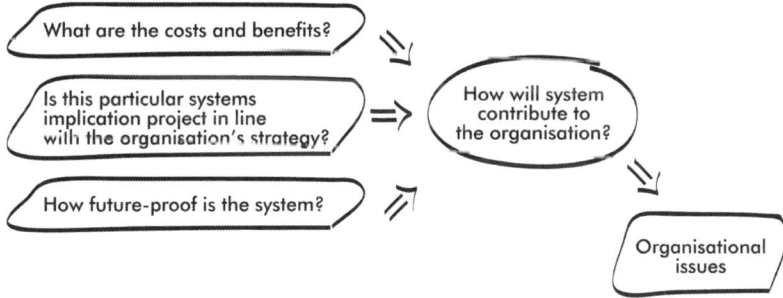

Figure 9.3
Factors affecting how a system contributes to an organisation

What are the costs and benefits?

You must think about both the visible costs of purchasing the new system and any necessary expertise and the invisible costs such as potential losses in productivity while people are learning to use the new system or potential resistance from employees or trade unions. Benefits will also be visible and invisible: reductions in data processing time and printing bills will be clear to see, but what value can you put on potential increased self-esteem within the Human Resources department and prestige of being a leading edge organisation?

 You can find more information about how to do this in the section entitled *Making the business case for an e-HR solution* in Chapter 3.

Is this particular systems implementation project in line with the organisation's strategy?

If your organisation has a vision or other form of strategic objectives, you should consider whether something such as e-HR does have a place within the strategy. Organisations are constantly looking for developments that will give them a competitive advantage over other businesses. Will the new system do this? How important is it for the organisation to be seen as a 'world-class business'? Is this one of the strategic objectives?

Also do not underestimate the importance of personal objectives of senior management. Projects need champions at senior management level, and if a board member sees a project as of benefit to their own personal agenda, they are much more likely to provide support. So decide which senior figures in the business want (or can be persuaded to want) e-HR.

How future-proof is the system?

As time goes by, needs will change and what seems to be the ideal solution now may prove to be inadequate when finally implemented. For example, headcounts may have grown considerably (or decreased). This is particularly an issue with e-HR systems where the technology and marketplace is changing very quickly. The modular nature of most suppliers' solutions will help make sure that systems can easily be upgraded as time goes by.

How will the system align with the organisation?

You next need to think about how the introduction of the system will affect the organisation in terms of its structure, culture and power distribution.

What impact will there be on the organisation's structure?

Less demand for data processing staff may mean that you may find yourself losing a particular grade of staff. Redeployment or redundancy will be called for. Other demands will appear, such as staff to manage helpdesks to support people having problems with the systems. Line managers may find themselves needing more support to help them with the increased demands being placed on their shoulders.

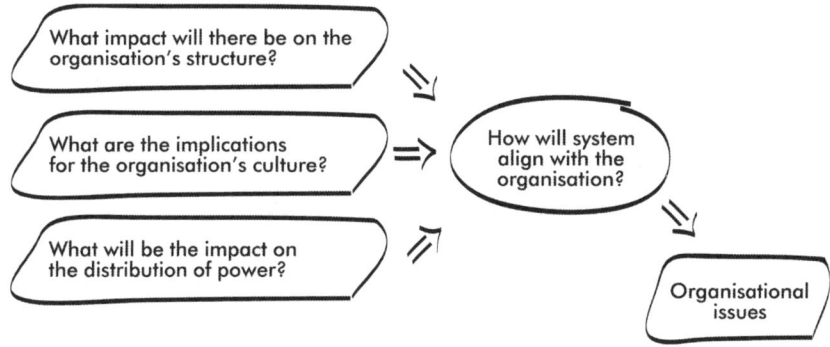

Figure 9.4
Factors affecting how a system aligns with an organisation

What are the implications for the organisation's culture?

E-HR systems generally mean a transfer of some responsibility from 'someone else' to each individual employee. Depending on the existing culture or the history of previous empowerment initiatives, this may cause greater or lesser difficulties.

As with changes in such things as fashion, an effective way of making changes to an organisation's culture is by focusing on people perceived as opinion-formers – those people who seem to be able to influence others around them. Note that they are not necessarily managers or experts. Identify who these people are and sell them the benefits of the new way of doing things. If you can convince them, they will spread the message throughout the organisation. Doing it in this way may take longer than using a top-down, hard-sell approach but it will almost certainly be more effective in changing potentially negative attitudes.

What will be the impact on the distribution of power?

If we think about the simple equation 'knowledge = power', two potential changes become apparent. Power may move horizontally to the HR Department and also downwards to junior management.

HR Departments can become a portal through which organisational information is disseminated. For example, HR can generate information or set up systems that channel information to other parts of the organisation on people-related factors.

Secondly, information will be available to people at lower levels than was previously possible, supporting empowerment of lower-level employees. For example, we mentioned earlier the ready availability of time and attendance information to departmental managers and how they could use this to monitor absence patterns. This can be of positive benefit to people who are ready and willing to use the information, but it will also increase expectations on junior staff and this will need to be addressed accordingly, perhaps through training or revised job profiles.

What are the human issues in systems implementation?

Although it seems blindingly obvious to state that for a system to be successful it must meet the needs of its users, most of us will have stories to tell about systems that have not been easy to use at all. The financial and technical pressures of systems implementation can often mean that basic human issues are overlooked or, at best, treated cursorily.

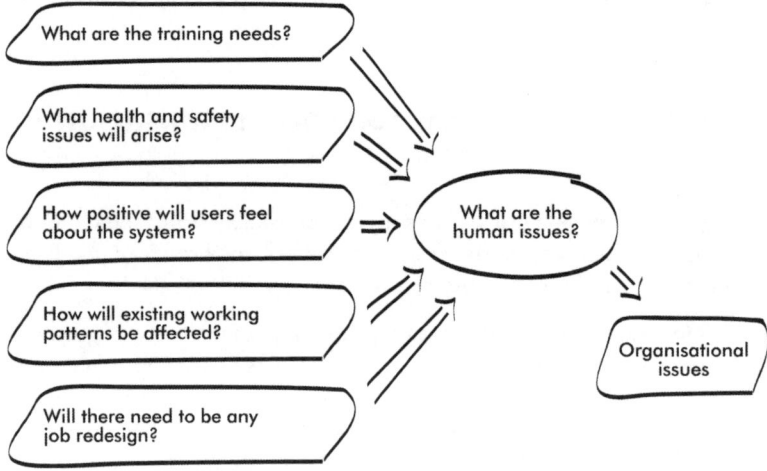

Figure 9.5
Human issues involved in systems implementation

Systems implementation needs to consider a range of human issues:

- Training issues - what training may be required?

- Health and safety issues - will people end up using a computer more and will new people start to use them?

- Will people be positive about the system?

- What effects may the system have on working patterns? Will this have a positive or negative effect and how will the change be managed?

- Will there need to be any job redesign and what are the implications of this?

Let us look at each of these in turn.

What are the training needs?

If people perceive a new system as being difficult to use, they will probably find that it is difficult to use. You must therefore make sure that the system you implement looks as user-friendly as possible and that the support and training provided are easy to access and are effective. Do not forget to include training costs in your budget and do not underestimate the cost of this: some observers have suggested that you should follow a 30/70 rule, where for every £30 spent on hardware and software, £70 should be spent on training and support.

Make sure that training is designed from a user's perspective, not from the system's. Focus on providing training in what users will need to do with the system, not on what features the system offers. The great majority of people will only need to use the system for a relatively small number of purposes, so make sure that you know what these are and plan your training accordingly.

So what training requirements will there be? The fact that browsers are used for a wide variety of commercial applications means that some people will be familiar with using them, but this hides some potentially difficult questions. Is it true that people will be comfortable with using a browser or will it be new technology for many or most people? What about the logic of the applications being delivered? How easy are they to follow? It may be easy to use the system to generate information, but what do you do with it once you have it? Will people need training in using information?

What health and safety issues will arise?

A great deal of attention has been focused in recent years on such things as workplace assessments and the ergonomic aspect of using computers. Many office workers now find that most of their work centres around using a computer, so the introduction of an e-HR system should make only a marginal difference to their degree of computer usage.

However, it is possible that you may be requiring completely new groups of people to start using a computer more regularly. This may mean introducing computers into potentially difficult environments, in which case you must make sure that you comply with all relevant health and safety regulations and provide new computer users with any information and training that they need.

How positive will users feel about the system?

In common with many other organisational initiatives, system implementation often fails to consider employees' reactions to changes introduced, deliberately or accidentally, by the system. There is an assumption that people are unchanging objects, responding predictably and consistently to changes around them. We see this in the analysis of organisations as being agencies for converting inputs to outputs by processes carried out in a 'black box'.

Figure 9.6
Organisations as black boxes

Simplistic analyses like this see organisations as:

- cast in stone, immutable objects with predictable behaviour
- independent of the actions of the people who make it work
- relatively independent of the environment within which they operate.

Similarly, employees are:

- unchanging one-dimensional characters
- behaving consistently and predictably, regardless of external factors.

In reality, inputs are converted to outputs as the result of a complex tangle of relationships, negotiations and expectations involving employees and the organisation.

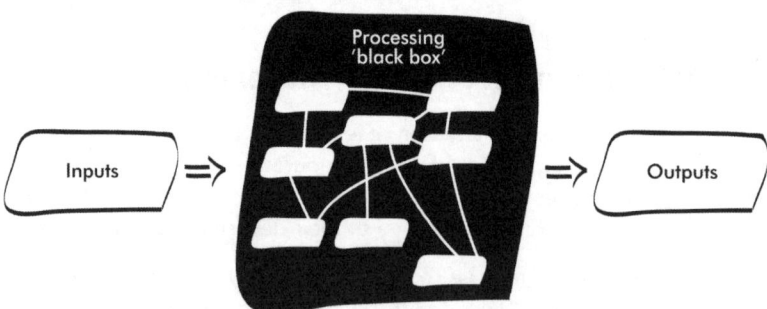

Figure 9.7
Looking inside the organisational black box

Analyses that acknowledge this level of complexity see organisations as constantly:

- changing what they do and how they do it in response to their environment and to internal influences
- organising and reorganising themselves
- reshaping themselves.

Similarly employees:

- continuously review and change their identities within the organisation

- see negotiations with others as a vital part of their everyday working life

- have ambitions (or not!) to acquire particular types of experience.

As Tansley and Watson put it[4]:

> An impoverished understanding of organisations ... [is] ... one that neglects the extent to which the organisation, in reality, has little existence separate from the ongoing social, political, cultural and economic processes of negotiation, sense-making and social construction involving human actors, all trading meanings and resources with each other as they simultaneously further their own personal projects in life and carry out organisational tasks for which they are contracted and rewarded.

In other words, ignore internal politics at your peril. Implementation plans should make sure that:

- the aspirations and anxieties of people involved in the implementation project itself are acknowledged and addressed

- changes to working procedures created by the system enhance the working lives of system users.

For example, in a small organisation where people tend to know most other people, even if only by sight, self-service HR may be seen as cutting off an important aspect of personal contact with someone in the HR office whom they see as a friend. On the other hand, people may see many aspects of an e-HR system as reducing the bureaucracy that they associate with HR. Be conscious of people looking for hidden agendas. People may (perhaps rightly) see an e-HR system as a way of cutting staffing levels or as a way of devolving (yet) more responsibility on to the shoulders of line managers.

People may have concerns about security of personal information. They may feel that, as it is easy for them to look at their own information, it must be easy for others to do so as well. This is a legitimate concern and, certainly according to the studies quoted in Chapter 1, is a major worry for many European businesses.

New e-HR systems will obviously make changes to the ways in which internal relationships work. If the implementation is to be successful, relationships that are cut or damaged must be replaced or repaired in some way. Think about what will capture the interest of your users: in Internet jargon, what will make the system 'sticky'? Potential solutions will depend very much on the nature of your organisation and the people working within it. Features that have been provided in e-HR systems in the past have included:

- child-cams, web cameras installed in the company crèche so that parents can see how their child is and what they are doing

- financial services information, such as stock market prices

- sports scores.

New e-HR systems should follow the same design principles that (should!) have been followed when designing the intranet itself. These include[5]:

- attractiveness – the intranet should be visually compelling so that users are drawn to it

- simplicity, so that training to use it is minimised

- speed – users should be able to find what they need quickly

- consistency – all pages follow the same visual design principles so they look part of a whole and users know where navigational features will be found

- accessibility – pages can be accessed from more than one route

- usefulness – the information available is valuable to users

- up-to-dateness – information is kept up to date

- practicality – information is designed for usability.

How will existing working patterns be affected?

Easier access to high-quality information and at lower levels within the organisation may be a catalyst for significant changes in working patterns. Line managers may be expected to look for significant pieces of information and to act accordingly: they will be expected to act proactively rather than waiting to be told what is happening. People throughout the organisation can therefore start to think more strategically.

Will there need to be any job redesign?

As a common primary driver for introducing self-service HR is to eliminate non-profit-generating data inputting by HR staff, it is clear that tasks (and perhaps jobs) will disappear. This can be handled by redundancy or by deploying staff to other areas within the business or by developing new roles within HR where they can use the information that will now start to be generated apparently automatically.

The spectre of job losses always hangs over automation projects and is a major factor contributing to employee resistance to new ways of working.

The analysis and use of new information is the area where employees may be able to find new and more interesting opportunities. Connected databases of information about the organisation's employees offer rich opportunities for analysing trends to help with planning for the future. For example:

- Which departments are currently experiencing the highest turnover rates? Has this changed recently? If so, why?

- What is the age profile of the organisation and of individual departments? What are the implications of this? Is an adequate succession planning strategy in place?

- What skills are available within the organisation for proposed new activities?

Unless information is sorted and interpreted it is really not information at all, just data. Failing to make quick and effective use of information collected by a self-service HR system will quickly discredit the system as well as costing people their jobs.

What about the transition from the old to the new?

Change is always difficult: somehow the status quo is always easier to deal with than the unknown future. Much of this is due to the transitional stage where things are having to change rapidly and perhaps unpredictably. You will need to manage the relationship with the suppliers carefully during this period to make sure that the implementation runs smoothly and that the final product works as per the specification. You will have to make decisions about timing: at what point will it be easiest to switch over from the old to the new? And of course, however well-managed the implementation there will be some disruption to normal working practices, and this must be dealt with.

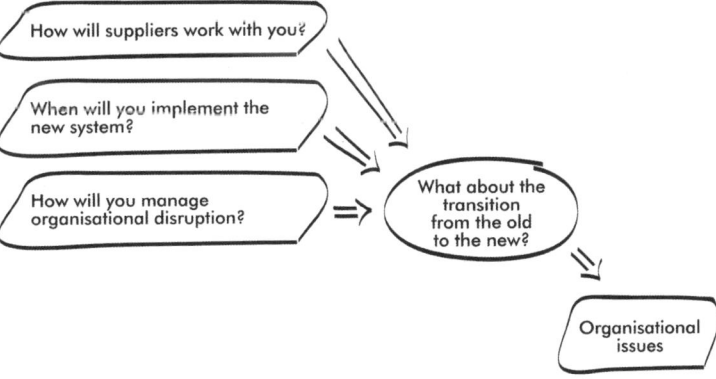

Figure 9.8
Transitional issues involved in system implementation

How will the suppliers work with you in customising and implementing?

However efficiently your supplier manages the installation and implementation of your new e-HR system, there will be teething problems. How well you cope with these problems depends to a large extent on your degree of understanding of the system and how it works. This, in turn, depends on what role you will have played in its specification, selection and implementation.

Here it is useful to consider different relationships that can exist between a customer and supplier during systems implementation projects. Dorothy Leonard-Barton[5] distinguishes between four different ways in which suppliers and customers can work together. These are shown in Figure 9.9.

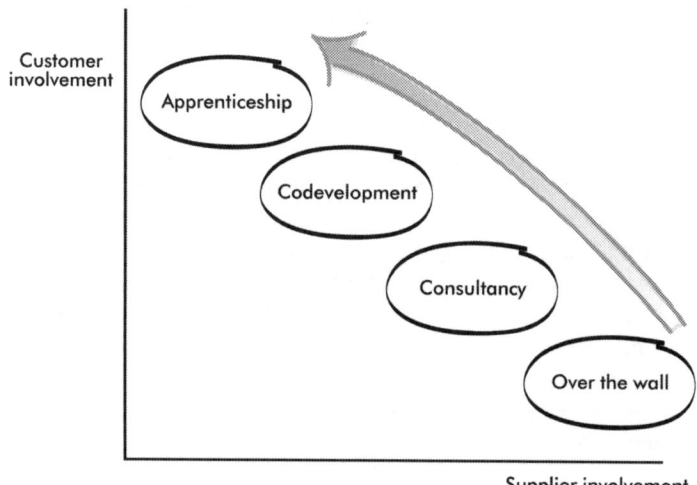

Figure 9.9
Different ways in which customers and suppliers can work together

The method with the lowest level of customer involvement is the 'over the wall' approach, so-called because the supplier basically throws the system over the wall and the customer catches it. This occurs where the customer tells the supplier what they want and has very little involvement in its development or customisation. Such an approach generally only works if the new system is so simple or self-explanatory that the customer does not need to understand how it works or if the customer is extremely skilled in the IT arena and can solve problems easily themselves.

The 'consultancy' approach describes development where the suppliers provide periodic opportunities for users to offer input to the development process. An approach like this is often used where processes are relatively well established.

In the 'codevelopment' model the customer and supplier work together to develop the system. The customer not only provides information about processes and procedures that must be captured, but also provides technical expertise to help with the development. Codevelopment is a useful model to follow if processes and procedures are to some extent unique to the customer and, of course, if the customer possesses the necessary technical expertise to be able to contribute to the development process.

The 'apprenticeship' model takes this to its logical conclusion. The supplier simply supplies technical advice to help the customer develop their own highly bespoke system.

As shown in Figure 9.9, the extent to which the customer learns about the inner workings of the system depends very much on the model employed. Customers following the apprenticeship model will find themselves having an intimate and detailed knowledge of every sub-routine and line of code needed to make the system work. If anything goes wrong they can easily lift up the electronic bonnet, tinker with a few bits and bytes and off they go again. However, it seems unlikely that many HR staff, or even internal IT experts, will want to have this degree of involvement in developing what is, after all, to a large extent a generic product. While every organisation will have its own specific requirements and will do things in slightly different ways, managing human resources information is reasonably similar from one organisation to the next, regardless of size or market sector. However, while the front end may be generic the back end of any e-HR system requires a considerable amount of integration with existing systems to enable it to work, and this can be extremely complex and difficult. It would therefore seem most appropriate for customers and suppliers to work together following the consultancy model.

But if the consultancy model is to work effectively you must make sure that there is an effective flow of information between the two parties. The customer must:

- make sure the supplier knows about any specific requirements they have due to particular working practices

- be confident that the generic model that the supplier uses is relevant to them.

The supplier must:

- have a clear understanding about any of the customer's specific requirements that deviate from the generic norm

- provide the customer with sufficient technical information so that they are able to solve minor problems themselves.

However, be aware that the further away from the safe and predictable world of human resources administration that your e-HR system moves, the more likely it is that you will need to adopt more of a codevelopment model. If, for example, you are looking to implement a knowledge management system you may find that the particular types of knowledge that are important in your organisation cannot be readily managed within an off-the-shelf system. You would therefore need to work with a supplier to use their expertise in systems development and knowledge management in general to design a system that is specific to your particular requirements.

Whatever the nature of the relationship that you establish with your supplier, there are several practical things that you can do to help the implementation process move smoothly. The Institute for Employment Studies' 1997 report on HR information systems[7] contained a number of suggestions made by the suppliers of such systems about what helps with the implementation process:

- give and take on both sides

- realistic timetables for implementation and adequate resources – in particular customers' staff available throughout the implementation process

- clear understanding about what constitutes best practice in HR information systems so that HR staff can realistically evaluate what suppliers are offering

- imaginative and forward-thinking procurement systems that relate the needs of HR to those of the organisation as a whole, and allow the appropriate investments to be made

- buy-in from the whole organisation rather than just from the HR Department so that potential barriers to implementation are lifted.

When will you implement the new system?

It is generally advisable to try to implement new e-HR systems incrementally, business unit by business unit.

If your business has periods when things are much slower than normal – for example, a summer shutdown – this may be a good time for bringing a new system on-line and making sure that it works.

Allow time for testing. An e-HR system can be installed and allowed to run in secret and in parallel to existing systems so that a small number of nominated staff can test it.

Involve someone with a communications or marketing background to help plan a communications strategy for the implementation. Keep them involved at all stages of the project.

How will you manage organisational disruption?

We all resist change to some extent. The status quo is a known quantity and, even if it is not perfect, it is comforting because it is predictable. The introduction of a new system, particularly one that may require completely different approaches to carrying out everyday tasks, is certainly going to be scary to many people. The introduction of a new e-HR system presents challenges to people that they will probably resist to some extent:

- They will have to learn how to use a new system ('Oh no! Not another new system!' they may well all chorus).

- They will have to change their ways of doing many different things. Remember that while introducing, say, a new stock control system will mean that people just control stock differently, a new e-HR system will touch on many different aspects of people's working lives.

Rebecca Frazee[8] discusses the issues involved in encouraging people to embrace new, technology-based ways of doing their jobs. She identifies a number of areas that need to be addressed:

- Make the clear benefits of the new system.

- Make sure there is strong leadership.

- Management must show strong commitment.

- Users must have the necessary skill.

- Users should be rewarded for using the new system.

Let us take a look at each of these in more detail.

Make clear the benefits of the new way of doing things

You must find ways of persuading people that the new system will be an improvement over existing methods. What has been found to be a particularly effective way of doing this is to focus on the problems of the old system rather than the wonderful features of the new system: you must make people feel dissatisfied about the status quo. Point out such things as the amount of paperwork involved in the current performance appraisal system or how people's names are often spelled incorrectly in the telephone directory. Once you have created this dissatisfaction it is much easier to say, 'Hey! Look what I've got here!' and to get people to listen.

Also think about what is important to people in the organisation. If keeping up to date with technology is important, stress the leading-edge nature of e-HR systems. If personal relationships between individuals and departments are seen as important, stress the value of better ways of communicating and the importance of more accurate information about people.

Provide strong leadership

Senior management must provide a clear vision about how the new system fits into the future of the organisation. This must then translate into the practical reality of people being given enough time to implement and learn to use the new systems adequately.

Invest money in a proper project manager with responsibility for overseeing the implementation process. Do not assume that someone can do this as another part of their already full job role. Project management is a time-consuming and potentially stressful activity and needs to be acknowledged and rewarded as such.

Make sure that management shows strong commitment

Management can show commitment by making sure that the implementation of the system is adequately resourced. Will everyone have sufficient access to a computer? Will training be available to everyone who needs it?

Give users the necessary skills and knowledge

As described earlier in this chapter, it is important to make sure that you provide access to whatever training and support people need in order to learn how to use the new system.

Reward people who embrace the new methods

You should think about encouraging people to use the new systems by providing intrinsic and extrinsic rewards.

Intrinsic rewards are those that come from seeing a job well done, perhaps from making sure that long-ignored mistakes in personal details have been corrected or from using an e-recruitment system to appoint a highly talented person quickly into position.

Extrinsic rewards are often more material in nature. For example, you could provide a prize for the first dozen people to use some part of the system.

Set milestones and measurable targets

You will only be able to assess how well the implementation of the system is proceeding by comparing it with targets and milestones agreed before implementation starts. The project team should therefore have a plan that identifies by what dates certain things should have been achieved. Without this, you cannot possibly have any idea about what progress you are making.

Do not rush the implementation process. Most organisations find that they need between three and 12 months to complete implementation. Of course, this will be influenced by how many new systems and processes you are introducing. Rather than introduce a comprehensive system that runs the risk of overwhelming and alienating people, consider introducing certain limited functions to start off with. If you start with functions that people will find very useful and will accept, you are well on the way to winning the hearts and minds battle. This will make it much easier to implement more comprehensive solutions.

Keeping your HR system working

Once the trials and tribulations of implementing a new system are over and everything is up and running, there is often a temptation to find a darkened room in which to lie down for several years. While some celebration is definitely due, implementation is really just the first stage in the system's life cycle. It is followed by operation and then, ultimately, by replacement. This is illustrated in Figure 9.10.

It is therefore important to move seamlessly into these stages and to carry out whatever tasks are needed to keep the system running at optimal efficiency. The maintenance schedule shown in Table 9.1 has been developed from one proposed by John Caplin[9].

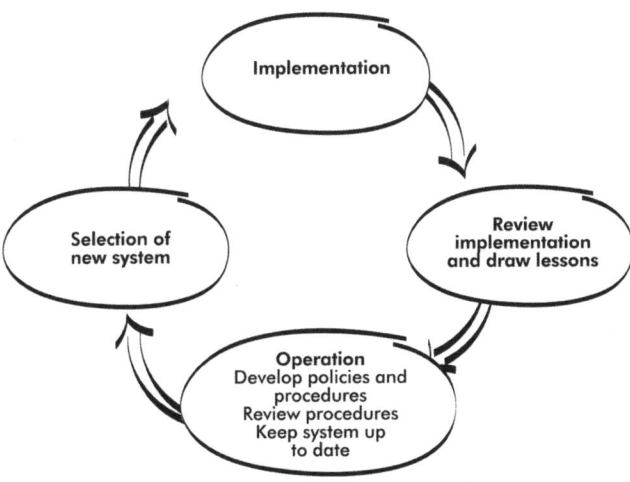

Figure 9.10
Life cycle of a typical computer system

It is important to keep in close contact with users to find out what they like about the system and what they think could be improved. One organisation with a large e-HR system organises regular focus group meetings that have proved instructive. For example, in one such session users revealed that their main use for the portal was to find information to help them deal with specific situations, one particular example mentioned being how to deal with members of staff coming into the office drunk. To do this they would look at the main page and then move on to the alphabetical Index and look under the letter 'D', a method which they preferred to using the search engine provided. The system administrator's response to this was therefore to move access to the index to the main page. Also, by looking at the statistics for which information was accessed most frequently they were able to provide direct links to this information from the main page.

They also found that users did not look at the HR portal for organisational news, although it was provided there. People looked at the on-line internal newspaper for this, so the administrator was able to release space on the portal page by removing news items that people never looked at any way.

Table 9.1
Maintaining a computer system

What to do	When to do it after implementation	How often
Review system implementation to celebrate success and identify what should be done better the next time	1 month	
Review security issues, policies and processes	1 month	Annually
Prepare schedule for subsequent installations	2-3 months	
Write internal procedures and policies guide	3 months	Update as procedures and policies change
Review that system is meeting business objectives used in business case	3 months	
Attend vendor's user group meetings	3 months	Continually
Install maintenance upgrades	As soon as is necessary	Continually
Review new products being developed by vendor	6 months	Annually
Develop plan for decommissioning obsolete systems	6 months	
Review system operation and streamline as necessary	6 months	Annually
Invite independent third party to review and suggest improvements to business processes	6 months	Every 2 years
Invite independent third party to advise on system maintenance	1 year	Every 2 years
Prepare return on investment report for new system	As soon as significant data is available	
Prepare for replacing the system	3 years	

Summarising ...

- Most systems implementation failures occur because organisational factors have not been considered carefully enough.

- When planning a system implementation you must think about:

  - how the system contributes to the organisation

  - how the system will align with the organisation

  - what human issues there are in the implementation process

  - how you will manage the transition to the new system.

- Once it is implemented, it is important to maintain the system properly.

Notes

1. Doherty, N. F. and King, M. (2001),'An Investigation of the Factors Affecting the Successful Treatment of Organisational Issues in Systems Development Projects', *European Journal of Information Systems*, December, **Vol. 10.**

2. Ibid.

3. *Cedar 2001 Human Resources Self Service/Portal Survey*, Cedar, http://usa.cedar.com/USA/whitepapers/

4. Tansley, C. and Watson, T., (2000), 'Strategic Exchange in the Development of Human Resource Information Systems (HRIS)', *New Technology, Work and Employment*, September. **Vol. 15**, No. 2, page 110.

5. 'Intranet Design Principles', www.hrtechnologies.com/hr_web.htm

6. Leonard-Barton, D. (1997), 'Implementing and Integrating New Technical Processes and Tools', in R.L. Ruggles (ed.), *Knowledge Management Tools*, London: Butterworth-Heinemann.

7. Robinson, D. (1997) 'HR Information Systems: Stand and Deliver', www. employment-studies.co.uk/summary/335sum.html, extracted from report of same name, Institute for Employment Studies.

8. Frazee, R.V. (2002), 'Technology adoption: Bringing Along the Latecomers' in A. Rossett (ed.) *The ASTD E-learning Handbook*, London: McGraw-Hill.

9. Gale, S.F. and Greengard, S. (2001), 'The HRMS Tune Up: Keep your System Running Smoothly', *Workforce*, July, **Vol. 80**, No. 7.

Implementation checklist

This checklist summarises the issues discussed in this chapter. Read through it and think about whether you have addressed, or if you need to address, the issues raised.

Addressed?

Contribution to the organisation

What are the costs and benefits? ☐

Is this particular systems implementation project in line with the organisation's strategy? ☐

How future-proof is the system? ☐

How will the system align with the organisation?

What impact will there be on the organisation's structure? ☐

What are the implications for the organisation's culture? ☐

What will be the impact on the distribution of power? ☐

What are the human issues?

What are the training needs? ☐

What health and safety issues will arise? ☐

How positive will users feel about the system? ☐

How will existing working patterns be affected? ☐

Will there need to be any job redesign? ☐

What about the transition from the old to the new?

When will you implement the new system? ☐

How will you manage organisational disruption? ☐

One of the challenges facing HR professionals moving into the world of e-HR is to become competent and confident when talking to IT experts. You may therefore find this brief explanation of network technology useful. However, if you want to find out more you would be advised to pay a visit to your local bookshop or explore reference sites on the Internet where you will be able to find other sources of information explaining many of these terms in more detail.

ASP (1)	Active Server Pages, a technology for connecting web pages with databases. See also CGI and PHP.
ASP (2)	Application Service Providers, companies who will host e-HR applications on their own servers and provide connections to a customer's intranet.
B2B	Business to business, a model for commercial transactions between businesses carried out across the Internet.
B2C	Business to customer, a model for commercial transactions between businesses and their customers carried out across the Internet.
B2E	Business to employee, Internet technologies used to mediate transactions between a business and its employees.
Bobby	A set of standards defining the accessibility of web pages to people with disabilities.
Bradford Factor	A way of quantifying absenteeism levels that attempts to quantify the reality that individual days of absenteeism are more damaging to an organisation than the same number of days taken off as a continuous period.

Bradford Factor $=$ number of days' absence $\times$ (number of absences)^2

For example, employee A takes ten individual days off a year while employee B is sick for a continuous period of ten days. Their respective Bradford Factors are as shown below:

Bradford Factor (A) $= 10 \times 10^2 = 1000$

Bradford Factor (B) $= 10 \times 1^2 = 10$

browser	Application such as Internet Explorer or Netscape Navigator on a computer linked to the Internet or intranet that allows the display of web pages.

bulletin board	A system similar to an e-mail system, but which allows messages to be linked together by subject matter. For example, a user could post a message on the bulletin board about some aspect of e-recruitment, and other people can then attach responses to this message. Such systems make it easier to conduct conversations about a specific subject.
CGI	Common Gateway Interface, a small program designed specifically to connect a web page to a database. Not to be confused with Computer Graphics Interface, something completely different. See also ASP (1) and PHP.
client-server	Network software where users' computers (the clients) contain software specially designed to connect to other software stored on a server.
digital signature	A technology that prevents unauthorised tampering with data sent from a user's computer to a server.
dynamic HTML	Written with a lower case 'd', this describes web pages written in such a way that they contain content drawn from a database. This will often be achieved by using technologies such as CGI, ASP or PHP.
Dynamic HTML	Written with an upper case 'd', this refers to an extension of the Web programming language HTML that offers extra functionality.
EPSS	Electronic Performance Support System. A sophisticated help system that tries to adapt itself to the particular task the user is attempting.
ERP	Enterprise resource planning, large software systems that integrate all the functions required within a business, such as sales, purchasing, stock control, finance and so on.
extranet	Section of an intranet that can be accessed by computers outside the internal network, typically by suppliers or customers.
firewall	Hardware devices or software applications that are designed to filter data flowing in and out of an intranet. They are essential security precautions to prevent unauthorised access to a network.
HPWS	High Performance Work System, term coined by Dave Ulrich to describe efficient and effective working processes.
HRIS	Human Resources Information System, applications designed to assist the HR function within an organisation.
HRMS	See HRIS.
HTML	Hypertext Markup Language, a programming language used to design web pages.

HTTP	Hypertext Transfer Protocol, a computer networking protocol used by browsers that allows them to translate data received into text and graphics on the screen.
hyperlink	Text or graphic on a web page that when clicked instructs the browser to load a different page.
Internet	Term generally used to describe the network of computers around the world linked together by telephone lines and network cables and using the TCP/IP protocol to exchange information.
intranet	Internal network within organisations or buildings using TCP/IP.
Java	Programming language used to write programs that can be run by a browser.
JavaScript	Programming language used to write programs that can be run by a browser.
LCMS	Learning Content Management System, applications designed to manage the content of e-learning systems.
Learning Management System	Systems designed to manage the administrative aspects of training within an organisation.
learning object	Small, generic item of training that can be used in a number of different applications.
LMS	See Learning Management System.
PHP	Personal Home Pages, a scripting language used to connect web pages to databases. See also CGI and ASP (1).
plug-in	Extra software installed in a browser that allows it to interpret special types of data, for example the RealPlayer® plug-in lets the browser receive and play sound files being streamed down continuously from a server.
portal	Web page that provides a user with access to a range of associated functions.
protocol	A set of rules used for transmitting and receiving data.
server	Computer storing files holding information such as web pages or databases.

streaming	Process where data is transferred from the server to the user's browser and is used immediately. If the browser has an appropriate plug-in it, can use the data as it is received and not have to wait until the download is complete. For example, it can play an audio file or display a video sequence.
TCP/IP	Transmission Control Protocol/Internet Protocol, a computer networking protocol (or language) that allows computers to send information to and from each other.
thin client	A hardware configurations where all data processing is carried out on a server and the users' computers (the clients) contain the minimum amount of software needed to display the results of processing.
URL	Universal Resource Locator, the address for every page on an intranet or the World Wide Web. This has two components: • the server name • the page name. For example, a URL could be 'intranet.acme.com/homepage'. The part of the URL before the '/', 'intranet.acme.com', is the name of the server while the name after the '/' (in this case 'homepage') is the file name of the particular page that the browser wants.
World Wide Web (or just 'Web')	One use of the Internet that allows the display of text and graphics using browsers and the Hypertext Transfer Protocol (HTTP).
XML	Extensible Markup Language, a programming language related to HTML that allows the data from any source to be displayed on a web page so that it looks exactly as it does in its native application.

 If you would like to find out more about any of the technical terms mentioned in this glossary, try looking at either of these two on-line sources of technical information:

- www.techweb.com/

- www.webopedia.com/

Index

How to Plan and Manage an e-Learning Programme

Roger Lewis and Quentin Whitlock

E-learning, as with many other aspects of the digital revolution, was hailed
as the panacea for training and development. In the intervening years and
following a number of, sometimes painful, lessons for learning providers, client
organizations and the learners themselves, we now have a more realistic view
of the opportunities provided by this medium and of the skills and processes
needed to make it work.

Roger Lewis and Quentin Whitlock's *How to Plan and Manage an E-learning
Programme* is a complete guide to best practice on managing the processes, the
content and all of the people involved.

Practising what they preach, the authors break the subject down into manageable
chunks and use a wide range of examples and plenty of checklists to give you a
rigorous and yet highly practical route map, from planning, designing and selling
the initial concept, through testing to launch and evaluation.

E-learning, despite its reliance on technology is a people-oriented process
and the authors include advice on managing and supporting learners
(and their expectations), building and managing the e-learning development
and support teams.

Commissioning effective materials and sustaining e-learning is an expensive, time-
consuming and risky business. *How to Plan and Manage an E-learning
Programme* is a must-have guide for those tasked with championing e-learning,
designing or commissioning programmes, and supporting and sustaining learners.

GOWER

How To Get Best Value From HR

The Shared Services Option

Peter Reilly and Tony Williams

An efficient and cost-effective HR function is essential to the successful running of any organization. And yet for many businesses it is impossible or costly to have HR staff in every office. This is particularly true for companies who have many branches, such as banks and building societies. So what are they to do? Increasingly they are turning to shared services by creating a unit within the organization that typically undertakes personnel administration and basic operational support. This may be delivered to managers and employees through some combination of call centre, personal contact or intranet.

Creating a shared services centre enables the HR function to redefine its relationship with its stakeholders. It can become more of a strategic player and make a more business-focused contribution. This book explains what shared services are and what they look like for the HR function. It describes why organizations opt for shared services and what activities are included. It sets out the relationship between shared services and the other HR activities, and between HR and line management. *How To Get Best Value From HR* outlines the process of introducing shared services, from identifying customer needs through designing the structure to implementation and monitoring. It also outlines the likely pitfalls and, importantly, offers possible solutions. In particular the book highlights the big design issues, including whether to outsource services, where a shared services centre should be located, how services should be delivered and organized, including through the option of e-HR. Crucially it features an extended case study of the Royal Bank of Scotland's experience of introducing HR shared services, providing a unique insight into the reality of this new way of working.

GOWER

Designing Computer-Based Learning Materials

Alan Clarke

Computer-based learning has the potential to provide a highly motivating learning experience. It also has the potential to achieve exactly the opposite. And the difference between these two extremes is the quality of the learning design.

The challenge for the learning designer isn't a simple one. You are being asked to prepare interactive learning for someone you can't see and with whom the only interaction you are likely to have is via limited written communication. Fortunately help is at hand in Alan Clarke's *Designing Computer-Based Learning Materials*.

Dr Clarke offers a definitive guide to each of the many elements involved in good design. This book explores the principles of adult learning, and relates to the potential, features and impact of computer-based learning.

This is not a 'how to…' book, but rather one seeking to help you understand the different elements which go into computer-based learning. If you are commissioning material, it will help you to understand the contractors' constraints. If you are designing materials yourself, it will allow you to avoid many of the errors it is all too easy to make when developing them.

Computer-based learning materials are not all the same: their range reflects the variety of learners that use them and purposes they are used for; the different learning environments that are available to people; the different subjects that they wish to learn and the level to which they wish to take them.

In the face of such a complex task, involving so many factors and variables, it is essential that the learning designer understands what is involved and uses a rigorous process for envisioning, planning, designing, implementing and testing their solution. This is a book about learning design and not about software production and, as such, it provides any aspiring designers with the fundamentals of producing the highly motivating learning experience, which should be their objective.

GOWER

The People Measurement Manual

Measuring Attitudes, Behaviours and Beliefs in Your Organization

David Wealleans

Understanding your organization is a pre-requisite of effective management: to move forward it is essential to know where you are now. This is true as much of your people as of your organization's processes and finances. However, measuring people is an imprecise science and as such is often overlooked or, if attempted at all, (carried out ineffectively or to an unrepresentative conclusion) ineffective and inconclusive.

The People Measurement Manual takes a systematic and objective approach to understanding human situations. As well as exploring the process of measurement and comparing the various methods open to HR managers – including how to create the right environment for measurement, how to select the correct measurements for your own organization, and the tools and techniques that can be used – the book focuses on how to make sense of, report on and use the results to bring real and lasting benefits to the organization.

The text is broken into topic headings and associated diagrams, and features a series of 'tips' which are highlighted from the text. Additionally, each chapter concludes with a summary of the key points covered.

GOWER